Rethinking American Electoral Democracy

Second Edition

While frustration with various aspects of American democracy abound in the United States, there is little agreement over—or even understanding of—what kinds of changes would make the system more effective and increase political participation. Matthew J. Streb sheds much needed light on all the major concerns of the electoral process in this timely book on improving American electoral democracy.

This critical examination of the rules and institutional arrangements that shape the American electoral process analyzes the major debates that embroil scholars and reformers on subjects ranging from the number of elections we hold and the use of nonpartisan elections, to the presidential nominating process and campaign finance laws. Ultimately, Streb argues for a less burdensome democracy, a democracy in which citizens can participate more easily in transparent, competitive elections.

This book is designed to get students of elections and American political institutions to think critically about what it means to be democratic, and how democratic the United States really is.

Part of the *Controversies in Electoral Democracy and Representation* series, edited by Matthew J. Streb.

Matthew J. Streb is Associate Professor of Political Science at Northern Illinois University. His books include *The New Electoral Politics of Race* (University of Alabama); *Academic Freedom at the Dawn of a New Century* (Stanford University); *Running for Judge* (NYU); *Law and Election Politics: The Rules of the Game* (Lynne Rienner); and *Polls and Politics: The Dilemmas of Democracy* (SUNY).

Controversies in Electoral Democracy and Representation
Matthew J. Streb, Series Editor

The Routledge series *Controversies in Electoral Democracy and Representation* presents cutting edge scholarship and innovative thinking on a broad range of issues relating to democratic practice and theory. An electoral democracy, to be effective, must show a strong relationship between representation and a fair open election process. Designed to foster debate and challenge assumptions about how elections and democratic representation *should* work, titles in the series present a strong but fair argument on topics related to elections, voting behavior, party and media involvement, representation, and democratic theory.

Titles in the series:

Rethinking American Electoral Democracy
Matthew J. Streb

Redistricting and Representation: Why Competitive Elections Are Bad for America
Thomas L. Brunell

Fault Lines: Why the Republicans Lost Congress
Edited by Jeffery J. Mondak and Dona-Gene Mitchell

In Defense of Judicial Elections
Chris W. Bonneau and Melinda Gann Hall

Congressional Representation and Constituents: The Case for Increasing the U.S. House of Representatives
Brian Frederick

The Imperfect Primary: Oddities, Biases, and Strengths of U.S. Presidential Nomination Politics
Barbara Norrander

Rethinking American Electoral Democracy, 2nd Edition
Matthew J. Streb

Forthcoming:

Helping America Vote: The Limits of Election Reform
Martha E. Kropf and David C. Kimball

Third Party Blues: The Truth and Consequences of Two-Party Dominance
Scot Schraufnagel

In Defense of Politicians
Stephen K. Medvic

Rethinking American Electoral Democracy

Second Edition

Matthew J. Streb

Routledge
Taylor & Francis Group

NEW YORK AND LONDON

First edition published 2008
This edition published 2011
by Routledge
270 Madison Avenue, New York, NY 10016

Simultaneously published in the UK
by Routledge
2 Park Square, Milton Park, Abingdon, Oxon OX14 4RN

Routledge is an imprint of the Taylor & Francis Group, an informa business

Typeset in Galliard by RefineCatch Limited, Bungay, Suffolk
Printed and bound in the United States of America on acid-free paper by
Walsworth Publishing Company, Marceline, MO

Library of Congress Cataloging-in-Publication Data
Streb, Matthew J. (Matthew Justin), 1974–
Rethinking American electoral democracy / Matthew J. Streb.—2nd ed.
p. cm.—(Controversies in electoral democracy and representation)
1. Elections—United States. 2. Democracy—United States. I. Title.
JK1976.S77 2011
324.60973—dc22
2010034983

ISBN13: 978–0–415–88201–9 (hbk)
ISBN13: 978–0–415–88202–6 (pbk)
ISBN13: 978–0–203–84815–9 (ebk)

Contents

List of Figures and Tables

Figures

Table

Preface

The idea for this book started with a conversation I had with a former student during the height of the effort to recall former California governor Gray Davis. During the spirited conversation, the student made a passionate defense in favor of recalling Davis and argued that the effort was "democracy in action," to which I blurted out, "It may be democracy, but it is dumb democracy!" Normally I would not be this direct with a student, but I was close to this particular student as I had him in several of my classes, I served as his thesis advisor, and we presented a paper together at a political science conference.

While we ultimately agreed to disagree, immediately after that conversation I began thinking about the many aspects of American electoral democracy that I considered to be "dumb"—some of which I had studied, such as nonpartisan elections and judicial elections, and some of which I had not, but always believed to be questionable, like the initiative process and the number of elected officials in the United States. I decided to write a book that would argue against many of these paradigms and the idea that "more democracy is always best." As I started thinking through the project further, however, I wanted to make sure I didn't take a tone that was too flippant—it could easily sound more like something that Ann Coulter or Keith Olbermann would write, and that was certainly something I did not want. And, to be honest, arguing that many of these practices and institutions were "dumb democracy" was not fair. The more research I completed, the more I realized that there are persuasive arguments supporting the status quo. While I ultimately may not agree with these arguments, they are far from "dumb."

Furthermore, revising the "dumb democracy" angle allowed me to write a more comprehensive book, permitting the inclusion of more than just democratic ideas that I questioned. This approach to writing the book naturally encouraged discussion of a wide array of subjects, some of which I supported, some of which I opposed, and some of which I either did not have a strong opinion on or on which I simply could not make up my mind. In other words, it allowed me to think about what a "model" electoral democracy should look like.

The reader should be forewarned. While I hope I have provided balanced coverage of the subjects that comprise this book, my point of view is clear. Certainly not everyone will agree with all arguments in the book; many will no doubt disagree with me entirely, and others will likely have strong opinions about topics that I do not. Some readers may support my position, but for different reasons than I advocate. What I hope emerges from this book is a dialogue about American electoral democracy. While I would like to persuade some of my skeptics, the more important goal is to get people to critically assess what it means to be democratic and how democratic the United States really is; hence the title *Rethinking American Electoral Democracy*. We are fortunate enough to be active participants in this wonderful democratic experiment. Unfortunately, few of us stop to wonder how well the experiment actually works. One of the basic but underappreciated features of a system like that of the United States is it is open to change. Few, if any, of the specific practices should mindlessly be continued if another practice can better serve the purposes of a democracy.

Acknowledgments

Of all the research projects on which I have worked, this one was the most challenging. As a political scientist, rarely do I "stick my neck out" and make normative arguments. Instead, usually I have some theory that allows me to develop testable hypotheses. I collect data and see whether my theoretical expectations hold. This is not to say that such research cannot be criticized—indeed, political scientists disagree all the time regarding the appropriate measurement of variables, whether a model is fully specified, and the like—but the nature of the criticism of such research is different. Normative arguments by definition are arguments about how the world should be, or, in this case, what makes a model democracy, and it must come as no surprise that many people have very different—and sometimes strong—views regarding such a question. Since this is the case, I have benefited enormously from the comments of many colleagues and the debates (and, in a few cases, heated arguments!) we have had about the subjects in this book.

First, I owe much to Michael Kerns at Routledge for his support of this project. I think Michael knew what I was trying to do in this book before even I did. He was instrumental in helping me think through the organization of the book. I was thrilled that he thought so highly of the book as to ask me to do a second edition. In addition to Michael, Beth Renner, Felisa Salvago-Keyes, Mary Altman, and the rest of the Routledge staff were a pleasure to work with. Beth, in particular, provided valuable feedback on the clarity of my arguments.

Several of my political science colleagues have been immensely helpful as well over two editions. Seth Thompson endured many long conversations in his office as I first started to envision writing a book on electoral democracy. Lee Goodman, Michael McDonald, Brian Schaffner, Mike Wolf, Curt Wood, and Mike Wyckoff provided critical, but fair comments about individual chapters in the first edition of the book. Brian Frederick was gracious enough to read the entire original manuscript; his suggestions were always extremely useful and helped me to hone my arguments. Of all the debates on issues in this book that I have had over the last several years, I have enjoyed my conversations with Melinda Gann Hall about judicial elections the most. Although Melinda and I disagree over the wisdom of electing judges, our conversations have been invaluable in the development of my thinking on the issue. Stephen Ansolabehere, Chris Bonneau, Kim Brace, Tom Brunell, Sharon Holmes, Jan Leighley, Bradley Smith, Charles Stewart, and Richard Winger all were kind enough to answer questions that I had about various subjects. In addition, Joshua Dyck, University at Buffalo, The State University of New York; Carl Klarner, Indiana State University; Charles Prysby, University of North Carolina at Greensboro; Stephen K. Medvic, Franklin and Marshall College; Mark J. Rozell, George Mason University; David Jones, James Madison University; Diana Dwyre, California State University, Chico; Audrey Haynes, University of Georgia; and Stephen Maynard Caliendo, North Central College all provided insightful and constructive feedback in their reviews of the book.

Marjorie Campbell, Andrew Foss, Ben Gross, and Neil Wright provided excellent research assistance. The Department of Political Science at NIU was kind enough to give financial support that allowed me to focus solely on finishing the first edition of the book over the summer.

Finally, my family deserves a great deal of thanks for their patience as I worked on the revisions to the book. As always, Page gave me immense support and was kind enough to explain to the neighbors why professors actually have to work during the summer. More importantly, she told me to stop complaining when I became frustrated with writing. Logan and Alex made sure that dad didn't work too hard, always talking me into hitting some balls off the tee or shooting some hoops. Fortunately, they don't appear to have my athletic genes. Neither appears to share my disdain for the Electoral College either.

Chapter 1

Creating a Model Electoral Democracy

At the beginning of every semester of my "Introduction to American Government" course, I can be sure that the class will comprise students who have a wide range of interests and views. Unfortunately, there will always be some students who have no interest in American government and are taking the class to fulfill a core requirement. There are many students who are curious but skeptical about the American government. Often cynical, they think politicians are corrupt and elites dominate election outcomes and the formation of public policy. In their eyes, their voices will never be heard. And, certainly included as well are a few idealists who believe that they can make a difference and that their involvement is essential to the functioning of a healthy America. While these students have different points of view regarding their interest in politics and their attitudes towards government, one belief unites almost all of them: the belief that democracy is a good thing, that people's voices *should* be heard, and that any attempt to limit democracy is bad. However, democracy is a complex concept and, while the students know they like democracy, when confronted with questions about what a model electoral democracy should look like, differences in opinion quickly emerge.

My students are no different than the country as a whole. Most Americans with rudimentary knowledge of government are adamant proponents of democracy; they believe that people should have control over their elected officials and be able to vote them out of office if the politicians fail to follow the popular will. But again, divisions develop when we move from an abstract concept of democracy to a more specific debate about what the rules and institutions of a well-functioning electoral democracy should be.

Let us assume that the students and most Americans are correct: democracy is a good thing. If we can agree on that, then the questions become how much and what kind of democracy should we have? Here is where differences in opinion become apparent. As political scientist Elisabeth Gerber writes, "All democracies face a fundamental problem in deciding how much political participation to allow and by whom."[1] Most Americans would likely agree that a direct democracy in which citizens are responsible for voting on all federal, state, and local policy is unworkable. But what about a limited direct democracy where citizens have the ability to vote on certain state or local issues? In a representative democracy it is obvious that we must elect some government officials, but specifically who? We must have some rules regarding who is eligible to vote, but what should those rules be and how difficult (or easy) should it be for eligible voters to cast ballots?

Other questions emerge as well. It seems relatively uncontroversial that everyone's vote should count equally, but how do we guarantee that and what trade-offs have to be made? What is the fairest way to best reflect the wishes of the people in primaries and general elections? Do we necessarily want competitive elections, and, if so, what is the best way to promote them? Would more or less money in the system be the answer? Who should appear on the ballot and how easy should it be for them to get on it? What mechanisms should be used to tally votes? The list of questions is nearly endless.

The goal of this book is to answer the question—If democracy, then what kind? The United States is the oldest, most established democracy in the world. Unlike emerging democracies, our Constitution is firmly embedded. We do not have to be concerned with creating the appropriate institutions to promote democracy; they have been in place for more than 200 years. Our challenge then is not to develop an electoral democracy from scratch, but instead, as prominent democratic theorist Robert Dahl writes, "to perfect and deepen [American] democracy."[2]

In this brief introductory chapter I discuss the criteria that drive the arguments for specific conditions of a model electoral democracy and provide an overview of the chapters to come.

Criteria for a Model Electoral Democracy

In his often-cited book, *On Democracy*, Dahl argues that democracy refers to both an ideal, which is probably unattainable, and an actuality. "In every democratic country a substantial gap exists between actual and ideal democracy," Dahl writes. "That gap offers us a challenge: can we find ways to make 'democratic' countries more democratic?"[3] Contrary to the common perception, however, making a country more democratic does not necessarily require more democracy. Indeed, as argued at several points in this book, "democratic" reforms enacted for the sake of creating more "democracy" are not always positive, and in fact can have negative effects, often making the country less democratic in the process. The solution isn't always more democracy — it's better, smarter democracy.

What is needed for that "better, smarter democracy?" The answer surely depends on an individual's values. "When we try to decide what political institutions democracy actually requires, we rely . . . on evidence and empirical judgments," Dahl continues. "Yet . . . what matters to us depends in part on our previous judgments about the meaning and value of democracy. Indeed, the reason we may be concerned with the shape of political institutions in the actual world is that the values of democracy and its criteria are important to us."[4]

There are several criteria that are needed for an ideal electoral democracy. Citizens must have the ability to speak freely, to criticize (or even support) those who are currently in office and those who are trying to get there. While it is impossible for every voice to be heard equally, we must make sure that certain voices do not dominate the discussion. Additionally, the people must believe that the institutions and rules of a democracy are legitimate. While these criteria are all important, throughout this book I focus extensively on four criteria for a model democracy in particular, all of which revolve around the concept of "free and fair elections."

One Person, One Vote

No criterion is more vital than the fact that people "should have equal and effective opportunities to vote."[5] It is imperative that different segments in society—the wealthy and the poor, the educated and uneducated, whites and racial or ethnic minorities—all have the same opportunity to vote and that barriers are not put in place to benefit one group at the expense of another. Along the same lines, a central component of a model electoral democracy is the idea of "one person, one vote." Each eligible voter in a democracy must have her vote weighted the same as everyone else, regardless of an individual's personal characteristics. All votes must not only count equally, but have the same probability of being counted as well. Moreover, the concept of "one person, one vote" applies not just to voting, but also to representation. In a system of government that includes a House of Representatives where seats are allocated based on population, it is essential that people receive equal representation. In other words, a system in which District A has 100 residents and District B from the same state has only 10 residents is flawed because the voices of residents in District B carry more weight than those in District A.

The Potential for Competitive Elections

"'A competitive struggle for the people's vote' is for many political scientists and political theorists the very definition of democracy," writes political theorist Dennis Thompson.[6] I concur. A model electoral democracy must have at least some competitive elections whose outcomes are in doubt before election day. Why? From a rational choice perspective, greater electoral competition should lead to higher voter turnout, which will contribute to the legitimacy of government.[7] According to rational choice theorists, citizens decide to vote by subconsciously computing the following equation, known as the "Calculus of Voting:"

$$R = PB + D - C$$

R equals the reward a person obtains from voting. If R is positive, then the person casts a ballot; if R is negative, then the person abstains. P equals the probability that the person's vote will determine the outcome of the election; B is the benefits a person obtains from having one candidate elected over another; D is often known as the "citizen duty term,"[8] and reflects the value that one places on voting as a duty of a citizen; C is the costs of voting, whether they be the informational costs of researching a person's vote or the time costs required to actually cast a vote (that is, register, wait in line at the polls).

Studies find empirical support for the Calculus of Voting. When elections are close, the outcome of the election may be in doubt, leading more people to cast their ballots.[9] Competitive elections produce greater media coverage and more efforts at voter mobilization, which provide citizens with additional information on which to cast their votes and hence lessen the costs of voting.[10] Furthermore, competitive elections provide the greatest opportunity for citizens to influence the outcome of an election, which means that turnout will be higher.[11] As important, competitive elections are more likely to produce moderate candidates;[12] this limits extreme polarization in government creating greater opportunities for compromise and making policy more reflective of public opinion. It promotes ethics in government because politicians who are corrupt are more likely to be removed from office or avoid corrupt practices in the first place. In other words, competitive elections promote government accountability and responsiveness.[13] Because of the enormous advantages that incumbents have we must look for ways to level the playing field and make elections fairer, which, in turn, will make them more competitive.

This is not to say that every election needs to be competitive. Indeed, as I argue later in the book, too much competition can have negative outcomes. But, the potential for competitive elections must exist to provide citizens with greater choice and to promote accountability. What do I mean by the *potential* for competitive elections? As one example, the cards should not be stacked against challengers who cannot compete with an incumbent's fundraising prowess. Incumbents must fear the possibility that a strong candidate could challenge and possibly defeat them.

Transparency

Voting should be private; other aspects of elections should not. Whether it is the selection of a party's candidate, the counting of votes, the drawing of congressional districts, or the contributions of individuals and organizations to candidates and political parties, citizens should be able to view the process. "When the requirement for transparency is violated," write political scientists R. Michael Alvarez and Thad Hall, "the fundamental tenets of democracy are violated."[14]

Rules that Are Not Burdensome

The previous three criteria are generally not controversial, although how one achieves those goals certainly can be. There is likely to be significant debate over whether this last criterion is essential—or even ideal—in a model democracy. In the eyes of many people, a model citizen should regularly participate in and deliberate about elections. Participation in elections is important, but the requirements for participation should not be overly onerous and—while some will disagree—I argue that they are.

Referring back to the Calculus of Voting equation, the costs of voting in U.S. elections can be excessive. Americans are required to go to the polls more often to vote for more offices than citizens in any other country in the world. Unnecessary barriers to voting are often placed in front of many citizens. In the majority of elections, citizens are not provided with important, reliable cues on the ballot that will help them determine their votes efficiently. We are faced with what seems to be never-ending campaigns where voters elect a candidate and then are almost immediately bombarded with campaign literature, television advertisements, and contribution requests for the next election. All of these occurrences lead citizens to become fatigued with elections, something that a system of government in which "the people rule" cannot afford.

This does not imply that the American public is not capable of making informed decisions. In this book I argue that we need to vote less, not because we are incapable, but because we are overwhelmed. I advocate a less burdensome democracy; not a simplistic democracy, but one in which Americans can more easily participate. Voting is important, but to expect Americans to be informed, even somewhat so, on all the issues we may vote on or offices we may vote for is unrealistic and, as I will argue, unnecessary.

A Few Comments

Before turning to the substantive chapters, it is important for me to make a few comments about what is, and is not, to come. First, writing a book such as this one means that inevitably some important topics will have to be left out. Including every possible aspect of the rules and institutions of U.S. electoral democracy would require a far longer book than I have the right to ask my readers to read. For example, questions such as whether those with mental disabilities or noncitizens should be able to vote will have to be left for another forum.

Additionally, the focus here deals with the rules, procedures, and institutions of our electoral democracy. It does not focus on several other aspects that no doubt influence the quality of democracy. For example, does negative advertising weaken democracy by making people cynical and less efficacious, which in turn keeps them from voting (i.e., weakens democracy), or does it lead to a more informed public (i.e., strengthens democracy)? Does the media do an adequate job of providing the public with the necessary information to cast an informed vote? Does the two-party system that exists in the United States promote or hinder democracy? These issues are important in a discussion regarding the health of a democracy, but all are beyond the scope of this book.

Along the same lines, in each chapter a concise and, I hope, persuasive case is made, but, due to space limitations, only the main issues within each subject can be covered and occasionally not in as much detail as I would have liked. Indeed, each of the topics covered here could be the subject of another book (and most have). Each chapter provides readers with the significant background on these issues and gives them enough information to establish opinions of their own on these topics.

Also, debates about the appropriate rules and institutions of a sound electoral democracy are frequently clouded by partisan politics. Certainly there are ideological divisions that separate the parties regarding the best electoral reform. For example, Democrats and Republicans are likely to have different beliefs regarding the role of government in financing elections because of their competing views of government. However, too often, Democrats argue in favor of what will most benefit the Democratic party and vice versa with Republicans and the Republican party. Unfortunately, this trend is understandable, given that politics is about power and the easiest way to get power and control the issue agenda is by winning elections. Certainly, then, partisans are going to want to shape the rules and institutions of electoral democracy in ways that make it most likely that their parties' candidates win elections. But partisan arguments can be problematic when thinking about electoral reform. Too often we become obsessed with protecting the party and not implementing reforms that would be fairest for the country. I have tried to be nonpartisan when making my case—and, fortunately, as a moderate partisan, this was not too difficult to do. When reading the book, I hope that you will do the same.

Overview of the Book

The book comprises three parts. Part I is devoted to rethinking the costs of voting. It is here where the strongest argument is made that the rules of voting are too onerous. Observed in Chapter 2 are some of the reasons that influence turnout, including the fact that Americans must go to the polls far more often than is needed, that election day is not a holiday or held on a weekend, and that most states require residents to register to vote several weeks in advance of the election. Chapter 3 focuses on the number of elected officials for which Americans are asked to vote and examines one type of election in particular: those for judges. There is no reason why citizens must vote for so many offices. In particular, judicial elections are problematic because they threaten due process and judicial independence, something that is crucial to protecting the rights of the minority. Chapter 4 looks at two types of direct democracy that exist in some states: the initiative and the recall. While both may be the purest examples of democracy, I argue that they should be used sparingly so as to not tie the hands of elected officials when creating policy.

Part II covers the mechanics of voting. Discussed in Chapter 5 are the laws required for a party's candidate to be placed on the ballot as well as the format of the actual ballot itself. The requirements for third-party or independent candidates to get on the ballot should not be arduous so that citizens have an adequate number of choices when deciding how to vote, and the actual ballot should be as simple as possible so as to reduce the number of errors people can make when voting. Chapter 6 examines the methods used for counting votes. While no voting machine is perfect, optical scanner and electronic voting machines offer the best chance to limit voting errors in the future. Less important than the machine that voters actually use, is that each voter in a state uses the same machine and that government conducts regular audits of election results.

Part III focuses on the rules of national elections. Chapter 7 questions the redistricting process in place in the majority of states and argues that redistricting should be conducted by a nonpartisan state commission. Chapters 8 and 9 focus on presidential elections. Chapter 8 examines the increasingly controversial presidential primary process, while Chapter 9 discusses the always contentious Electoral College. In both cases, substantial reform is needed. The current primary process should be eliminated in favor of a national primary, while the Electoral College should be abolished in favor of a popular vote election with an instant runoff. Chapter 10 looks at one of the most complex aspects of electoral democracy: campaign finance. In order to promote more competitive elections, we should consider lifting the restrictions on campaign contributions. However, contributions by individuals and political organizations must be disclosed for transparency and to provide voters with important information when deciding how to vote. Finally, Chapter 11 concludes with a brief discussion of how the arguments made throughout the book are consistent with the criteria listed for a model democracy in this chapter.

Part I

Rethinking the Costs of Voting

Chapter 2

Factors that Influence Voter Turnout

One day, shortly after we had voted in a November midterm election, my wife was sorting the mail. She suddenly stopped when she came across her sample ballot for that March's primary in Los Angeles. She looked at me incredulously, as though as a political scientist I was somehow responsible for scheduling elections, and said, "This is ridiculous. Didn't we just vote?" Apparently most Angelenos felt like my wife did, because when the March primaries to vote in certain districts for city council, board of education, and community college seats came, less than 13 percent of the eligible electorate voted. Slightly more than two months later, when people were asked to go to the polls yet *again* to vote in the runoff election, barely more than 9 percent turned out to vote.

One of the most cherished rights we have as American citizens is the right to vote. And, though many of us may not use that right often, we certainly have plenty of opportunities to do so. Few countries in the world hold as many elections as the United States. As political scientist Ivor Crewe notes, "The average American is entitled to do far more electing—probably by a factor of three or four—than the citizen of any other democracy."[1] In fact, the average American is likely to be called to the polls more than twice a year, every year.[2]

The number of times Americans are asked to vote raises the costs of voting discussed in Chapter 1. The more we are asked to vote means the more we have to be informed and take the time to cast our votes. However, the number of election days is not the only barrier to voting that Americans face: in all states but one, citizens must register to vote, and in most cases must do so well before election day; the times and days in which citizens are asked to vote may make it difficult to do so; several states still have restrictive absentee voting laws or do not allow residents to vote early. Other states require identification to vote or prohibit felons from doing so. This chapter examines these barriers to voting and argues that many should be eliminated.

"Didn't We Just Vote?"

The American electoral system is unique. We elect our president and lower house more often than any country. That, in and of itself, is not a problem. A four-year term gives the president time to enact his agenda while still keeping him accountable to the people. The House of Representatives was designed by the framers of the Constitution to be the people's "House." Two-year terms, while I'm sure annoying to members of the House who constantly have to run for reelection, again promote accountability. But, as Crewe writes, the differences between the United States and other countries do not stop with more frequent elections for president or the lower house. "No other country popularly elects its state governors *and* town mayors; no other has as wide a variety of nonrepresentative offices (judges, sheriffs, attorneys general, city treasurers, and so on) subject to election. Only one other country (Switzerland) can compete in the number and variety of local referendums" (emphasis in original).[3] On top of that, few countries hold primaries to nominate party candidates.[4]

This problem becomes further exacerbated when one considers that a solid majority of municipal elections are held at different times than presidential elections.[5] As noted, in Los Angeles, voters are not only asked to vote in the even-year primaries and general elections for federal and state offices, but also in odd-year elections for local offices, such as mayor or city council. If no candidate receives a majority of the vote in the first electoral round, then voters are asked to go to the polls again to determine the runoff winner.

Los Angeles is not alone. Growing up in New Jersey, I had just assumed that campaign season was all year long. I would see candidates' political signs on the neighbors' front lawns. As soon as those came down, new signs would be placed for a different office. New Jersey is one of the few states (Kentucky, Louisiana, Mississippi and Virginia are the others) that elect its governor in odd years. As a result, New Jerseyans are asked to vote for high-profile races, both in a primary and general election, every three out of four years. Because the primaries are held in June and the general election in November, the following campaign starts almost immediately after the previous election.

The number of election days in California and New Jersey pale in comparison to the state of Georgia. In 2008, for example, some Georgians had the good fortune of going to the polls five times in one year, and potentially more! Georgia held its presidential primary on February 5th, which was on a different date than its general primary, July 15th, for offices like the House of Representatives. Georgia law states that candidates must receive a majority of the vote in the primary or they must face a runoff election, which was August 5th. The general election, like in the rest of the country, was held on November 4th and a runoff election for a U.S. Senate seat and the Public Service Commissioner was held on December 2nd. The statewide turnout for the general election runoff was under 30 percent, down from 54.7 percent in the November general election.[6] Georgia also had two special elections to fill open state house and state senate seats, both of which also went to a runoff election.

The problem with holding so many elections is that it leads to what some scholars call "hyper-democracy;" voters become fatigued and information costs increase greatly. Voting is not perceived as being special anymore.

Instead, voters are overwhelmed with election information. The constant campaigning is likely to turn off people to the political process. As I have mentioned, from a rational-choice perspective, potential voters measure the benefits and costs of voting as well as the likelihood of their vote making a difference. With so many elections, the costs of voting increase and, as a result, voter turnout is likely to decline. In fact, several studies have attributed the low turnout in the United States partially to the frequency of elections.[7] To be fair, consolidating elections would probably have a minimal effect on voter turnout in November elections, which is the election the cited studies analyzed.

However, consolidating elections would have an enormous effect on voter turnout in local elections.[8] You certainly would not see roughly 10 percent of the public voting for their city council as was the case in the previously mentioned Los Angeles election. Some may argue that the 2003 Los Angeles municipal election is an outlier, and that voter turnout is really much greater in other local elections. Although turnout is higher in some cases, it usually remains quite low. In a study of turnout in Californian municipal elections, political scientists Zoltan Hajnal and Paul Lewis find that the mean turnout for eligible voters in city council elections is only 32 percent.[9] In many cases, turnout consistently falls below 10 percent of the voting-age population.[10] According to political scientist Louis DeSipio, turnout in local elections is no more than 10 to 20 percent of eligible voters.[11] Even statewide elections suffer from extremely low voter turnout. Jack Doppelt and Ellen Shearer note that the *combined* turnout for two statewide 1998 Texas primaries (a regular one and a runoff) was 14 percent of registered voters.[12]

It is tough to argue that democracy is functioning well when turnout is so low in so many different elections. While I have never been a proponent of increasing turnout for the sake of increasing turnout, we do run the risk of becoming an elite democracy in which only a small number of citizens partici- pate regularly. Some people might charge that as long as everyone is eligible to vote, there is not a problem. No one is keeping citizens from voting and if only 10 percent of the public care enough to vote, then so be it. My students often make this argument, to which I respond that I will hold the review session for the midterm at 6:00 a.m. Tuesday and change my offices hours to Saturday and Sunday mornings from 7:00 till 8:00 a.m. All can come, but it is likely that even strong students who normally take advantage of review sessions or office hours will not attend. Due to this inconvenient scheduling, good students are disadvantaged. Similarly, good citizens are disadvantaged when so many elections are scheduled.

To make matters worse, turnout in these inconveniently scheduled elec- tions is highly skewed. Studies find consistently that the costs of voting are greater for the poor or less educated.[13] Little information is usually accessible in these races and they are often nonpartisan (see discussion in Chapter 5), creating a huge information gap. Thus, we are electing officials based on what a few thousand (and in some cases less) citizens believe. Even many people who normally participate, who regularly vote in presidential elections or midterm elections, may find the number of elections overwhelming and the lack of information available daunting. "[A]t the local level where policies are most likely to be implemented and where a majority of the nation's civic leaders are being elected," write Hajnal and Lewis, "important public policy decisions are being made without the input of the most affected residents."[14] And, while empirical studies question whether higher voter turnout matters at a national level,[15] Hajnal and his colleague Jessica Trounstine find evidence that it does at the local level.[16]

Even if the 10 percent turnout was reflective of the general population and voting was not so taxing, there are other reasons to oppose holding so many election days. Conducting elections is expensive. For instance, an April 2009 election in Cook County, IL in which turnout was only 21 percent cost $4.85 million, roughly $16 per voter. Per capita spending in neighboring Kane County was even higher ($17.30 per vote). The expense of the election was not lost on Kane County Clerk John Cunningham. "It bothers me as a businessman when I see the cost of each vote," Cunningham said shortly after the election. "It's not good business."[17] And, remember, this is money that may be spent multiple times in one year.

However, consolidating elections is difficult because of federalism. The U.S. Constitution gives Congress the power to control the "Times, Places, and Manner" of holding elections for Congress or the president, but it has no power over state or local jurisdictions regarding when or how many state and local elections are held. Some county and local governments are reluctant to merge their election days with those for federal offices. If a presidential election is held in conjunction with a mayoral election, for example, many voters may go to the polls intent on voting for a presidential candidate and, at the same time, vote for a mayoral candidate of the same party for no other reason than partisanship. One could imagine an election in which the Democratic presidential candidate excites and mobilizes party members who otherwise might not vote. Those people who are mobilized might then vote for the Democratic mayoral candidate simply because the person is a Democrat, not because of the person's qualifications or ideas. In other words, some fear that a Democratic presidential candidate's popular platform will influence the outcome of a local election. Were the local election to be held on a different date, they feel that the influence of national politics would be less strong.

It is possible that national trends could influence state or local races, but empirical evidence indicates that, recently anyway, they have not. Presidential coattails have basically disappeared in presidential elections.[18] In 1992, the Democratic party lost 10 seats in the House and had no gain in the Senate, even with Bill Clinton's convincing victory over George H.W. Bush. In 1996, Democrats gained a small increase in the number of representatives, but lost two Senate seats. In 2000, George W. Bush's razor-thin win did not bring with it an increase in congressional seats. In fact, the Republicans lost two seats in the lower chamber and four seats in the upper chamber. In 2004, while Republicans picked up four seats each in the House and Senate, gains in the House could be attributed largely to a controversial redistricting plan in Texas designed to weaken several incumbent Democrats. In 2008, although Democrats did gain seats in Congress, it is not clear what effect Barack Obama had on these gains. However, anecdotal evidence from his home state of Illinois indicates that the answer is "not much." In the state's Tenth congressional district, a vulnerable Republican incumbent held on to his seat even though Obama solidly carried the district. Certainly, congressional races are not the same as local races and unfortunately little empirical research has examined the effects of presidential coattails on local elections, but it is not unreasonable to think that the effects of national elections on local races might not be as pronounced as some people believe. And, even if national trends affected local elections, I am not sure that is such a bad thing. As I argue in chapter 5, local government is not simply administrative in nature. It matters whether Democrats or Republicans control office. If the public mood swings in one direction or another at the national level, it only makes sense that it should do so at the local level as well.

Another concern of state and local election officials is that, by consolidating elections, voters will be less informed about state and local elections; they will not cast thoughtful votes. If state and local elections are held separately from national elections, opponents of consolidating elections argue, only those citizens who care enough to inform themselves will vote. Those who can't be bothered will stay home. If local elections were held at the same time as presidential elections, then many uninformed voters about local elections would be mobilized and, once at the polls, may vote in the local elections just for the sake of voting. Opponents also argue that consolidating municipal elections with federal and state elections will create a long, confusing ballot. Yet, some empirical evidence indicates that voters pick and choose which offices they vote for, based on the information they have regarding the office.[19] Voting tendencies are such that people often refrain from voting when they are not familiar with the candidates running for a particular office. According to this data, the idea that voters will jump on the party bandwagon and vote for all the candidates belonging to one party is certainly not a guarantee. As likely is that voters simply will not vote for elections they know nothing about.

Moreover, while in a democracy the quality of a person's vote is always a concern, separating state and local elections from federal elections is not a guarantee of smart voting; and it is not a reason to purposely lessen voter turnout. First, as argued in the next few chapters, the number of offices for which we vote should be reduced drastically, initiatives should be restricted, and nonpartisan elections should be eliminated. All of these actions would lessen the costs of voting immensely, allowing citizens to focus more energy on local elections, even when they are held in conjunction with state and federal elections. Second, as Hajnal and Lewis assert, the concern about voter attentiveness and knowledge is a strong argument "for civic education, voter outreach campaigns, higher quality media coverage of local races, and intensive campaigning by candidates for mayor and council. They are . . . not good arguments for scheduling local elections so as to knowingly reduce public participation."[20]

While a discussion of the quality of election news coverage would fill an entire book and is not the focus here, local newspapers and news stations could do more to cover local races. The trend away from locally owned television and radio stations is a concern because coverage of local races may become even sparser.[21] Nevertheless, the media needs to focus on municipal elections more than it currently does. Often around the Superbowl, World Series, or NCAA basketball tournament, newspapers create a section devoted to coverage of that event. This same thing could be done for elections. Citizens would then have a convenient place to turn for election coverage. The section need not focus just on federal or state elections, although those elections would still likely command the most coverage, but could also include regular commentary on elections for mayor, city council, and school board. As it stands, the coverage of most nonpresidential races is extremely sparse. The news media has an obligation to inform the public about contested races, and is failing to do so. Fortunately, with the rise of the Internet, the media's limited coverage of local politics becomes less of a concern because voters now have access to more information than ever before online.

Though it is unlikely that all localities will combine their elections with those for federal and state offices, at least one study uncovers a trend in a positive direction. In a survey of Californian county clerks, Hajnal and Lewis find that more than 40 percent of the cities have changed the timing of municipal elections recently "with the vast majority of those switching from stand-alone elections to elections concurrent with statewide contests."[22] This is a step in the right direction and hopefully one that other localities will follow.

Other Barriers to Voting

It is not just the number of times people are asked to vote that makes American elections different from most other countries' elections, but the fact that other institutional obstacles to voting exist in the United States that do not in many other countries. Now, let's turn to a discussion of many of these barriers.

Voter Registration and Election Day Registration

One voting requirement that separates the United States from most other countries is that, in all states but North Dakota, citizens must register to vote. The registration requirement makes voting a two-step process: citizens must first register before they can vote. Opponents of voter registration argue that it lessens turnout because the costs of voting increase.[23] For example,

G. Bingham Powell finds that automatic registration would increase voter turnout in the United States by 14 percentage points.[24] As Steven J. Rosenstone and Raymond E. Wolfinger note, "Registration is often more difficult than voting. It may require a longer journey, at a less convenient hour, to complete a more complicated procedure—and at a time when interest in the campaigns is far from its peak."[25]

Although registration requirements have generally been left for the states to decide, in 1993, President Bill Clinton signed the National Voter Registration Act (NVRA) into law. Among other things, this act, also known as the Motor Voter Law, was designed to make it easier for people to register by allowing them to do so at various government offices including the Department of Motor Vehicles. While roughly 22 million people have registered to vote under NVRA, the success of the legislation is not clear.[26] In 1996—the first presidential election since the implementation of the law—voter turnout was the lowest it had been since 1924.[27] Turnout rates in midterm elections since the law was passed have not risen significantly. And, while the last two presidential elections did see an uptick in voter turnout, it is not clear that the increase was due to Motor Voter.

However, states are continuing to develop ways to make voter registration easier. Six states, including Arizona and Washington, now allow people to register to vote online. Measures are put in place to ensure that fraudulent registration does not occur. For example, in both states, citizens are required to enter information such as their date of birth, driver's license number, eye color, and social security number. If the information entered does not match the information in the state's driver file, the person may not proceed. In addition to being popular with citizens, online registration saves states significant money.[28] According to the United States Election Assistance Commission, nearly 700,000 people registered to vote on-line in the 2008 presidential election.[29] The implementation of online voter registration seems to be a step in a positive direction.

Another registration modification that reformers have pushed to increase turnout is election-day registration (EDR), also known as same-day voter registration. Under EDR, potential voters must still register, but they can do so on the day of the election. Nine states, including most recently Montana and Iowa, allow same-day voter registration. The remaining states all have registration closing dates of several days before the election up until 30 days before the election. In 2009, a bill was introduced in the Senate by Wisconsin Senator Russell Feingold and in the House by Minnesota Representative Keith Ellison that would implement EDR nationwide; the bill has made little headway.

One result of EDR that seems clear is that voter turnout is higher in states that allow for same-day registration than in states that do not. In 2008, turnout in states with EDR was roughly 10 percent higher than in states without EDR. Similar results occurred in 2000 and 2004.[30] This analysis is admittedly simplistic; after all, it does not allow for a wide array of factors that influence voter turnout. However, numerous multivariate analyses of EDR and voter turnout indicate that same-day registration can increase turnout rates anywhere from roughly 3 to 10 percent.[31]

There are a few reasons why same-day registration leads to higher voter turnout. First, as the election draws nearer, interest in the election rises. Political scientist Thomas Patterson, an advocate of EDR, finds that people increasingly think about and discuss the election as election day gets closer.[32] In other words, by the time people are paying attention to the races, the deadline to register may have already passed.

Second, EDR makes it easier for various groups of people, including the young and those who regularly move, to vote. According to one analysis, voter turnout rates of 18–24-year-olds who lived in EDR states was 18 percentage points higher than their counterparts in non-EDR states.[33] Younger people generally do not have the history of voting that older people do and may not follow the campaign season until near the end. Those who go away to college also may decide that they want to register to vote in their college town, but fail to do so before the registration deadline. Same-day registration helps those who have recently moved as well. For example, roughly 40 million people moved between 2002 and 2003.[34] These people tend to be young, nonwhite, and poor—groups that are already less likely to be registered.[35] With the exception of a few people who may have moved but remained in their original precinct, everyone else must reregister. If the move occurred close to the registration deadline, people may forget to register because of the chaos of the move and some may have actually moved after the registration deadline. This is a mistake that I almost made. When I moved to Illinois several years ago, being a good political scientist, I immediately registered to vote. A few months later we moved into our new house, in a different city from where we were temporarily staying and where I was registered. Being a bad political scientist, I forgot to reregister right away. Fortunately, I remembered to do so the day before the registration deadline.

Few people, even opponents of EDR, question whether voter turnout increases when same-day registration is allowed, although there is disagreement over how large the effects will be. The debate is not over whether turnout increases, the debate is over at what costs. Critics of EDR assert that it increases voter fraud, is expensive, imposes significant burdens on election officials, and that people should not be able to vote at the last minute when they have thought little about the election.

One of the most outspoken opponents of EDR is journalist John Fund. In his book, *Stealing Elections: How Voter Fraud Threatens Our Democracy*, Fund contends that same-day registration is a bad idea because it opens up the possibility for all sorts of voting irregularities. He notes, for example, that the U.S. Postal Service returned roughly 3,500 election day registration confirmations as undeliverable; in other words, a significant number of people cast ballots on election day in precincts in which they did not live.[36]

We must consider the possibility that EDR could lead to more voter fraud, but the concern over voter fraud is exaggerated. With proper identification requirements and access to computerized records, voter fraud is far less likely to occur and certainly not likely to be rampant. People who register on election day should be required to show proof of residence such as a recent utility bill, credit card bill, or closing or leasing documents.[37] For example, New Hampshire requires its residents to complete an affidavit and show proof of age and residency. These requirements work to eliminate the possibility that people can "move into" an area for a day to vote, as Fund contends.

If EDR is implemented, then more hiring and training of poll workers will be necessary. In fact, former Montana Secretary of State Brad Johnson supported eliminating same-day voter registration in the state because the lines to vote in some precincts in the 2006 midterm election were so long.[38] The hiring and training of more poll workers would no doubt lead to greater costs. However, I am often amazed on what governments are and are not willing to spend money. The costs would not be prohibitive; if they were, no state would have EDR, and the benefits could be great.

The biggest concern that I have with same-day voter registration is that people might decide to vote at the last minute, based on a thirty-second commercial they saw on television or because their friends encouraged them at the last minute to do so. I would like to think that people spend time weighing the pros and cons of candidates and deliberate about the election with family, friends, and colleagues. In fact, in 2004, residents of California had the opportunity to vote in favor of same-day voter registration. I was one of the 59 percent of people who voted against the measure and residents of Colorado also voted down a similar initiative in the same year. At the time, I agreed with Californian Governor Gray Davis, who felt that "voters who go to the polls ought to have a minimum amount of information about what they are voting on."[39] (Perhaps the larger concern I had was that the proposition had no provision for separating the ballots of those who registered on election day from those who did not, which would keep election officials from verifying that the person registering on election day is indeed an eligible voter in the precinct.)

After more reflection, though, I realized that my argument was flawed. To go back to Davis' quote, there is nothing guaranteeing that people who register early to vote have a minimum amount of information on what they are voting. In fact, people often vote based on nothing more than a candidate's partisan affiliation, gender, race, or ethnicity, even when they have not registered on election day.[40] These cues are usually available to voters, regardless of when they registered. Finally, telling someone what they should or should not be basing their votes on is elitist. If people want to cast votes based on one 30-second spot they saw before they left for work on election day, then that is their right. This is no different than people who cast votes for someone because the candidate is good looking or because they like the candidate's name.

People regularly cast votes based on nothing more than the advice of family, friends, or colleagues. Why does it matter if my wife tells me who to vote for 30 days before the election or on election day? In hindsight, same-day registration is something that states should seriously consider. Evidence indicates that it will increase turnout, especially among groups who are less apt to vote, and the elections in states that have implemented it appear to function well and certainly no worse than states that have not instituted the reform.

No-Excuse Absentee Voting and Early in-Person Voting

The easing of voter registration laws is not the only proposal reformers advocate to ease the burdens of voting. A great number of states are passing laws that make it more convenient to vote absentee or allow you to vote in person before election day. Voters are taking advantage of those reforms. It is estimated that roughly 30 percent of the electorate voted before election day in 2008.[41]

Initially, in most states absentee voters had to provide evidence that they would be unable to get to the polls on election day (for example, because they were away at school, away on business, disabled). Today, 28 states have no-excuse absentee voting laws; in other words, a person can request an absentee ballot for any reason.[42] In 2001, California went one step further by allowing registered voters to permanently request that absentee ballots be sent to their homes. Before, although voters were not required to have an excuse for voting absentee, they still had to go through the process of requesting an absentee ballot. In California, and now fourteen other states as well, that is no longer the case; when people initially request an absentee ballot, they can also ask that one be sent permanently.[43] By 2008, roughly one third of California's registered voters had requested absentee ballots permanently.[44]

Similar to same-day voter registration, the goal of less restrictive absentee voting laws is to expand the electorate. Using California as an example again, it is clear that more people are voting absentee. Figure 2.1 shows the percentage of the electorate in California voting absentee in presidential elections covering 1980–2008.[45] While slightly more than 5 percent of Californians cast their ballots by absentee in 1980, that percentage grew steadily to roughly 40 percent in 2008. It is not clear, however, that absentee voting is actually expanding the electorate. As Figure 2.1 also illustrates, the percentage of eligible voters casting their ballots has not increased. The results in Figure 2.1 are similar to what more rigorous studies of the influence of liberalized absentee voting laws find regarding voter turnout. While less restrictive absentee laws change the kinds of people who vote absentee,[46] they have a minimal effect at best in terms of increasing voter turnout.[47] There is some speculation that the lack of a significant increase in voter turnout is because the costs associated with mobilization make it more difficult for parties to muster voters over such a long period of time.[48]

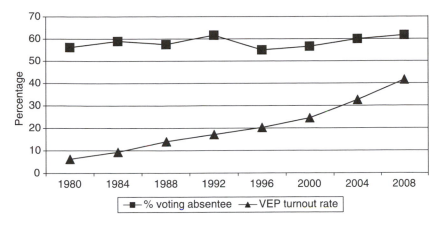

Figure 2.1 Absentee Voting and Voter Turnout Rates in California, 1980–2008
Source: California Secretary of State webpage.

In addition to less restrictive absentee laws, other states allow voters to cast their ballots early in places such as clerks' offices, libraries, or supermarkets. Again, the goal here is to make voting more convenient by giving people more opportunities to go to the polls. As with less restrictive absentee laws, most studies find marginal effects of early voting on turnout rates.[49] The people who take advantage of such reforms are people who are already likely to vote.[50] In other words, no-excuse absentee laws and early in-person voting are not expanding the electorate; they are simply making it easier for people who usually vote to do so.

Oregon has gone one step further, requiring that all Oregonians vote by mail. Roughly 30 days before an election, ballots are sent to registered voters who then have the option of sending back their ballots via the mail or dropping them off with an election administrator before election day. The process of voting cannot get any easier than having a ballot sent directly to you in the mail. While there is some evidence that all-mail voting does increase turnout, it too seems to benefit those who are already more likely to vote.[51] Once more, habitual voters benefit by lowering the costs of voting; however, apparently the costs of voting are not lessened enough to bring many new people into the electorate.

Even if turnout did increase significantly as a result of the less restrictive absentee laws, early in-person voting, and vote by mail, some people have questioned the wisdom of encouraging more voting not done at a precinct. With the opportunity to vote early, election day now becomes *election days* or an election period. In Maine, voters can cast ballots three months before election day![52] The problem with this, opponents argue, is threefold. First, the nature of campaigns changes immensely. Because voters can begin voting so far before election day, candidates must get their message to the public that much faster. This means that candidates must raise money earlier and campaigns are likely to become negative sooner, as well. Second, early voters have not had the opportunity to consider all of the facts that arise during the election. Fund goes so far as to argue that the inability of voters to take into account all the information that arises during a campaign may have cost Al Gore the presidency. While Fund has no empirical evidence for his claim, he notes that the revelation the weekend before election day of George W. Bush's "driving under the influence" (DUI) charge in 1976 convinced many voters to cast their ballots for Gore. Absentee or early voters who may have changed their minds because of the charge could not change their votes. While it is true that the nature of campaigning is different and that voters cannot evaluate the candidates based on the entire campaign, these problems are lessened by the fact that most early voters tend to be highly partisan.[53] Because their minds are likely made up well before election day, it is unlikely that they would vote differently if they were exposed to new information. The third problem with allowing people to vote over a period of a few weeks is that it undermines the ideal of an important civic ritual. There is something to be said for having a day where everyone votes. John Mark Hansen writes:

> Election Day is one of the few opportunities Americans have to do something important together as a nation. It is the one time when the American people come together to govern themselves through the choice of their leaders. To critics, to make participation in this important civic rite a matter to be pursued at an individual's convenience is to undermine the sense of our nationhood, our common experience in the government, of, by, and for the people.[54]

However, many Americans do not seem to share Hansen's values as convenience is often listed as the main reason why people vote absentee.[55]

Political scientists R. Michael Alvarez and Thad Hall argue that the concerns of people like Fund and Hansen are exaggerated.[56] For instance, they note that there is no research that indicates that people who vote early have diminished civic values compared to those who do not vote early. Nor does research find that early voters are less informed than precinct voters.

Yet, there are other issues with non-election day voting than the expansion of an election period and the undermining of a civic rite, especially regarding absentee voting. First, there is concern about the possibility for increased fraud and voter coercion. In the privacy of a voting booth, the ballot is truly secret; that is not necessarily the case when one votes absentee. Moreover, it is possible that someone who is not the voter herself completes the absentee ballot. While several states require signatures to verify who the voter is, "most states do not routinely check signatures either on applications or on returned ballots."[57] As Hansen concludes in his report for the Task Force on the Federal Election System, "Certainly, the potential for fraud is present, and all the more so because so much of the process is beyond the supervision of election officials."[58]

As important, the propensity for a voter to commit an error and not have his or her ballot counted increases substantially with absentee voting. According to Michael McDonald, "perhaps as many as 500,000 to 750,000 mail-in ballots were rejected in the 2008 election" because of voter error, including failure to sign the ballot or properly sealing the envelope.[59] When voting in person, an election official can alert a voter to a potential error on the ballot. No such opportunity exists when voting absentee.

Times and Dates of Elections

Another obstacle to voting that Americans face that citizens of many other countries do not is that in the United States election day is neither a holiday nor is it held on the weekend. As a result, it may be difficult for some people to get to the polls. When I lived in Los Angeles, I experienced this firsthand. I lived about 45 minutes from campus and had to teach an 8:00 a.m. class. I also had a late afternoon class and by the time I got home (after fighting Los Angeles traffic) I almost arrived after the polls had closed.

Support for making election day a national holiday appeared to gain some momentum after the National Commission on Federal Election Reform, created after the 2000 elections and headed by former Presidents Gerald Ford and Jimmy Carter, endorsed the idea. The Commission supported moving Veterans Day to the current election day, arguing that making election day a national holiday would make it easier to recruit poll workers and for some people to vote. However, the proposal was opposed vehemently by veterans groups such as the American Legion and Veterans of Foreign Wars, and the idea quickly lost traction. Furthermore, business leaders would not be apt to support a national election-day holiday because of the loss of revenue that would come with it. Even the public is not strongly in favor of the idea. Democrats and independents are more likely to support an election-day holiday, while Republicans are more likely to be opposed.[60]

Another possibility is to hold elections over the weekend. There is no reason why voting in precincts has to be limited to one day. Weekend voting would have all of the benefits of making election day a national holiday without upsetting veterans or business leaders, both of which are powerful lobbies. Conflicts would not exist because of religious beliefs since people could vote on either Saturday or Sunday. Surely weekend voting would increase the costs of conducting elections because precincts would have to be open two days instead of one, but, as I argued earlier, consolidating the number of times people are asked to vote will help lessen the costs of adding an extra day of voting. Moreover, while some people claim that voter turnout would actually decline because people are busy over the weekend, empirical evidence shows the opposite.[61]

Going to weekend voting would be a major change from the status quo and likely difficult to enact. In fact, a bill to implement weekend voting was introduced recently in Congress but failed to gain any traction. And, given the expansion of the election period discussed earlier, many people argue that weekend voting is now unnecessary. One reform that is simple to pass and would have similar effects as weekend voting is to keep polls open longer. In 2010, 52 percent of the states had poll closing times of 7:30 p.m. or earlier, with three closing at 6:00 p.m. Furthermore, 92 percent of the states had closed their polls by 8:00 p.m. Only in Iowa, New York, North Dakota, and Rhode Island did polls stay open until 9:00 p.m.

Expanding the hours in which polls are open would make situations like my voting experience, described earlier, less likely. In fact, according to US Census Bureau, approximately 1 million people reported that long lines, *inconvenient hours*, or polling-place locations were the main reason they did not vote in the 2000 election (my emphasis).[62] It would cost more to keep the polls open longer, but the cost of staying open an additional two or three hours does not seem burdensome. Perhaps the only real problem with keeping precincts open longer is that more poll workers, who are difficult to recruit in the first place, would be needed. Staying open later, however, would allow people who work during the day to volunteer at night. Most important, one study of closing times determined that turnout is higher in states whose polls are open longer, even when controlling other factors that influence turnout.[63] This rise in turnout does not come at the expense of increasing possible fraud or voter errors as is the case with absentee voting. Additionally, the public strongly supports the idea of later poll closing times. Close to 80 percent of the public believes that the polls should be open later than 7:00 p.m.; 34 percent, the modal category, thought they should close at 10:00 p.m.[64]

Voter Identification

The previous reforms mentioned, such as same-day voter registration or no-excuse absentee voting, are designed to eliminate perceived barriers to voting by lowering costs. However, opponents of another reform that has gained traction in the past several years argue that it creates an unnecessary barrier to voting. In several states, including Indiana and Georgia, people are required to show a government-issued photo identification in order to vote. The debate over voter identification has become one of the most heated, controversial issues related to election reform in recent years.

Supporters of requiring a person to show photo identification in order to vote, usually Republicans, argue that such a law is needed to combat voter fraud. People are required to show photo identification for all kinds of things, such as flying on an airplane, to prove that they are who they say they are, the argument goes, so they should have to do so when voting as well.

Opponents of voter identification, usually Democrats, argue that the reform essentially amounts to a poll tax placed on voters, especially the poor, disabled, elderly, and minorities.[65] Not everyone has a government-issued photo identification and, in order to obtain one, people have to pay a fee. For example, in Indiana if people cannot present a passport or a driver's license, then they must supply an official document to get a free photo identification card. However, that official document is usually something like a birth certificate, which, if a person does not have, costs money to obtain. Opponents of voter identification also argue that the reform is not needed. Evidence of in-person voter fraud is extremely rare and is not enough to justify the implementation of additional burdens on potential voters.

Because of the controversy over photo identification laws, they have been challenged in court, both at the federal and state levels. Perhaps most importantly, in *Crawford v. Marion County Election Board* (2008), the Supreme Court weighed in on the issue.[66] In a 6–3 decision, the Court ruled that Indiana's identification law was justified because of the state's interest in preventing fraud, even though no case of actual in-person fraud was documented. The Court also held that voter identification laws promoted confidence in elections, which encouraged participation. However, the Court did leave open the door to future challenges to photo identification laws if other state laws provide too much of a burden on voters.[67]

The controversy over photo identification is one of the most frustrating election reform debates to follow. Neither side appears to be willing to give an inch, yet both have difficulty providing persuasive empirical evidence for their claims. It does not seem unreasonable to require people to show photo identification at the polls—if, as scholar Norman Ornstein says, "it's done properly."[68] Ornstein argues, and I agree, that if a state has a voter identification law, then that identification must be free (and, unlike in Indiana, so must the documents, such as birth certificates, that are needed to obtain that identification) and easily accessible. Ornstein promotes the idea of mobile vans to transport people who otherwise cannot get there to sites that provide identification.

However, I also agree with Ornstein that in-person voter fraud is not the problem. As Ornstein writes, "I do not have any Pollyannish notion that most people in politics are good and fair ... But, frankly engaging in systematic in-person fraud is way too much effort for way too little payoff. To be sure, there are occasional instances of either sloppiness or chicanery in voter registration drives, and individual instances of wrongdoing. But every allegation of big-time fraud ends up being defeated by the evidence."[69]

If voter fraud is a problem, then it is a problem with absentee voting not in-person voting. Ironically, voter identification laws like Indiana's do not apply to absentee voting. Therefore, it is not clear how effective such laws are likely to be. If implemented properly, I do not see a problem with voter identification laws. Yet, I am not convinced that they are needed (at least the way the laws on the books are currently written) either.

Felon Voting

Convicted felons present another controversy regarding voter eligibility. As with the other issues discussed in this chapter, decisions regarding felon voting are left to the states. In all states but two (Maine and Vermont), people who are incarcerated are prevented from voting. Several other states reinstate voting rights after a person has completed his or her time in jail or after he or she is off on parole and/or probation. Nine states, including Alabama and Tennessee, permanently disenfranchise at least some felons.[70]

Like the voter identification debate, the controversy regarding felon voting often breaks along partisan lines, with Democrats more likely to oppose permanent disenfranchisement than Republicans. It is easy to understand why the issue is so partisan. According to one study, felons are significantly more likely than the pubic as a whole to support Democratic candidates. In fact, this same study argued that three U.S. Senate elections as well as the 2000 presidential election would likely have had different outcomes, had previously incarcerated felons had the right to vote.[71]

Supporters of permanent disenfranchisement of felon voting argue that voting is a privilege and that by removing voting rights it sends the message that committing a crime can have serious consequences. Opponents claim that once felons have served their debt to society, they should have their rights restored. "We let ex-convicts marry, reproduce, buy beer, own property and drive," writes columnist Steve Chapman. "They don't lose their freedom of religion, their right against self-incrimination or their right not to have soldiers quartered in their homes in time of war. But in many places, the assumption is that they can't be trusted to help choose our leaders ... If we thought criminals could never be reformed, we wouldn't let them out of prison in the first place."[72] Moreover, there is some evidence that allowing felons to vote may reduce recidivism rates.[73]

Perhaps the greatest controversy over felon disenfranchisement laws is whether such laws are unconstitutional. Because one in six African American males is ineligible to vote as a result of a current or past felony conviction[74] some reformers argue that felon disenfranchisement laws violate the Voting Rights Act (VRA) of 1965, which is designed to protect the voting rights of racial or ethnic minorities. Under Section 2 of the VRA, voting practices that discriminate on the basis of race or color are not permitted. Until recently federal appellate courts have provided conflicting rulings on this issue. In previous cases, including *Simmons v. Galvin* (2009),[75] circuit courts upheld felon disenfranchisement laws. In *Simmons*, for example, the First Circuit held that Congress never intended the VRA to have any relevance to felon disenfranchisement. However, in January of 2010, in the case *Farrakhan v. Gregoire*,[76] the Ninth Circuit overturned Washington's felon disenfranchisement law because it violated Section 2 of the VRA. In both the *Simmons* and *Farrakhan* cases, the courts were divided 2–1, an indication of how contentious the issue is. However, because of the controversy surrounding the initial ruling, the Ninth Circuit heard the *Farrakhan* case, *en banc* (meaning all of the judges on the circuit hear the case) in September of 2010. In that ruling, the court overturned the Ninth Circuit's earlier decision. As a result, federal courts are no longer divided on the issue.

Even with the Ninth Circuit's *en banc* ruling, permanent felon disenfranchisement laws may still become extinct because there has been movement in recent years away from such laws. Numerous states have loosened their felon disenfranchisement statutes. According to ProjectVote, an organization dedicated to eliminating felon disenfranchisement laws, since 1997 "nine states either repealed or amended lifetime disenfranchisement laws; two states expanded voting rights to persons under community supervision (probation and parole);[and] six states eased the restoration process for persons seeking to have their right to vote restored after completing sentence."[77] Public opinion supports this trend. One study found that, although only 31 percent of the public favors giving prisoners the right to vote, 80 percent support restoring the franchise to felons who have served their time and are no longer on probation or parole.[78]

I am ambivalent on allowing people who are currently incarcerated to vote. When convicted of a crime, it does not seem unreasonable that people relinquish certain rights while serving their punishment. Whether such laws violate the Voting Rights Act is a difficult question in which judges on the courts are divided. I see no reason, however, to deny a person who has completed his or her sentence the right to vote. Felons owe a debt to society. Once that debt has been paid, they should have the ability to participate in a process to determine who represents them in government. Some may question the judgment of convicted felons and wonder why they should potentially have the ability to influence the outcomes of elections. However, there are many people whose judgment can be questioned, not just convicted felons. I abhor people who cheat on tests, and question their judgment. Yet, no one prevents cheaters from voting in an election. Determining whether a person has the right to vote based on his or her judgment is dangerous. Moreover, one would hope that felons might be rehabilitated and become productive members of society. Although one should interpret these results with caution, empirical evidence exists that allowing felons to vote may contribute to that rehabilitation.[79]

Compulsory Voting

Most of the reforms in this chapter have the goal of increasing voter turnout. One final possibility to increase voter turnout is to simply make it the law that one must vote. To most Americans this concept is foreign, but countries including Australia, Belgium, and Greece require their citizens to cast a ballot, although they do not have to actually vote for a candidate. The punishments vary by country for not voting and some countries do not enforce the law, but usually people are fined the equivalent of a parking ticket. At one time, the names of Italians who did not vote was posted outside the local town hall as punishment.

Perhaps the greatest advocate of compulsory voting in the United States is noted political scientist Arend Lijphart, who argues that compulsory voting may provide stronger incentives to participate in other political activities, reduce the role of money in politics, and discourage attack advertising.[80] It would also likely eliminate the socioeconomic differences that currently exist between voters and nonvoters. Furthermore, Lijphart argues that "mandatory voting *may* serve as an incentive to become better informed" (my emphasis).[81] However, Lijphart only provides anecdotal evidence for this last claim.

The most frequent argument against compulsory voting is that it violates a person's right to not vote, either out of protest or because they do not want to take the time to be informed. Lijphart notes that the "right *not* to vote remains intact" (emphasis in original; remember, you only have to cast a ballot not actually make a vote) and that "compulsory voting entails a very small decrease in freedom compared with many other problems of collective action that democracies solve by imposing obligations: jury duty, the obligation to pay taxes, military conscription, compulsory school attendance, and many others."[82]

Compulsory voting is an interesting idea. Other countries have used it and seem to have done so with few problems. However, most Americans are not likely to agree with Lijphart (my students certainly do not). To them, the right not to be engaged or informed is too important. I am skeptical of forcing people to vote because I am not as convinced as Lijphart that people will become more engaged and informed as a result of compulsory voting; I have yet to see any empirical evidence that this claim is true. It is sad to think that many Americans view it as their right not to be politically informed or engaged, though. Also, if nonvoters were charged with some monetary punishment, the poor (people who are less likely to vote) would be hurt most by compulsory voting.

One of the themes that resonates throughout this book is that we need to enact reforms that will allow citizens to participate more effectively in the political process. To go back to the Calculus of Voting, the reforms suggested here generally deal with lowering the costs of voting and removing barriers to voting. We definitely should consolidate the number of election days held and increase the hours that the polls are open. We should consider making election day a national holiday or holding it over the weekend, although given the expansion of early voting in many states this reform becomes less pertinent. Same-day voter registration is worth enacting as long as safeguards, such as provisional voting, are put in place to prevent fraud. The movement toward early in-person voting appears to be positive as well. Though early in-person voting does not appear to expand the electorate, systematic empirical evidence has yet to show that it has adverse effects on the quality of voting or the administration of elections.

Compared to no-excuse absentee voting, early in-person voting is the better option. Voting in person ensures privacy when voting and lessens the probability that voters will commit an error. Additionally, voter fraud is much less likely to occur with early in-person voting than with absentee voting. In general the more voting that is completed in the presence of an election official, the better. One concern that I have with early in-person voting, however, is that it extends an election season that is already too long by forcing candidates to campaign for votes earlier. If states are to enact early voting, then voting centers should only open a week before election day to minimize the length of the campaign season.

No-excuse absentee voting is trickier. As someone who lived in a state where I had to show proof that I attended a university outside of that state in order to get an absentee ballot, I know how much of a pain it was to do so. Moreover, early in-person voting is not an option for a student who is registered in another state. So, young people in particular benefit from no-excuse absentee voting. However, no-excuse absentee voting brings with it problems that early in-person voting does not. First, the opportunity for fraud to occur is greater. Ironically, the voter identification statutes discussed earlier do not apply to absentee balloting, only in-person voting—a reason why many question the effectiveness of voter identification laws. Second, voters are more likely to have their ballots rejected because they commit an error such as forgetting to sign their ballots or by filling in their ballots incorrectly. The former is not a problem and the latter is a correctable error with in-person voting.

The reforms discussed in this chapter will make it more convenient for those who already vote to do so, which is certainly positive. However, we should not expect an enormous jump in voter turnout rates, even if we enacted all of them. Lowering the costs of voting is only one part of the equation; we need to determine ways to increase the benefits citizens see in voting. One empirical study finds that lowering the costs of voting does boost turnout, but that increasing the benefits is much more important.[83] How this can be done is difficult to say and beyond the scope of this book, but if the goal is to expand the electorate, although not everyone is convinced that this is a worthwhile goal, the best way to do so is to convince people why they should vote, not simply make it easier for them to do so.

Chapter 3

The Offices We Elect

Do you know the job responsibilities of the public weigher? How about the public service commissioner or the corporation commissioner? Can you list the qualities of a good coroner or insurance commissioner? What would be the difference between Democratic and Republican candidates for constable or commissioner of public utilities? In states and localities across the country, citizens have the opportunity to vote for candidates for those offices and many more. Not only are Americans constantly called to the polls as mentioned in the previous chapter, when they get there they are asked to vote for an amazing number of offices. For many of these offices, not only do voters have very little information about the candidates, but the responsibilities of the elected official may not even be entirely clear to them. In many cases, these offices are neither responsible for policymaking nor have much influence over policy. Moreover, the majority of the time a cheap, reliable cue—the candidate's party affiliation—is not listed on the ballot. As political scientist Martin Wattenberg writes, "[I]t would probably take an individual approximately the amount of time required for one or two college-level courses a year in order to cast a completely informed vote for all of these offices in all of these elections."[1]

In this chapter, I argue that the number of elected offices at the state and local levels should be reduced dramatically. Doing so would significantly lower the information costs facing voters, making it easier for them to participate more effectively in elections. Since one could debate forever exactly which offices should be elected, I spend most of this chapter addressing one particular type of elected office: judge. Because of the nature of the position, few elections are more controversial than those for judgeships. Supporters of judicial elections argue that they are needed to hold judges accountable, but that is exactly the problem. We do not want judges who slavishly follow public will. Furthermore, judicial elections create the potential for significant conflicts of interest, which can undermine due process and the justice system. As a result, Americans should not vote for state judges. However, before making my argument against judicial elections, I want to briefly discuss why it is that Americans vote for so many offices in the first place and why this fact is not necessarily good for democracy.

Do We Really Need to Vote for Coroner?

A quick look at the number of statewide elected offices shows the daunting task that many American voters face (see Table 3.1). The average state elects 6.38 statewide offices; voters in Maine, New Hampshire, and Tennessee are least taxed, electing only the governor statewide, while North Carolina takes the prize for the most elected statewide offices (12). The average number of statewide elected offices understates the amount of voting that is actually done by Americans because it is number of elected *offices* not elected *officials*. States that elect their supreme courts, for example, usually hold elections for several different seats. The number also does not include retention elections, nor does it include lieutenant governor candidates who are chosen by voters in a primary but then run on a ticket with the gubernatorial candidate in the general election. In addition, this number excludes the four federal offices for which citizens must vote: president, representative, and two senators; state representatives and senators (two in every state but Nebraska); and numerous local offices

Table 3.1 A Sample of the Elected Statewide Offices

Office	Number of states electing office
Governor	50
Attorney General	42
Secretary of State	35
Treasurer	35
Auditor	24
Supreme Court Justices	22[a]
Lieutenant Governor	19[b]
Intermediate Appellate Court Judges	18[a]
Superintendent of Public Instruction	14
Commissioner of Agriculture	11
Commissioner of Insurance	10
Comptroller	6
Commissioner of Public Service	5
Commissioner of Public Lands	4
Commissioner of Labor	4
Controller	3
Corporate Commissioner	2
Commissioner of Public Utilities	1
Commissioner of Railroads	1
Mine Inspector	1

Source: Compiled by author from states' secretary of state or elections division webpages.

Note: Some offices may have slightly different names in certain states (e.g., Commissioner of Agriculture, Secretary of Agriculture).

a Does not include states that hold retention elections.

b Does not include states where the gubernatorial and lieutenant gubernatorial candidates run as a ticket in the general election.

including everything from county commissioner and mayor to community college trustees and coroner. In other words, Americans are voting for a large number of people![2]

Why do Americans elect so many people to office? The answer is simple: accountability. As with many of the topics discussed in this book, the rise in the number of elected officials can be attributed to the progressive movement and its attempt to eliminate corruption and cronyism during the heyday of the city and, in some cases, state political machines. City bosses not only controlled the electoral process, but they determined who would fill a variety of local positions. The practice of patronage—politicians rewarding supporters with jobs—was rampant. Appointed officials often were not qualified to perform their duties and were accountable to the politician or boss who appointed them, not to the people they were supposed to serve.

As a result of patronage, we now elect an enormous number of elected officials, many of whose job responsibilities are only administrative in nature. Yet, the American public is skeptical of giving up its right to vote for these offices. For example, in the fall of 2006, the city of DeKalb, IL, voted whether to keep its clerk as an elected official or instead make it an appointed position. Among the responsibilities that fall under the clerk are the keeper of the city's records and seal. The clerk is not responsible for any policymaking decisions. Yet, 62.5 percent of voters wanted to retain the city clerk as an elected position. When running for office a few years later, candidates for the city clerk position ran on platforms that included updating the city clerk's webpage, opening the clerk's office during the lunch hour, and posting the minutes of city council meetings online earlier.[3]

As the DeKalb city clerk case illustrates, Americans are reluctant to give up their right to vote for a wide range of offices. When I discuss the option of eliminating elections for a variety of offices with my students, they usually retort that doing so is "undemocratic" or "un-American." But is an election where few people know what the responsibilities of the office are, much less the qualifications of the candidates, really democratic? If we know virtually nothing about these offices, then can we really hold elected officials accountable?

Appointment of government officials is not a perfect system. One would be naïve to argue that patronage no longer exists, although it certainly has been curtailed since its heyday. But, governors, mayors, or other elected officials responsible for appointments must be careful to appoint qualified people to positions or else *they* will face the wrath of the voters. Moreover, if people are worried about patronage, then, similar to the federal level of government, checks on the appointment powers of governors and mayors can be easily implemented. The president nominates members of his cabinet and other federal officials, but his nominees must be confirmed by the Senate. Nothing keeps the state legislatures or city councils from performing a similar function. Furthermore, there is no reason that appointed officials must be appointed for life.

Interestingly, there has been virtually no research, to my knowledge, conducted regarding the differences in qualifications of elected versus appointed officials, although scholars have conducted some research on this question as it relates to judges. One can surmise that there are probably not great differences between the qualifications or the performance of elected versus appointed officials. Even so, American voters become unduly taxed by a system that asks them to vote for so many people. Only a small number of people can participate effectively when voting in so many elections. And, as I discuss in Chapter 5, electing so many offices creates an unnecessarily confusing ballot as well as makes it more difficult to consolidate elections. Exactly which positions should be appointed and which should be elected are beyond the scope of this book, but there is no reason why the number of elected officials should not be decreased significantly.

The Case of Judicial Elections

Instead of making a case for which officials should be elected and which should be appointed, I want to spend the rest of this chapter focusing on one specific office, that of judge. Questions about whether judges should be elected are especially contentious because of the nature of the position. Unlike most other elected officials, there is great debate about whether judges should be held accountable by the people because accountability may sacrifice the cherished notion of judicial independence that was so important to the founders. As a result of controversy over elected judges, a more thorough discussion is warranted.

Why Do We Have Judicial Elections?

Before turning to the arguments for and against judicial elections, it is important to understand how they came about in the first place. Federal judges do not have to run for their seats on the bench; the Constitution makes clear that they are appointed for life by the president and confirmed by the Senate.[4] However, because of federalism each state decides the rules of its judicial system. Since variation exists across states, the judicial selection process at this level is far more complex. There are literally 50 different sets of rules regarding selection process, term length, and reappointment. Maine and New Jersey simply follow the federal model with the state's executive appointing the judge subject to confirmation by the state Senate. Other states, such as Hawaii and New Hampshire, create nominating committees composed of state lawyers and judges who make recommendations to the governor. Then, the governor appoints one of the candidates put forth by the nominating commission. South Carolina follows essentially the same process, but the actual appointment is made by the state legislature, not the governor. Virginia continues to use the plan adopted by the majority of the states after the ratification of the Constitution; its judges are appointed (and reappointed) by the state legislature.

Nonetheless, the appointment of state justices without an electoral component is infrequent. Thirty-nine states use some sort of electoral process to choose at least some of their judges and 87 percent of the general jurisdiction appellate and trial judges run in popular elections.[5] Judicial elections are usually nonpartisan, meaning that the candidates' party affiliations are not listed on the ballot (see Chapter 5 for a critique of nonpartisan elections), but a few states, including Alabama, Illinois, and Texas, hold partisan elections just like those held for Congress or the state house.

The quirkiest electoral aspect of the judicial selection process is the retention election, also named the Missouri Plan, after the state that first adopted it. In retention elections, judges are initially appointed to the bench, usually by the governor, in some cases with nominating committees, and in some cases without them, to serve a certain length of a term, say 12 years. After the term expires, voters have the opportunity to retain the justice. The judge does not run against an opponent; voters simply vote "Yes" if they would like to keep the justice and "No" if they want someone new. If a judge is not retained, a new one is appointed and the process starts over again.

To complicate matters more, not all states use just one of the three electoral components of judicial selection. Instead, some states incorporate different rules for different judicial positions. In California, for example, judges for the supreme and intermediate appellate courts are appointed to 12-year terms and then must face retention elections, while candidates for the superior court must run in nonpartisan elections and are elected to six-year terms. Arizona appoints justices to its appellate courts via a nominating commission. For superior court seats in counties with populations greater than 250,000, a nominating commission is used. In counties with populations less than 250,000, nonpartisan elections are held.

While judicial elections are quite common today, it has not always been that way. In fact, after the ratification of the Constitution, following the argument of Hamilton and others about the importance of judicial independence, no state elected judges. Instead, the state legislature or governor appointed judges. In states where the governor appointed judges, the legislature or a commission made up of state legislators approved the appointment to act as a check on gubernatorial power. It was not until the election of Andrew Jackson and the rise of "Jacksonian democracy" that states began to consider electing judges, although the idea was hinted at by Jefferson as early as his writing of the Declaration of Independence. What set Jackson's presidency apart was the movement toward granting the "common person" more political influence. Also, around the time of Jackson's tenure, more states began to enter the Union. These states questioned the appointment process because it limited the accountability of judges to the people and, therefore, was perceived as being undemocratic. In 1832, Mississippi became the first state to amend its constitution to require that all state judges be elected. By the time of the Civil War, 24 of 34 states had an elected judiciary.[6] In fact, every state that entered the Union between 1846 and Alaska's admission in 1959 allowed for the election of some, if not all, of its judges.[7]

"He's not that Gene Kelly"

Public support for judicial elections is quite strong. A survey sponsored by the Justice at Stake Campaign, a nonpartisan organization comprising more than 30 judicial, legal, and citizen organizations, found that 52 percent of respondents supported merit selection followed by a retention election. Another 19 percent favored holding nonpartisan elections, and 7 percent believed that judicial elections should be partisan. Only 18 percent responded that there should be no electoral component to the judicial selection process.[8]

Even though people want judicial elections, one criticism of holding them is the argument that voters are uninformed in these contests. My own classrooms over the years have provided some support for this claim. Throughout my years in academia, I have had the pleasure of teaching more than a thousand students. Every semester I ask them if they recall the name of a judicial candidate for whom they voted; only once has a student been able to answer "yes." It turned out his girlfriend's mom had just run for a judgeship. To be honest, I am no different from my students. If I were quizzed upon leaving the voting booth, I am not sure that I could recall the names of judicial candidates on the ballot. Anything I knew about them was based on nothing more than a few lines in a voter information guide or the recommendation of a trusted friend.

There is far more systematic evidence than just me and my students that voters in judicial elections are not very informed. A study of judicial elections in Washington and Oregon finds that an overwhelming majority of people reported not having enough information to cast an informed ballot.[9] Like my students, most people do not even know who the candidates are. Surveys discover consistently that voters do not recall, or even *recognize*, who they voted for in judicial contests, much less why. In one study, only 14.5 percent of people interviewed immediately after voting could identify a single judicial candidate on the ballot.[10] Not only can people not remember who they voted for, they do not remember the winners either. A study of the Ohio State Supreme Court finds that only 4 percent of Ohioans could name a justice on the highest court in the state.[11]

Voting in judicial elections becomes even more problematic when one considers that few states hold partisan judicial elections, taking away a cheap, reliable signal from voters. Instead, voters are forced to rely on a candidate's ethnicity[12] or gender[13]—hardly dependable cues. There is evidence that people consult voter pamphlets distributed by the secretary of state before the election.[14] While certainly better than nothing, these pamphlets often provide little meaningful information to help people decide how to vote. For example, in the five 2004 Californian judicial races in which I voted, only four of the 10 candidates provided statements; in only one race did both candidates give a write-up.[15] In that race, the candidates listed endorsements of a wide range of individuals and groups, but the information was of little help. They each received endorsements from law-enforcement agencies and were rated "well qualified" by the Los Angeles County Bar. Prominent Democrats backed both. While Los Angeles County Sheriff Lee Baca endorsed one, he said about the other, "Judy Meyer has shown herself to be a person of honesty, integrity, and sound judgment." From the candidates' statements, it is extremely difficult to determine which candidate is more qualified and would do a better job. At least one study of intermediate appellate court elections finds that providing information guides to voters does not increase the number of people casting votes in an election.[16]

There have certainly been funny (or scary, depending on one's perspective) examples that call into question the rationality of judicial election voters. Perhaps this is best illustrated by a 1997 Texas Supreme Court race. A man named Gene Kelly beat an intermediate appellate judge who was supported by both the plantiff's bar and the defense bar—a rare happening—in the primary. Kelly then spent less than $8,000 in the general election against an opponent who exhausted more than $1,000,000, mostly on ads reminding voters "He's Not That Gene Kelly." Kelly still captured 44 percent of the vote. Had his name been Fred Astaire, I am sure he would have won. The Kelly race may not have been Texas' most dubious judicial election. In 1976, an unknown lawyer named Don Yarbrough—who just happened to have the same last name as the state's longtime popular Senator, Ralph, and the *same name* as a man who had run two competitive campaigns for governor—beat a well-respected judge who had strong support from the state bar. Yarbrough won, despite numerous ethics complaints that were filed against him, and later resigned due to criminal charges. In another questionable judicial election, a Washington man who had the same name as a popular Tacoma television anchor raised $500 and did not campaign. This noncampaign was still effective enough to beat Washington's sitting chief justice.

Not everyone believes that judicial election voters are incompetent. In fact, two of the most vocal defenders of judicial elections and my co-authors on another project, political scientists Melinda Gann Hall and Chris Bonneau, argue that people are able to make fairly sophisticated decisions in judicial elections. Analyzing aggregate data in supreme court elections, Hall and Bonneau find that quality challengers—measured by whether the candidate had previously served on a lower court—do better than non-quality challengers.[17] They also note that participation is greater the closer the election. Based on this evidence, they assert that people are capable of distinguishing between the qualifications of judicial candidates. However, my research with Brian Frederick on intermediate appellate court (IAC) elections finds that voters are not able to distinguish between quality and non-quality challengers and that only the most competitive of IAC races lead to more participation.[18] Moreover, because Hall and Bonneau use aggregate data, they cannot know for certain that people are actually voting based on the candidates' qualifications. It could be simply that name recognition is driving a person's vote—not qualifications—and people who are considered to be quality challengers just have more name recognition.

Whether voters are able to make sophisticated decisions in judicial elections is an interesting empirical question, but, even if they cannot, there are more significant problems with judicial elections. If states would simply hold partisan judicial elections, then voters would be able to rely on a cheap, reliable cue to cast a somewhat informed vote. While party identification is not a perfect cue, it is far better than other alternatives, such as gender, race, or name recognition. Moreover, for all the concern about the information-levels of judicial voters, surprisingly little—if any—difference exists between the quality of elected and appointed judges.[19] The real problem with judicial elections is not the ability of the voter, but the fact that judicial elections create the strong possibility for conflicts of interest, which can undermine due process, and threaten minority rights—integral components of a free society. I turn to both of these issues now.

Justice for Sale?

Running in elections requires candidates to campaign and campaigns cost money—usually lots of it. Judicial campaigns are no different and are becoming much more expensive. Here is an astonishing number. In one 2004 Illinois state supreme court race, two candidates spent a combined total of roughly $10 million, the most expensive judicial race in history. The contest was more expensive than 19 of the 34 US Senate races held that year.[20] The amount of money spent in supreme court elections has been on the rise. Between 2000 and 2009, judicial candidates for the high courts raised $206.4 million compared to only $83.3 million from the previous decade.[21] The substantial spending is not limited to the supreme court level; one candidate for a Georgia intermediate appellate court seat spent more than $3 million of his own money in 2004.[22]

Campaign spending in judicial elections is not inherently negative. Indeed, the more money the candidates spend, the greater the likelihood that a person will learn something about the candidates. The problem is where the money is coming from. Not surprisingly, business and trial lawyers, two groups who are likely to appear before the court, are the biggest donors to judicial candidates.[23] In 2006, they combined to donate 65 percent of money given to state supreme court candidates (roughly $22.5 million).[24] The Florida Bar Association estimates that 80 percent of all campaign contributions to its state judges comes from lawyers.[25] In the 2004 Illinois race mentioned previously, one group estimated that national tort reform groups contributed more than

$1 million to one candidate, while the other received money primarily from trial lawyers.[26] And, while controversial 527 organizations played a major role in the 2004 presidential election, they were not silent in judicial elections either. In West Virginia, one 527 group spent at least $4.5 million to successfully beat an incumbent.[27] The organization, known as "And for the Sake of the Kids," accused Justice Warren McGraw of being lenient on child molesters and was funded primarily by the chief executive officer of Massey Energy. With the Supreme Court's ruling in *Citizens United v. FEC* (2010), in which the Court held that corporations and labor could not be barred from independent spending on election campaigns, many people are worried that the influence of these groups in judicial elections will only grow (see chapter 10 for a more detailed discussion of the *Citizens United* case).[28]

Advocates of judicial elections argue that candidates for all offices accept money; therefore, a conflict of interest always exists. But, the difference between a congressperson who cannot wield much influence without the help of a couple hundred of her colleagues, and a judge who simply has the power in many instances to rule on a case or significantly influence the outcome of a case because of her rulings during the case, is enormous. Tort reform organizations or trial lawyers giving money to judicial candidates is the equivalent of allowing a student to donate money to help fund a professor's research project and then take the professor's class. Even the most honest professor is likely to be slightly influenced by the monetary contribution. The idea that individuals or groups can give money to a judicial candidate's campaign and then appear before that judge, who is expected to be an objective arbiter of justice, is extremely problematic.

The dangers of campaign contributions are duly noted by Deborah Goldberg, the former Director of the Democracy Program at the Brennan Center for Justice and a leading expert on judicial elections. "High candidate spending . . . means that special interest groups are giving substantial amounts directly to judicial candidates, furthering the impression that justice is for sale," says Goldberg.[29] Public opinion surveys support Goldberg's point. Though the public backs judicial elections, 72 percent reported concerns that the money raised by judicial candidates compromised the judges' impartiality. Even judges acknowledged they were not immune. Twenty-six percent of judges *admitted* that campaign donations have at least some influence on their decisions; this does not include those judges who would refuse to publicly say that donations influenced them even in an anonymous survey.[30] Moreover, political scientist Jim Gibson finds evidence that campaign contributions and the appearance of impropriety generated by contributions have the capacity to diminish citizen perceptions of impartiality in courts.[31]

Of course, whether campaign contributions and independent spending in judicial elections influence judicial decisions is a different matter, and a complex issue to study. Some empirical evidence—limited as it may be—exists indicating that contributions could influence judicial decisions.[32] Additionally, anecdotal evidence exists that campaign donations limit judicial independence. In a study of judicial elections in Cook County, Illinois, a commission reported:

> Given the method of judicial selection in Cook County, it is not surprising that the testimony before our Commission indicates a serious lack of judicial independence in Cook County. Along the way to the bench, judicial candidates become embroiled in reciprocal obligations to political sponsors, ward and township committeemen, as well as to campaign contributors, many of whom are likely to be attorneys who appear before the judge. Too many judges feel obliged to return these favors . . . One aspect of judicial elections—campaign fundraising—has a particularly corrosive effect upon public perceptions of judicial independence.[33]

There is also substantial evidence that judges fail to recuse themselves from cases in which they have received campaign contributions from one of the parties appearing before the court.[34] The failure of judges to recuse themselves from cases received public scrutiny after a controversial ruling made by the West Virginia Supreme Court. In the 2004 West Virginia Supreme Court election mentioned earlier, Don Blakenship, the CEO of Massey Coal, spent roughly $3 million independently in support of the campaign of a little-known attorney, Brent Benjamin, and in opposition to incumbent Justice Warren McGraw.[35] Benjamin defeated McGraw, winning 53 percent of the vote.

Blakenship's independent spending was controversial because it highlighted the increasingly expensive and negative nature of judicial elections. It became all the more contentious, however, once Blakenship and Massey Coal found themselves before the state supreme court on which Benjamin now sat. That court, in a 3–2 decision, overturned a $50 million verdict against Massey Coal. Benjamin failed to recuse himself from the case and cast the deciding vote.[36]

The controversy over Benjamin's refusal to recuse himself led all the way to the U.S. Supreme Court. In *Caperton et al., v. A.T. Massey Coal Co.* (2009), the Court ruled that the Due Process Clause required Benjamin to have recused himself "given the serious risk of actual bias." Yet, how exactly effective recusal laws will work remains unclear to me. How much money is needed to be spent for a conflict of interest to occur? What if that money is spent only in opposition to a candidate's opponent, but not in support of the candidate? Also, what happens if all of the justices on the bench have received donations from a certain person or group, something that possibly could happen given the money that some organizations are spending on elections and the small number of justices on the high court in some states?

Some states have tried to remove the conflict of interest by adopting public financing of judicial campaigns similar to the system used in presidential elections (see Chapter 10). Citizens check off a box on their income-tax returns, which provides money to be distributed to judicial candidates who qualify for public financing. Candidates are then given funds if they agree to limit their spending to that amount of money. The goal is to keep candidates from having to raise money from individuals or groups who might appear before the court.

In 2002, North Carolina became the first state to adopt full public financing for all appellate-level judicial campaigns. Many claim that the system is a resounding success. In the first judicial elections after its implementation, for example, all but two of the 16 candidates for five appellate court races enrolled to receive public funding. Of the five winners, four received public money; the fifth failed to qualify for it. Given the success of the program in North Carolina, New Mexico followed suit in 2007 and Wisconsin did so in 2009; several other states, including West Virginia, are considering public financing of judicial elections.

While public funding might seem like a step in the right direction, and it certainly is better than the alternative of candidates relying solely on donations, it is unclear how successful the program will be. The results of the North Carolina races are positive, but it has been only tested for a few election cycles. Whether the system might work over a long period of time remains to be seen. There certainly is evidence that speaks to the contrary. In the landmark campaign finance case, *Buckley v. Valeo* (1976), the Supreme Court held that campaign spending limits were unconstitutional because limiting spending "would necessarily restrict the quality and quantity of political discourse."[37] As a result, candidates cannot be forced to accept public funding and abide by spending limits. The *Buckley* decision allows for massive amounts of money to be spent, even in cases where candidates received public money. Unless the Court reverses its decision in *Buckley*—an unlikely occurrence—public financing will not be the beacon judicial reformers would like it to be.

Even if candidates were forced to accept public funds, conflicts of interest would not entirely disappear. Groups can still run issue advocacy ads and support or oppose a judge without directly contributing to a campaign. As I noted previously, noncandidate spending in judicial elections has grown enormously. Although a conflict of interest may not be direct, it remains. Indeed, public financing of judicial elections would not have eliminated the Massey Energy controversy in West Virginia mentioned earlier, because most of Blakenship's spending occurred independently of Benjamin's campaign. The best way to alleviate the conflict of interest is to eliminate judicial elections entirely.

Furthermore, it is not certain that public financing programs are sustainable. In the 2004 North Carolina judicial elections, only 7 percent of North Carolina taxpayers chose to allocate $3 of their taxes for the public funding of campaigns.[38] There is an ideological barrier to public financing with conservatives being far less likely to support public funding than liberals.[39] Perhaps most importantly, the constitutionality of such programs remains up in the air at the time of this writing. In June 2010, the Supreme Court barred Arizona from providing matching funds to candidates who accepted public financing (Arizona has a so-called Clean Elections law on its books for state legislative races). In Arizona, and in many other states with Clean Elections laws, the state provides "rescue funds" to candidates who accept public financing but run against candidates who do not. The Court is likely to hear whether such a provision is constitutional. If the rescue funds are declared to be unconstitutional, then the future of public financing laws is dubious.

The Problem with Judicial Accountability

Supporters of judicial elections argue that democracy demands accountability and the only way to keep representatives accountable is to hold elections. There are a few holes in this argument. First, judges are not representatives; they have no constituency. Second, accountability may sacrifice a judge's ability to remain impartial and fair, and to protect the rights of a minority. As Justice Anthony Kennedy said, "The law is a promise ... It is a promise of neutrality. If the promise is broken, if neutrality does not prevail, then the law, as we know it, the law as we respect it, ceases to exist. The reason for judicial independence is to preserve neutrality."[40] There is compelling empirical evidence that judges do not remain neutral if they are elected. Political scientists Paul Brace and Brent Boyea find that elected judges are less likely than appointed judges to overturn death penalty sentences. Moreover, in an election year, elected judges are less likely to overturn death penalty cases than they are when it is not an election year.[41] Additionally, a study of Pennsylvania trial court judges finds that judges become more punitive in criminal cases as their elections approached.[42] This is not justice.

Judges must look at the facts of the case when making their rulings, not be concerned with public outrage in an election year. There should not be a difference between appointed judges and elected judges in terms of the length of sentencing or how often death penalty sentences are overturned. The fact that there are differences implies a lack of equal protection under the law; people in states that elect their judges are not treated the same as people in states whose judges are appointed.

All of this likely has Alexander Hamilton rolling over in his grave. Hamilton, of course, argued for justices to be appointed and to serve lifetime terms. He was convinced that judges had to remain independent in order to "guard the Constitution and the rights of individuals."[43] Hamilton, like many of the founding fathers, believed that that the Constitution was the will of the people and that the job of justices was to protect that will from the momentary passions of a fickle public. Judges had to be insulated from politics, and if they were required to run for reelection their ability to protect the Constitution, and especially the rights of the minority, would be threatened. If judges were elected, instead of defending the Constitution, they would be forced to heed public opinion and make popular rulings to save their jobs.

Hamilton may have been wrong about life tenure on the bench; serving on a court for over 30 years as recently retired Justice Stevens did, as did Chief

Justice Rehnquist before his death, gives one person too much power, and often judges remain on the court well after they should, purely for political reasons. Set terms without the possibility of reappointment would stop judges from "hanging on" until a new president of the other party is elected. The ability to only serve one term would also keep a justice from making political decisions in order to boost her chances of being reappointed. However, Hamilton was absolutely right about the need for judicial independence. The job of a justice is to protect people's rights and freedoms, not to promote the popular will. As Fareed Zakaria powerfully argues in his book, *The Future of Freedom*, freedom and democracy do not always go hand in hand.[44] A country where 51 percent of the population votes to eliminate the civil liberties of 49 percent of the population is a democracy, but it certainly is not free. Minorities need protection and, in the United States, the courts offer that protection. If judicial elections are held, courts may cave when faced with protecting the rights of a minority. For example, had the Warren Court been forced to run for reelection, it is likely that the *Brown* ruling, declaring segregated schools to be inherently unconstitutional, would not have been decided for many more years. "It is hard to give voice to a political minority when officials are beholden to an electoral majority," notes former Californian supreme court justice Cruz Reynoso.[45] It is the courts that protect that voice.

Certainly Hamilton is not the only person to argue for judicial independence. In her concurring opinion in *Republican Party of Minnesota v. White* (2002), which declared unconstitutional the state's announce clause that prohibited judicial candidates from stating their views on disputed legal or political issues, Justice Sandra Day O'Connor, the only justice on the Court at the time to have run in a judicial election, cautioned against holding judicial elections.[46] "We of course want judges to be impartial, in the sense of being free from any personal stake in the outcome of the case to which they are assigned," writes O'Connor. "But if judges are subject to regular elections they are likely to feel they have at least some personal stake in the outcome of every publicized case. Elected judges cannot help being aware that if the public is not satisfied with the outcome of a particular case, it could hurt their reelection prospects."[47] O'Connor mentions only closely followed cases, but a ruling on a case that is not highly publicized at the time could still be made an issue in a later campaign and come back to haunt the judge.

I have never understood why people are so adamant about judicial accountability at the state and local level, but it seems to be of little concern at the federal level. If judicial accountability is so important, then shouldn't we elect federal judges? Presently, there is no movement to amend the Constitution to elect federal judges. Certainly, federal judges who serve for life are less likely to be held accountable (although in rare cases they can be impeached) than state judges. Why is it that judicial accountability is so important at the state level, but not at the federal level? If we were to elect any judge, one could argue that it should be federal supreme court justices, because the stakes are so high. People know how they feel about abortion; they know where they stand on the death penalty. They have strong views about gay marriage, affirmative action, the use of marijuana for medical purposes, assisted suicide, the Patriot Act ... the list is endless. In a federal supreme court election, people could actually make informed votes. They would be voting based on a different view of constitutional interpretation instead of who went to a more prestigious law school. Wouldn't conservatives have loved to have a shot at electing strict constructionists when Justices Breyer and Stevens retired? Wouldn't liberals jump at the chance to stack the Court with loose constructionists who would uphold cases like *Roe v. Wade*? Many would argue that we do not want people voting based on judicial candidates' positions on issues because we want the judges to be neutral when they are sitting on the bench. But that is exactly the problem on the state level; it is extremely hard to be neutral when you are facing reelection! In reality, the whole notion of voting for a supreme court justice runs counter to our ideas of judicial neutrality; why is it not the same when voting for a state superior court judge?

One attempt to try and balance the tension between accountability and independence is to hold retention elections. As noted earlier, a retention election is not like most elections because the judge is not running against an opponent. Retention elections are seen as a compromise between promoting independence and accountability because a judge is not facing an opponent who is trying to use that judge's decisions against her. Also, sitting justices generally do not raise money to be retained—alleviating the conflict of interest. At the same time, judges cannot make rulings that are inconsistent with the public's wishes because they still must face the voters after their terms are up.

To be fair, an overwhelming percentage of judges who are up for retention are retained. On average, more than 70 percent of voters in state supreme court and intermediate appellate court retention elections reaffirmed judges.[48] Between 2000 and 2006, of the 524 appellate court retention elections, only two judges were not retained.[49] In Florida, a judge has never lost a retention election.[50] In fact, voters in South Dakota and Nevada recently rejected amendments that would have changed the state's method of selection for state circuit judges from popular election to merit selection/retention elections, largely on the argument that the plan would basically appoint judges for life and lessen accountability.

The fact that judges are generally retained does not mean that they are immune from the threat of removal. Melinda Gann Hall finds that "retention elections are not impervious to partisan pressures, contrary to the claims of reformers."[51] It is not simply the threat of removal from the other party that could influence judges. Interest groups have taken a more active part in retention elections. During the 1990s, justices in Tennessee and Nebraska were not retained after they made controversial decisions. Two justices in Florida survived only after extremely expensive campaigns. More recently, in Arizona, an organization named No Bad Judges targeted two superior court justices who were up for retention. While both judges were retained, one of the judges said the challenge could influence future judges' decisions. "I'm not sure it will have an impact on me or Judge Sargeant," said Judge Ken Fields, "but a for a brand-new judge looking to make a career out of this, it could have some effect."[52] The Arizona case was not an isolated incident in 2004; judges in Kansas and Iowa also faced strong challenges to their retention. In 2005, citizen groups targeted Pennsylvania Supreme Court Justices Russell Nigro and Sandra Schultz Newman, after the state legislature voted to enact pay raises for the legislature and judges. Neither justice had anything to do with the vote, but since no one in the legislature was up for reelection in 2005, groups such as Clean Sweep and Democracy Rising targeted Nigro and Newman in their retention elections. While Newman was barely retained, Nigro was not as lucky. And, in 2010, three Iowa supreme court justices lost their retention elections as a result of the court's controversial ruling declaring same-sex marriage to be constitutional. Anti-same-sex marriage organizations spent at least $1 million urging voters to oust the justices. With the recent heightened interest in judicial elections and the increasing amount of money spent on them, it is likely that we will see a growing number of justices challenged as they come up for retention.

An Imperfect Solution

If judicial elections and retention elections are not the answer, then what is? Certainly no solution is perfect; perfection, when it comes to selecting judges, is an unattainable goal. That does not mean we cannot do better than the status quo.

The most interesting and unique idea for judicial selection that I have seen is put forth by noted defense attorney Gerry Spence. In his book, *With Justice for None*, Spence argues that the only way to select judges is to draft them. According to Spence, qualifications for potential judges would be set by the state legislature and differ depending on the level of the judiciary. As an example, Spence says that the qualifications for a trial court judge might be that the lawyer is a member in good standing with the bar of the state, practiced law for no less than five years, and tried at least five jury trials to verdict. Once a lawyer meets those qualifications, they are then selected at random to be a judge for a particular case. Matters of disqualification because of a conflict of interest would be resolved by an assigning judge.

Spence claims there are many advantages of drafting judges:

> Suddenly our court dockets would become current, because the assigning judge can appoint as many judges as are needed to get the work done. Lawyers can only be better lawyers for having experienced the justice system from the side of those whose duty it is to make heavy decisions, and judges will never forget how it was to once be a lawyer, because

tomorrow they will be back in their law offices again. No longer will the judges' decisions be tempered with political considerations, because they will never stand for reelection or have political debts to pay.[53]

The argument for drafting judges is intriguing. According to Spence, when he discusses the idea with his colleagues, they argue that they could not afford to take an assignment as a judge in a prolonged case. As Spence notes, if we can expect jurors to leave their jobs in the name of protecting justice, we certainly can expect lawyers to do so.

One concern with Spence's plan is that unqualified people could be sitting on the bench. It does not take an extremely bright person—the kind that we hope would be presiding over cases—to be in good standing with the bar, practice law for five years, and try five cases. In fact, a lot of poor lawyers can meet those criteria. Spence states that there is no evidence "that the average intelligence of the bench as a whole is better than that of the bar."[54] Neither he nor I have the data to test whether his assertion is true. The argument that judges are no smarter than lawyers misses the mark, though. Intelligence is an important component of being a good judge, but so is experience. This is the one area where comparisons can be drawn between a legislator and a judge. To be a good legislator, one needs to understand how the system works. Legislators are likely to be far more successful passing their bills the fifth time than the first, because they will have learned something about the process. The same can be said for judges. Like legislators, judges benefit from on-the-job training. Judges are unlikely to look at their first murder trial the same way they will look at their fifth. This type of experience will be sorely missed if we draft judges. Still, even with some potential flaws, Spence's argument is one that should be considered.

Another possible option is to simply follow the federal system in which, in this case, the governor would appoint and the state Senate would confirm. This option is better than the election method because judges are not subjected to a conflict of interest, but it too is far from perfect. As the current federal appointment process shows, politics plays a major role here as well. Presidents Clinton and George W. Bush both struggled to get their appointees confirmed by a Senate controlled by the other party. Because of the filibuster, President Obama has not found the process to be smooth sailing either. Putting the most qualified person on the bench is not the goal of the Senate. If it had been, Robert Bork would have been easily confirmed and Clarence Thomas would have not. Still, there is little evidence that the federal courts do not have extremely qualified people sitting on the bench even with partisan politics involved in the appointing process.

How about another solution? For superior court seats, a nonpartisan nominating commission comprising former judges, lawyers, and citizens would present the governor with five options; the governor would then choose one. The same system would be in place for municipal judges. A nominating commission would present names to the mayor who would then make the appointment. If the municipal court includes more than one city, the appointment process for state judges would be followed. Judges would then serve one set term. Similar to the arguments made by opponents of term limits, some might claim that limiting judges to only one term would lessen the number of experienced judges on the bench. Term limits for judges and for members of the state legislature are not comparable, however. First, the term for a judge would be much longer, say 15 years. The number of years state legislators may serve is usually significantly less. Most states limit representatives to six to eight years in one house of the legislature. Second, as I will discuss in a moment, appellate court justices would not lack experience because they would be promoted from below.

The nominating commission system is already in place in several states, although no state limits its judges to only one term. It, too, is not perfect. For example, in January 2005, the governor of Colorado refused to fill a supreme court vacancy because he was presented with only two options, neither of whom he felt was qualified. Furthermore, the nomination committee is not always immune to partisan decision-making.[55] Spence also notes the possible problems of a nominating commission. He uses the analogy of choosing a referee for a football game. Three options are presented. One candidate is blind, one is confined to a wheelchair, making the third the only viable option. A nominating commission has some flaws, but its potential problems are less insidious than the conflict of interest in judicial elections. And, nominating commissions allow citizen input, which makes the process at least somewhat democratic.

Appellate court justices would be selected by their peers. If an intermediate appellate seat opened, district court judges, through a secret ballot, would elect one of their members to fill the vacancy. The same process would occur when a supreme court seat opened, but intermediate appellate court judges would cast votes to fill the vacancy. As with district court judges, appellate court judges would serve one set term, with the possibility of serving an additional term on a higher court if appointed. Under this plan, judges could remain impartial because they would not face election and, unlike Spence's draft option, appellate court judges would be experienced. Also, a true peer review would occur and the most qualified judge more likely would be promoted. Certainly politics would not disappear from the process completely, but it would play much less of a role than under existing options.

The likelihood of such a proposal being implemented is, admittedly, not great. People are likely to resist any attempt to take away their ability to vote for judges. That being the case, if we are going to insist on having judicial elections, then let judicial elections be like other elections. This is where I differ from most of my colleagues who oppose judicial elections. Their view is that, if we are going to have them, then judicial elections should be different from other elections. Candidates should be limited by what they can say and political parties should be removed from the process. I disagree. While I think that judges should not be elected, if we are adamant about electing judges, then we need to hold partisan judicial elections to give voters a better chance of making an informed vote. As Hall finds, nonpartisan judicial elections are not insulated from politics, the very reason why we hold them in the first place.[56] And, my research on the involvement of political party organizations in nonpartisan elections indicates that parties are still quite active in everything from get-out-the-vote efforts to fundraising.[57] Nonpartisan judicial elections appear to be nonpartisan in name only, not in spirit. Yet, it is not clear that voters are picking up the partisan cues provided in an election and, given the evidence discussed previously, seem to struggle to cast an even somewhat informed vote.

Furthermore, candidates must be able to take stands on issues. I agree with the Court's verdict in the *White* case mentioned earlier. Certainly, voters should consider the qualifications of the candidate, but it is often difficult to determine who the most qualified candidate is. And let's be honest—qualifications are not the only thing we care about regarding our judges. Certainly, both Antonin Scalia and Ruth Bader Ginsburg are qualified to sit on the highest court in the land, but they differ greatly in their views regarding how the Constitution should be interpreted. Those differences allow them to be loved by some people and loathed by others. The same can be said for state judges.[58] There are clear differences between how some judges view the criminal justice system and the appropriate sentencing for some crimes (when their hands are not tied because of state statute); voters deserve to know a judicial candidate's positions on issues like these before they vote for the person. Some people might counter that a voter's right to information is less important than the integrity of due process. It would seem unfair, for instance, for a person to appear before a judge on a DUI charge when that judge is on record as saying she will have zero tolerance for drunk driving. Certainly we must be concerned about a person's right to due process. Perhaps I have just watched too many episodes of *Law and Order*, but it seems to me that certain judges already have reputations as being strict, lenient, or whatever. Most lawyers already know a judge's tendencies even without the judge making her positions clear on the campaign trail. That being the case, I am not sure that due process is threatened as much as some believe if the canons in the ABA Model Code of judicial conduct discussed earlier are removed or declared unconstitutional (and all indications are that most will no longer pass constitutional muster given recent court rulings).

Finally, many judicial organizations are concerned about the threat that the *White* ruling presents to the public's perceptions about the legitimacy of the courts. As one example, after the decision, New York State Bar Association president, Lorraine Power Tharp, said, "This is going to open up the doors to so many campaign abuses that have been documented around the country. The public loses its trust and confidence in the judiciary. Judicial campaigns should be conducted with dignity and integrity."[59] If true, this result would be worrisome because no institution is more reliant on legitimacy than the judiciary. As Hamilton noted in *Federalist 78*, the courts have the power of neither the purse nor the sword but "merely judgment" and therefore depend upon widespread support to implement rulings.[60] The problem is that no empirical evidence exists for Tharp's claim. In two separate studies (one a survey of Kentucky residents and the other a nationwide study), political scientist Jim Gibson fails to uncover any evidence that policy pronouncements diminish individual perceptions of judicial impartiality.[61] According to Gibson, "[w]hen judges express their policy views during campaigns for elected judgeships, no harm is done to the institutional legitimacy of courts. Indeed, the data even indicate that policy *promises* have no untoward effects on court legitimacy."[62] Moreover, Gibson's data indicate that citizens actually *expect* candidates in judicial elections to make pronouncements. Finally, no evidence, at this point anyway, exists that the *White* decision has fundamentally changed key characteristics of judicial elections, including contestation and competition.[63] In short, there are definitely good reasons to oppose electing judges, but concern over the effects of the *White* ruling is not one of them.

Chapter 4

Direct Democracy

In the summer of 2000, I moved to California to begin a job at Loyola Marymount University. One of the things that really intrigued me about moving to California, besides the warm weather, was that it is a state that allows for direct democracy including initiatives and recall elections.[1] With initiatives, citizens get to vote directly on policy issues like lowering taxes and increasing education spending. As someone who grew up in New Jersey and went to college and graduate school in Indiana, I had never experienced the initiative process before. Studying American politics, specifically political behavior, I was interested in learning more about voting on initiatives and could not wait to do it myself. Then I actually did, and it wasn't easy. I had the opportunity to vote on eight statewide initiatives, ranging from issues dealing with drug treatment to the funding of public works projects.

However, the 2000 general election was relatively easy compared to the 2004 general election when California voted on an astonishing 16 initiatives (and this did not even include several local measures). I had spent several hours the night before the election going over the voter information guide that provided the pros and cons of each initiative, in addition to the considerable amount of time I took to follow the initiatives throughout the election season. I voted at 7:30 a.m. on the morning of election day. By 9:30 a.m., I had already changed my mind regarding one of the initiatives.

I further had the opportunity to experience direct democracy firsthand when, in 2003, the residents of California voted to recall the governor, Gray Davis, less than a year after he was reelected. Californians were upset by, among other things, Davis's handling of the energy crisis in the state and the perception that he flip-flopped on issues in order to benefit politically.

The initiative and recall election were two of several reforms pushed by both populists and progressives around the turn of the twentieth century to give the average person a greater voice in government as well as to limit corruption by party bosses and elected officials.[2] In a sense, they are democracy at its purest; the public has a direct say in the types of policies passed and can remove corrupt or unresponsive elected officials from office without having to wait for the next election.

There is something to be said for the idea of direct democracy. Certainly we do not want corrupt individuals running government and the opportunity to vote on issues such as school vouchers or same-day voter registration is, in many ways, exciting. But both the recall and the initiative process have flaws, too. Recall elections do not guarantee greater accountability and create political environments that are more divisive than usual. The initiative process undermines the legislature and courts, making legislators' and judges' jobs more difficult. Because of these reasons, along with a few others that I raise throughout the chapter, eliminating the recall and the initiative process, or, at the very least, dramatically reforming the rules behind each, is necessary for a stronger, more effective democracy.

The focus of much of this chapter will be on the initiative, since it is more common on a statewide level than the recall and, perhaps, more interesting. This chapter begins with a discussion on how the initiative process works and points out some common misperceptions about citizen lawmaking. Next, we move to the arguments made in favor of the initiative process and note the troubles it creates. Then, I offer a few reforms that might make citizen lawmaking less problematic. Lastly, I give some brief comments on recall elections.

What is the Initiative Process and How Does it Work?

The initiative emerged around the turn of the twentieth century. During the early 1900s, large amounts of money entered the political process and the common belief was that politicians were beholden to special interests. While this view is still popular among some people today, concern about corruption was even worse then because campaign contributions were unregulated. By implementing the initiative process, reformers believed that big money would be less influential, party bosses could be controlled, and grassroots organizations would have a greater voice. If the elite legislatures were not responsive to the people, then the people could take matters into their own hands by passing an initiative. In 1898, the initiative was first passed in South Dakota and several states, mostly in the West, quickly followed. Today, 24 states have some form of an initiative process, with Mississippi as the last to enact one in 1992. Figure 4.1 shows the states that allow for initiatives and recall elections.

Unlike most of U.S. democracy that is representative in nature, the initiative process gives citizens a direct vote on public policy. If people can obtain a certain number of signatures of registered voters based on turnout in the previous gubernatorial election, then the initiative is placed on the ballot. The rules regarding initiatives vary immensely by state. For instance, in South Dakota the number of signatures equal to 5 percent of the number of voters in the previous gubernatorial election is required for statutory initiatives, compared to 15 percent in Wyoming.[3] Some states require a certain percentage of signatures to be obtained from each congressional district, while others do

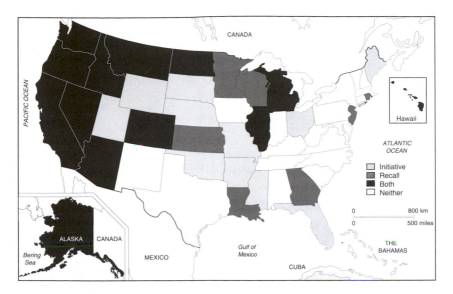

Figure 4.1 A Map of States that use the Initiative and Recall

Source: National Conference of State Legislatures.

Note: Initiative states include states that either have a direct or an indirect initiative and/or allow initiatives for statutes or to change the state constitution. Virginia is not listed as a recall state because its process, while requiring citizen petitions, allows a recall trial rather than an election.

not. The amount of time proponents have to get signatures, or whether a time constraint exists at all, is different from state to state as well. For example, Oklahoma only allows signatures to be gathered for 90 days, but Arkansas, Idaho, Nebraska, Oregon, and Utah allow for unlimited time. Some states allow the proponents to title the initiative, others do not. Some states limit the subject matter of initiatives, such as not allowing the appropriation of money, or require them to address only one issue, others do not.[4]

There are different types of initiatives as well. Most states use the direct initiative—the process I have discussed so far—but a few also allow for indirect initiatives. Under an indirect initiative, the state legislature has the option of adopting an initiative once it makes the ballot or can create an alternative initiative that would be placed on the ballot alongside the original.[5]

Often, many people are confused by the differences between an initiative and a referendum. While initiatives are placed on the ballot by obtaining signatures and then voted on directly by the people, bypassing the legislature altogether, referenda are passed by the legislature and then presented to the people for a "yes" or "no" vote. Although referenda are interesting to study, my primary focus in this chapter will be initiatives since, as political scientists Shaun Bowler and Todd Donovan note, "they have the greatest policy impact and generate the most heated discussions among observers of state politics."[6]

The initiative process might generate heated discussions among scholars and practitioners, but one thing is quite clear: the public favors the initiative process. A 2010 poll found that 59 percent of Californians thought that public policy decisions made through the initiative process are "probably better" than decisions made by the governor or state legislature. The same poll found that 55 percent were either "very satisfied" or "somewhat satisfied" with the way the initiative process was working.[7] Support for initiatives is not limited to California. A 2001 national poll found that almost 57 percent of the public favored a national initiative.[8]

Some Misconceptions About the Initiative Process

Before discussing why the initiative process is flawed, it is necessary to refute a few common arguments against the process. It is easy to discount the use of initiatives, but it is important to avoid the knee-jerk responses some people often make as to why citizen lawmaking should be abandoned. We must look at empirical evidence and, for some frequent criticisms of the initiative process, the empirical evidence is scant at best or simply does not exist. Three arguments against the process in particular are highlighted in this section: special interests are able to buy the passage of initiatives, voters are completely uninformed, and minority rights are threatened.

The Role of Big Money

One of the most common concerns about the initiative process is that it allows powerful interest groups to simply circumvent the legislature by spending enormous amounts of money to convince voters to support their issues. It is easy to understand why people would believe that the initiative process allows interest groups essentially to buy laws or changes to the states' constitutions. It is impossible to deny that substantial amounts of money are often spent on initiative campaigns, and certainly money matters in elections. In fact, one could argue that nothing is more important, especially in low-information campaigns. Name recognition can be enough for a candidate to win an election if little information exists about the race. The same rationale can be applied to the initiative process. If limited information is available about the initiatives—and in many instances this is the case—and one side of the initiative is well funded while the other side is not, which is, again, not uncommon, then it would seem logical that special interests could pass initiatives easily. If the public is only hearing one side of the story, then that side is likely to win.

The appearance of corruption becomes even greater when one considers that, unlike in candidate campaigns, the courts have refused to regulate money in initiative campaigns. In the landmark case, *Buckley v. Valeo* (1976), the Supreme Court ruled that while candidate spending could not be restricted, because to do so would limit the marketplace of ideas, individual donations to campaigns could be capped to root out the appearance of corruption.[9] Two years after *Buckley*, the Court struck down a Massachusetts law that banned corporate expenditures in initiative campaigns.[10] "Referenda are held on issues, not candidates for public office," wrote Justice Powell. "The risk of corruption perceived in cases involving candidate elections simply is not present in a popular vote on a public issue."[11] A few years later, again using a lack of corruption argument, the Court overturned a law limiting contributions to ballot measure campaigns to $250.[12]

The lack of regulation regarding financing of initiative campaigns opens the door for vast amounts of money to enter the process ... and vast amounts of money have entered it. For example, in Ohio and Colorado in 2008 total spending on ballot measures was greater than $70 million in each state. However, this number pales in comparison to California, where more than $470 million was spent on 21 ballot measures. More than $100 million was spent on Proposition 8 alone, which banned same-sex marriage in the state. Altogether, ballot measure committees raised more than $813 million in 2008, 69 percent of which came from business or other special interest groups.[13]

While there is no doubting that large sums of money are behind many initiative campaigns, empirical evidence actually indicates that money is not a significant predictor of whether an initiative passes.[14] In fact, money spent by opponents of initiatives is likely to keep an initiative from passing while money spent in support has a limited effect. According to one study, the side that spends the most money only has about a 25 percent success rate in promoting ballot issues, but a 75 percent rate in stopping ballot initiatives.[15] In other words, interest groups may be able to preserve the status quo, but they are limited in their ability to change it. For example, in 2002, supporters of a same-day voter registration initiative in California spent close to $11 million, much of it donated by heir to the Taco Bell fortune, Rob McKay, compared to just over $500,000 by opponents. The measure failed overwhelmingly.

The fact that campaign spending by interest groups has a limited impact on whether an initiative is passed does not mean that money plays no significant role in the initiative process. First, without money there is no chance of getting an initiative placed on the ballot. It generally costs about $1 million, sometimes more, to get a measure put before voters. Initiative campaigns face great legal fees in writing the actual proposition and must spend more money collecting signatures. As a result, many argue that an "initiative industrial complex" has emerged where initiative campaigns are run not by grassroots organizations, but by experienced campaign professionals. As one Californian initiative campaign professional stated, "There is no such thing as an amateur [initiative]. The best example is this affirmative action one [Proposition 209 in California]. Two amateurs came up with the concept. And they wrote it . . . but, behind the scenes there are a lot of professionals involved in making sure it happens."[16] Supporters of initiatives often argue that the process allows the concerns of all people, not just special interests, to be heard. Based on the costs of putting an initiative on the ballot, it is hard to believe that this is the case.

Indeed, it is difficult to argue that the populists' notion of grassroots organizations promoting initiatives exists. Political scientist Daniel Smith claims that, in the case of tax limitation measures, generally perceived to be pushed by populist-like movements, it was "faux" populist movements that backed the initiatives. According to Smith, his case studies "reveal how three tax crusaders did not draw the bulk of their financial and organizational support from ordinary citizens and volunteers, as the conventional wisdom suggests, but rather from vested special interests with the assistance of top campaign consultants."[17]

Because of the money it takes to start up an initiative campaign, it is possible that only some elite groups can set the issue agenda. However, the fact that initiatives supported by these groups are rarely successful makes this problem less of a concern. It is conceivable, though, that even if the initiative fails at the polls it may be placed on the legislative agenda and passed, which would mean that money has an indirect effect on the success of an initiative. Political scientist Elisabeth Gerber notes this possibility in her research on the initiative process. Looking at economic groups, Gerber finds that the ability of groups to achieve indirect influence is "severely limited."[18] Those groups who can indirectly influence the legislature, Gerber's research shows, are those who already have the resources to do so directly.

Others argue that money is problematic in initiative campaigns because it keeps ballot measures that the public otherwise would have supported from passing. As mentioned earlier, there is evidence that money is more likely to matter when initiatives are defeated than when they pass. This result indicates that powerful groups can keep the status quo they favor and subvert the will of the people simply by spending money. But it is important to point out that this finding should not be an argument against direct democracy. Instead, what it shows is that direct democracy might not be all that democratic. The role of money can only be used as an argument against the initiative process if there is evidence that groups can pass their measures by simply spending money. Again, the empirical evidence that this happens is scant.

Voters are Ignorant

Another common critique of the initiative process is that voters are uninformed and incapable of making rational decisions. As someone who has voted on several initiatives, I have experienced firsthand how difficult it can be, especially when there are multiple propositions on which to decide. Ballot measures are often technical, which makes voting complex, far more so than voting in candidate elections. As one state official who prepares Colorado's pamphlet on initiatives maintains, "I write the pros and cons that go into the official state booklet and I also work for the state legislature, but, in all honesty, I sometimes don't know what's [sic] the guts of an issue; that is, what the consequences of it would be if voters passed it."[19] The election official is not the only one to struggle with understanding the benefits and drawbacks of initiatives. "Making sensible judgments on [initiatives] would have required bringing a lawyer and an accountant into the booth with me," writes columnist Russell Baker.[20]

Indeed, voting for ballot measures can be challenging because the information costs are so large. First, unlike in many candidate elections, there is no identifiable party cue on the ballot. Second, while there is evidence of retrospective voting in candidate elections where voters make their decisions based on the performance of the incumbent, it is impossible to vote retrospectively in initiative elections. Third, the voter information guides on which citizens may rely to obtain the pros and cons of an initiative are not always easy to read and can be lengthy; for instance, the 1990 Arizona ballot pamphlet was 224 pages![21] Moreover, the overwhelming majority of states do not require that voter information guides be sent to registered voters. As a result, some research finds that people rarely rely on voter information guides when voting on initiatives.[22]

Furthermore, political scientist David Magleby, in his routinely cited book on direct legislation, finds that interest in initiative campaigns is generally much lower than for candidate races at the top of the ballot.[23] This disinterest leads to a lack of motivation to become informed about the proposals. "Substantial proportions of the electorate report not having seen or heard anything about even very controversial or highly publicized propositions."[24] To be sure, there is some anecdotal evidence that voters are unaware of exactly what they are voting for or against on ballot measures. In his book, *Democracy Derailed*, respected political columnist David Broder informally interviewed people regarding a recent set of California initiatives. Several of the people he interviewed actually had their voting backwards; the interviewees thought that they supported a proposition when in fact they sided with the position of the other side, or vice versa.[25] In California's heated battle to end affirmative action in the state, there were instances where people thought that they voted to save affirmative action when in fact they had voted to eliminate it.[26] The title of the proposition was the "California Civil Rights Initiative," which made some people believe it protected affirmative action when it did not. In fact, supporters of Prop. 209 purposely did not include the words "affirmative action" in the summary that appeared on the ballot for fear that people would vote against the measure because preelection polls showed that the people supported affirmative action.[27] Also, Magleby finds that voters' preferences are less stable on initiatives than they are on candidates. According to Magleby, 70 percent of voters changed their opinions on ballot measures, compared to only 26 percent who did so in candidate elections.[28]

It should not come as a surprise that there are varying levels of voter interest and knowledge regarding initiatives. As Magleby writes, "Direct legislation is a political process best understood and utilized by those voters who are better educated or better-off financially."[29] If an education and income bias exist in initiative voting, then it is hard to argue that direct democracy is truly democratic.

There is no doubt that voting for ballot measures is complex; as noted earlier, I have often struggled to decipher what is really at stake in some initiatives. There is also no doubt that we are not as informed as either the progressives or the populists envisioned. That does not mean, however, that uninformed voting is a reason to scrap the initiative process. First, while most of the information cited above relies on anecdotal evidence, more recent empirical works discover that people can vote rationally, even if they are not well informed. In his study of Californians who voted on five insurance reform initiatives—hardly an easy topic—political scientist Arthur Lupia finds that badly informed voters are able to use shortcuts to help them cast votes similar to relatively informed voters.[30]

Lupia is not the only person to make such claims. Jeffrey Karp finds that citizens are able to use the cues of elites when voting.[31] For example, if I have similar views as my congresswoman, and I know she opposes a measure, chances are that, if I were fully informed, I would oppose it as well.[32] Bowler and Donovan also present empirical evidence that initiative voters can use heuristics. According to the authors, voters may use elite cues, look at the strength of the state's economy, or, when in doubt, vote "no" to be safe.[33] Susan Banducci even uncovers evidence of ideological consistency in voting on ballot measures.[34] "[W]hile direct democracy has its failings," write Bowler and Donovan, "the flaws do not necessarily lie with citizens being 'duped,' nor with voters approving things they do not want or do not understand at some basic level."[35] They later conclude:

> The mass electorate engaged in direct democracy is not likely to be fully informed, nor do they deliberate long, nor do they always evaluate policy from an objective, public-regarding perspective, but many have an ability to respond to the steep information demands presented to them. They are likely to reason in ways that conserve cognitive resources, time, and energy, and they often vote on the basis of subjective, instrumental concerns.[36]

Finally, Bowler and Donovan argue that even if we are not as engaged or as informed as classic democratic theorists would insist, it is difficult to think of any examples of initiatives passing that voters really did not want or that they would reject with the benefit of hindsight. This is likely because initiative voters seem to be cautious. If they are unsure about the implications, then they usually do not approve the measure.

It is not that we should not be concerned about voter competence on ballot measures, but the situation is not as grave as many make it out to be. Perhaps political scientist Tom Cronin sums it up best when he asks, "How competent, informed, and rational are ballot issue voters? Not as competent as we would like them to be, yet not as ill informed or irrational as critics often insist."[37]

Violating the Rights of the Minority?

Because the initiative inherently means that a majority will win at the expense of a minority, one concern about the process is that it restricts minority rights. It may not be problematic if a minority loses on tax cut, school voucher, or redistricting initiatives, but if the minority's civil rights or liberties are consistently violated, it is certainly cause for concern. In the most extensive analysis of the effects of the initiative on minority rights, Barbara Gamble finds that ballot measures that restrict civil rights are far more likely to pass than other types of initiatives. Gamble's data indicates that voters approve more than three-quarters of initiatives dealing with five major civil rights issues compared to only one-third of all other initiatives and popular referenda.[38] "Our representative government, with its admittedly imperfect filtering mechanisms, seeks to protect the rights of minorities against the will of majorities," writes Gamble.

> Minorities suffer when direct democracy circumvents that system. Not only do they lose at the polls, the very act of putting civil rights to a popular vote increases the divisions that separate us as a people. Instead of fortifying our nation, direct legislation only weakens us.[39]

Gamble's results are certainly worrisome, but they are not as severe as she makes them seem. First, other empirical evidence refutes Gamble's findings. One study notes that only 18 percent of statewide initiatives aimed at restricting gay rights passed, a lower percentage than the pass rate for all other initiatives.[40] Another study of Californian propositions looks at whether certain groups are more likely to end up on the losing side of an issue. With the exception of Latinos, there are no significant differences in the probability of groups winning, and Latinos still fell on the winning side 58 percent of the time.[41] Furthermore, public opinion polls indicate that minorities support the initiative process, which would imply that they do not see it as hurting their rights.[42] Second, the courts have regularly overturned initiatives that violate civil rights or liberties although, as I argue later, this fact creates a dilemma for the courts.[43] Third, the real assessment that should be made regarding whether citizen lawmaking violates minority rights is not comparing the success rate of civil rights initiatives to other initiatives, but comparing the record of the initiative process on civil rights to the legislative process. Legislatures have had a history of limiting the rights of minorities; whether that record is better or worse than initiatives, to my knowledge, no one has studied. As Cronin writes about the issue of minority rights:

Since 1900, when various direct democracy procedures were enacted in several states and countless local governments, few measures that would have the effect of narrowing civil rights or civil liberties have been put forth by voters, and most of those have been defeated. On those occasions when limiting or narrowing measures have been approved, there is little evidence state legislatures would have acted differently, and some evidence state legislators actually encouraged the result.[44]

After 11 states overwhelmingly passed anti-same-sex marriage initiatives in 2004, more concerns were raised about the effects of the initiative process on minority rights. In many of these states, however, it was actually *state legislators* that pushed to get the "defense of marriage" initiatives on the ballot. In Pennsylvania, for instance, state legislators sought to obtain a court declaration that would prevent the recognition of same-sex marriage. Moreover, 42 states and the federal government had already passed "defense of marriage" legislation, which indicates that direct democracy has been no harsher to same-sex marriage than representative democracy.

When voters in California passed Proposition 8 in 2008, which amended the state's constitution to recognize only marriage between a man and a woman, opponents of direct democracy once again raised the charge that initiatives infringed on minority rights. However, Proposition 8 overturned a state supreme court ruling that same-sex couples had a constitutional right to marry; that right was not extended by the legislature. Again, the point is not that direct democracy has never infringed on minority rights, just that its record appears to be no worse than representative democracy.

I do not mean to imply that the role of money in the initiative process, the intelligence of voters, and the impact of initiatives on minority rights are not reasons to be apprehensive about citizen lawmaking. It would be just plain wrong to argue that money does not matter in initiative campaigns and that voters are as informed as we want them to be. Also, while the records of the state legislatures on issues like same-sex marriage may be no better than the initiative process, it is no reason to defend the direct democracy. I simply want to point out that the many reactions people have to the initiative process may only be partly true, or overstated, and in some cases they may be completely wrong. Citizen lawmaking has many flaws, and while the role of money, voter competence, and the limitations of minority rights may be somewhat worrisome, they are not the real problems with the initiative process.

Why the Public Supports the Initiative Process

Proponents of the initiative process like to point out the exaggerations of the above criticisms. In turn, they give a wide variety of reasons that the initiative process works. However, these contentions, too, have flaws. Perhaps the most common argument in favor of the initiative process is that it embodies democracy. The initiative, supporters claim, allows for participatory democracy where grassroots organizations are able to shape public policy, and the power of special interests and political parties is limited. The problem is that the public is not nearly as empowered as supporters of the initiative believe. While large interest groups have a limited ability to pass legislation that the public does not agree with, as I said, they *do* have the ability to keep initiatives that the public supports from passing. Because of the immense costs of simply getting an initiative on the ballot, much less passed, it is difficult for many grassroots organizations to have a voice come voting time. Furthermore, it is not apparent that the public cares about the issues on which they are voting. As Magleby writes:

> Essential to the claim that more democratic governments result from direct legislation is the assumption that the issues placed on ballots are representative of the issues people have on their minds and would like submitted to a public vote. Very few voters, however, can spontaneously name any particular issues on which they would like to see the public vote. Those issues that do appear on the ballot are typically not the same issues that voters list as the most important problems facing their state or the nation.[45]

Political scientist Richard Ellis agrees with Magleby. In his scathing critique of direct democracy, Ellis writes, "The initiative process enables people to express opinions on things that matter to initiative activists but it does not necessarily empower people to express themselves on the issues that they care most deeply about. The initiative literally belongs to the few who write the measures, not to the many who vote."[46]

Another favorable argument for the initiative process is that it allows the public to act when legislators evade tough issues. It is true that occasionally this can be a benefit of the initiative (see Chapter 7 for an example). The potential to force the legislature to act, or to circumvent the legislature when it does not act, exists, but is rarely the reason behind an initiative. "While direct democracy can be a safety valve against the failures of representative democracy," writes Magleby, "comparatively few initiatives fall into the 'safety-valve' category."[47] The most common policy that people note when discussing an inattentive legislature is term limits. Twenty of the 24 states with initiatives have limited the terms of state legislators.[48] Ironically, this is the one area where people did not need the initiative; they already had the ability to vote their representatives out of office.

Because people believe that direct democracy forces legislators to act on issues that are salient to the public and because, if legislatures do not do so, people can bring the issue to a vote, supporters of the initiative argue that policy responsiveness is greater in initiative states than in noninitiative states. However, empirical evidence challenges this belief. Although Gerber notes that parental consent laws for teenage abortions more closely reflected the state's median voter's preference in initiative states than in states without the initiative,[49] others fail to discover empirical evidence that differences exist across a broad range of policies. In their path-breaking work on representation in the state legislatures, Erikson, Wright, and McIver find strong policy representation across the board. While they say little about differences between initiative and noninitiative states, their results indicate that people's preferences generally mirror policies in all states.[50] Lascher and his colleagues specifically compare initiative and noninitiative states and uncover no evidence that initiatives make for more responsive policy.[51] The reason that legislators in initiative states are no more likely to respond to public opinion than legislators in states without citizen lawmaking is clear; they all must face reelection. As Erikson, Wright, and McIver conclude, "Ultimately, our message about representation in states is a simple one. At the ballot box, state electorates hold a strong control over the ideological direction of policies in their states. In anticipation of this electoral monitoring, state legislatures and other policymakers take public opinion into account when enacting state policy."[52]

Proponents of citizen lawmaking also assert that the process will raise people's political efficacy, make citizens more knowledgeable about politics, and increase voter turnout. The progressives first put forth these arguments, and the theory behind these claims makes sense. After all, there is no democratic process that should make people feel more involved than direct democracy. If citizens cannot get excited about participating when they get the opportunity to vote directly on legislation, then it is hard to imagine them getting excited about politics at all.

Perhaps surprisingly, early research found little or no support for these claims. Magleby notes that initiative voter participation rates are lower than in many candidate races and that, on average, 15–18 percent of those people who turned out did not vote on statewide propositions. He also concludes that many of these people who rolled off were poor. He writes, "The evidence . . . disputes the claim that direct legislation fosters more effective citizen participation or more adequately expresses the public sentiment than conventional devices of representative democracy such as candidate elections."[53] Political scientist David Everson's results regarding voter turnout and the initiative process are similar to Magleby's.[54]

Magleby also questions whether direct democracy lessens citizen apathy and alienation. He believes that the complex, technical language of many propositions does nothing more than frustrate potential voters and, in turn, alienate them. Nor is he convinced that citizen lawmaking raises levels of political interest. "Most people are not very interested in politics most of the time," Magleby claims, "with or without the initiative."[55]

While Magleby's book is regularly cited by scholars of the initiative process, recent empirical work challenges some of his early findings. In *Educated by Initiative*, political scientists Daniel Smith and Caroline Tolbert uncover evidence that voter turnout is higher in initiative states, that citizens are more informed about politics in states with more frequent initiatives, and that greater citizen efficacy and confidence in government exists in states with frequent exposure to ballot initiatives.[56] Several others have concurred with Smith and Tolbert's findings.[57]

However, Smith and Tolbert are careful not to overstate their results. Using multiple regression analysis (unlike Magleby and Everson), they find that citizens with frequent exposure to ballot initiatives are more likely to vote, but only under *certain conditions*. Midterm elections and noncompetitive presidential elections produced differences in turnout between initiative and noninitiative states, after controlling for a variety of variables. However, no significant difference in turnout emerged during the extremely close 2000 presidential election.

Smith and Tolbert's results regarding civic engagement are also election-specific. They discover that "people in states with frequent ballot questions are more informed about politics in the 1996 presidential election, more interested in politics in the 1996 and 1998 elections, and more likely to discuss politics in the 1996 presidential election."[58] Again, significant results exist in election years that have little information (midterm elections) or in years with noncompetitive presidential contests. Increased political knowledge only happens when initiatives are closely related to campaign issues in state or local elections, such as California's Proposition 209 in 1996. The only measure that is statistically significant across all years is citizen confidence in government.[59]

Smith and Tolbert's results indicate a potential positive of citizen lawmaking. While most of their results are election specific, initiatives do create the possibility of a more active citizen (although still not nearly as engaged as classical democratic theorists would like). It should not come as a surprise that there are positive aspects of direct democracy; after all, some strong arguments exist for almost every subject discussed in this book. Although Smith and Tolbert deliberately avoid the question of whether ballot initiatives undermine representative democracy by weakening the legislature, they do leave open the possibility that the negative effects of the citizen lawmaking could outweigh their findings. And that is exactly the case.

The Problems with the Initiative Process

Citizen lawmaking may lead to greater civic engagement, but it also creates significant harm. First, the initiative process is not conducive to good lawmaking. Unlike in a legislature, there is no opportunity for compromise or deliberation. Citizens have no choice but to vote an initiative up or down; there are no other possible options. This is a dangerous way to create laws. As Magleby notes, correctly:

> While the reformers' call to "let the people rule" rings an immediate and positive chord, the actual experience with direct legislation demonstrates

that the process is structured in ways that limit effective participation for some voters, and the agenda of issues may only serve to intensify conflict and lead to a politics of confrontation. In contrast, indirect democracy is generally structured to facilitate compromise, moderation, and a degree of access for all segments of the community.[60]

David Frohnmayer, the former Oregon attorney general, says of the initiative process, "Initiative campaigns enhance the new tribalism in our politics. It's an up-or-down choice between extremes, all-or-nothing, take-no-prisoners deal. I have no idea how we're supposed to live together in a civil society with a system like that. It plagues us."[61] Elizabeth Garrett and Matthew McCubbins argue that the inability to amend initiatives may result in outcomes that do not actually reflect the wishes of the average voter.[62] Finally, political scientists Bruce Cain and Kenneth Miller note the irony of the initiative process. They write, "[D]irect democracy can actually be less democratic than representative democracy in that it fails to maximize democratic opportunities for refinement, informed deliberation, consensus building and compromise, and violates democratic norms of openness, accountability, competence, and fairness."[63]

In addition to limiting debate and compromise, Cain and Miller argue that direct democracy poses a threat because it undermines the courts. State judiciaries often are forced to invalidate initiatives because the measures are unconstitutional. This can create great resentment against judges—after all, their ruling goes against the wishes of the majority of the state's voters—and exacerbates many of the problems discussed in the previous chapter regarding judicial independence. Judges who are forced to make unpopular rulings to uphold the rights of minorities may be targeted when they come up for reelection or retention.

The initiative process does not promote compromise or deliberation and, moreover, threatens judicial independence, but perhaps even more problematic is the fact that initiatives often tie the hands of legislators and undermine the legislature. If voters were only asked to vote on issues such as same-day voter registration, same-sex marriage, or affirmative action, some might not like the results, but they generally would not restrict the legislature's flexibility when it comes to issues of taxing and spending. Issues become far more complex once government spending is tossed into the equation.

A good example is California's Prop. 71 that dealt with funding for embryonic stem-cell research, an issue on which most people probably have a strong opinion. If the proposition was simply a "yes" or a "no" on supporting stem-cell research, the vote would have been easy enough. The problem, however, was that people had to decide whether they wanted to spend $300 billion, or nothing at all, on the issue. This proposition is a good example of the lack of flexibility with the initiative process. A voter could support stem-cell research, but only want to spend, say, $150 billion on it. But the bigger question is, does the state of California have $300 billion to spend on stem-cell research? That is a difficult question for the average person to answer.[64] Even though initiative voters tend to be reluctant to vote for measures that have significant costs, people are basically getting a free credit card to decide what they want to spend money on and how much they want to spend without necessarily understanding what the consequences of the spending are. In the end, state governments may run a tab that they cannot afford. California certainly has found itself in that situation. Because of Californians' unwillingness to vote to cap state spending (and because of the difficulty the legislature has raising taxes because of previous initiatives, a subject I return to momentarily), the state found itself with a $21 billion budget deficit in 2010.

The potential to use the credit card unwisely is a concern. However, the bigger worry is not that initiatives will lead to uncontrollable government spending, but rather that propositions will prevent legislatures from spending as much as the people would like and limit the amount of revenue that states receive. Citizens often want to have their cake and eat it too. We generally want government services and programs, but we do not like to pay taxes—two obviously conflicting goals. If government takes in less revenue, then one of two options emerge, neither of which is positive. Like California, states could run up large budget deficits, or they could spend less money on the programs citizens want. In this way, citizen lawmaking often puts politicians in a bind; tax cut measures are likely to pass, meaning there is less money to spend on other popular programs. As Donovan and Bowler write, "Responsiveness on one level (changing tax rules) hinders responsiveness at another level."[65]

One excellent example of this problem is California's Prop. 13. Passed by voters in 1978, Prop. 13 rolled back property values to their 1975 levels and then allowed them to be reassessed only when the property changes hands. It was an extremely popular measure at the time, and many Californians still fiercely defend it today. The measure is also often attributed to igniting a new wave of initiative proposals.

However, Prop. 13 has had many negative consequences. For example, a family who bought a house in the 1990s paid as much as five times more in property taxes than their neighbor who had been living in an identical house since 1978.[66] The disparity has only grown since the turn of the century. While one can certainly question the fairness of the measure, it is not the proposition's biggest flaw. The worst aspect of Prop. 13 is that it has limited government spending on health, welfare, and, education—issues that the public also supports—and has shifted spending away from localities to the state government.[67] As Broder notes, the happening of the latter is ironic since the goal of the reformers was to take power *away* from the state legislatures.[68]

Peter Schrag, one of the harshest critics of Prop. 13 (and the initiative process in general) and former *Sacramento Bee* editorial page editor, argues that the process has made it "harder to write budgets, respond to changing needs, and set reasonable priorities."[69] In other words, the initiative ties the hands of the legislatures. Legislatures are often restricted because states enact tax or expenditure limitations (TELs) or require a "supermajority" in the legislature in order to raise taxes. Neither of these is unique to initiative states, but they are more likely to be instituted in states with citizen lawmaking.[70] TELs and supermajorities make it increasingly tough for legislators to do their jobs. In Colorado, for example, changes in tax policy are only allowed with voter approval. It is extremely difficult for government to function if it does not have control over collecting revenue. A few studies find that TELs lead to higher long-term state debt.[71]

There is also some evidence that initiative states have less progressive taxation, and that the poor bear a greater share of the burden of funding services.[72] If participants in direct democracy are more likely to be the educated and the wealthy, then the voices of the less educated and the less well-off are not heard. At least in a legislature, there are generally some representatives fighting for the interests of these constituencies. Furthermore, initiative states are more apt to rely on user fees than noninitiative states, the burdens of which may fall more heavily on the poor.[73]

Donovan and Bowler best sum up the problems with the initiative:

> Direct democracy does allow citizens the ability to change rules about how legislatures do business, and it might be highly responsive to voter hostility to the property tax. But contrary to what classical democratic theorists might have feared about direct legislation, it does not cause a state to have more redistributive policies (i.e., progressive taxation). Contrary to what Progressive advocates might have expected, it does not necessarily cause more "responsible" budgeting in the long run. The problem is not simply with direct democracy as a process, but how it interacts (or fails to interact) with the legislative process. By frequently presenting voters with only part of the fiscal equation (cutting taxes, maybe borrowing, but rarely spending choices or raising new revenue), direct democracy places state legislatures in a position where it might be extremely difficult for them to write a budget.[74]

Some Potential Reforms

Citizen lawmaking can undermine the legislatures and the courts, limit the ability to compromise and deliberate, place undue burdens on the less well-off, and lead to greater state indebtedness. However, the initiative process remains extremely popular with the public and any attempt to eliminate it is likely to fail. Since that is the case, there are some reforms that states could adopt to make the process fairer, easier to navigate, and more democratic. I only address a few of the hundreds of proposals that reformers have suggested. According to the National Conference of State Legislatures, an astounding 188 reform bills dealing with the initiative were offered during 2001–2002 alone.[75]

If states choose to keep citizen lawmaking, then they must consider reforms that at least control the process. Mississippi, the last state to adopt the initiative (in 1992), created a limited process. Under the state's initiative rules, no more than five initiatives can appear on one ballot, laws of the legislature cannot be negated, one-fifth of the signatures to place an initiative on the ballot must come from each of the five congressional districts, and, for an initiative to pass, at least 40 percent of voters who cast ballots in the election must support it. In addition, every initiative that has revenue implications must identify the amount and source of revenue required to implement it. If taxes are cut or funding is reallocated, the initiative must specify which programs will be affected.[76]

Mississippi's initiative rules are a step in the right direction. For example, limiting the number of initiatives makes it less likely that voters will be overwhelmed and even more likely that they will be able to participate intelligently. However, I would argue that the Mississippi rules do not go far enough. The revenue implications requirement is better than nothing, but still gives the public too much control over the budget process. If citizen lawmaking is to exist, it should only be for nonrevenue or nonexpenditure measures. Critics may argue that this reform would significantly limit the number of initiatives proposed, something I think is actually a good thing, but it will keep legislators from having their hands tied and lessen the possibility that unintended consequences occur.

We must also make citizen lawmaking more open to deliberation and compromise. One particularly interesting reform was suggested by the Commission on Campaign Financing, a bipartisan group that studied the use of the initiative in California. The Commission recommended that the legislature hold a public hearing on any qualifying initiative and then allow proponents of the initiative to offer amendments. The legislature and the initiative proponents would also be able to negotiate and compromise. These reforms could open up the initiative process, allow for deliberation, and potentially have citizens and legislators working together on legislation.[77] The indirect initiative mentioned earlier could be one way to accomplish these goals, although the effects of this procedure have been limited largely because of noncooperative legislatures. Others have recommended having a judicial or administrative review of the petitions before they circulate. This reform might lessen the number of initiatives that courts must overturn later as well as save initiative proponents and opponents a great deal of time and money because they will be less likely to challenge the initiatives in court.

Finally, states must make information more easily available to voters. For all of its problems with the initiative process, this is one area where California has taken a positive lead. The Secretary of State sends every registered voter a booklet before the election that outlines the pros and cons of each proposition. The booklet is not perfect; as mentioned earlier, it did not keep me from struggling with one of my votes, but it is certainly better than nothing.

Surprisingly, very few states require voter information guides, and the quality of these guides varies.

Citizen lawmaking is an intriguing idea. The ability to have a direct say in the laws of one's state is exciting, but giving citizens too much of a say can be harmful. It undermines the abilities of the legislatures and the courts to perform their duties and can result in policies that protect the wealthy at the expense of the poor. In the end, what appears to be democracy in its purest form is really no more democratic—and perhaps even less so—than representative government. As Cronin writes in the introduction of his respected book on direct democracy, "The idealistic notion that populist democracy devices [such as the initiative] can make every citizen a citizen-legislator and move us closer to political and egalitarian democracy is plainly an unrealized aspiration."[78]

Recall Elections

Before concluding this chapter, it is important to comment briefly on another controversial form of direct democracy: the recall election. A recall election is simply an election to remove an elected official from office during the middle of her term. While the 2003 Californian gubernatorial recall election referenced earlier may seem to be unique, recall elections are common for lower-level elected officials, such as members of city councils and school boards. Writing roughly 20 years ago, Cronin estimated that between 4,000 and 5,000 recalls had been held at the time and thousands more never made it to the ballot.[79] Obviously, that number has grown in recent years. Again, Figure 4.1 shows which states allow for the recall of statewide elected officials.

The main argument in favor of the recall is simple: it provides a continuous opportunity for voters to hold elected officials accountable. With the recall, incompetent, corrupt, or unresponsive politicians can be removed from office without the public having to wait for them to come up for reelection. "With the sword of the potential recall hanging over them, elected officials will remain alert, honest, and responsive," Cronin writes. "In this sense, the recall can be viewed as a remedy for the defects of representative government."[80]

On the other hand, opponents argue, the recall could keep politicians from making tough choices for fear of being removed from office early. It encourages short-term thinking (what is best for the politician's political career) over long-term thinking (what is best for the locality or state). The recall also undermines the notion of trustee representation, the view that elected officials who may have access to information that the general public does not should exercise their own judgment on issues that come before them. People also criticize recall elections because they, by nature, promote divisiveness and conflict. Furthermore, in some states, such as California, an official can be recalled simply for political reasons, not because they are corrupt or have violated the law.

In general, we should be skeptical of recalls. First, representatives already appear to be accountable to the people, even when the recall is not an option; policy tends to mirror public opinion.[81] Second, a system by which politicians are constantly being recalled can create chaos, both in the government that has to deal with the constant turnover of politicians and in the electorate that must continuously go to the polls to vote. However, it is far from clear, at the state level anyway, that recall elections are undermining government and placing an undue burden on the electorate. In fact, perhaps the aspect of the 2003 California recall election that contributed most to the circus-like atmosphere surrounding it was the uniqueness of the election in that few attempts to recall statewide officials ever make it to the ballot. While critics of the Davis recall argued that the partisan nature of the recall would spark similar efforts across the country, this has not happened.

Also, there is little evidence that the recall is keeping politicians from making tough choices because of the constant threat of facing reelection. As Cronin notes:

> A few officials probably minimize the risktaking because of the recall. It is doubtful, however, that the recall device encourages this any more than the fact that they must stand for reelection. Politicians are generally cautious. By definition they want to retain majority and plurality support. Democratic elections encourage this. Recall is merely an additional device—a form of insurance.[82]

However, Cronin also states that there is little evidence that the recall really improves democracy:

> The recall device, often viewed as a direct democracy device, has not significantly improved direct communication between leaders and led and has not ended corruption in politics. Neither has it produced better-qualified officeholders or noticeably enriched the quality of citizenship or democracy in those places permitting it. Whether it has strengthened representative government in any measurable way seems doubtful.[83]

In the preface, I referred to my conversation with a student about the recall of Gray Davis in which I referred to the recall efforts as "dumb democracy." In the case of the Davis recall, I considered it to be nothing more than a political maneuver to ouster a politician that the public had reelected just a few months earlier. Davis violated no laws and, while many in the state may have perceived him as slimy, he did not face any corruption charges. In my view, then, this is the recall at its worst. Democracy occurred in November of 2002; what happened roughly a year later was a successful attempt by wealthy politicians to remove someone they did not like from office.[84]

There may be times when a politician legitimately needs to be removed from office because of graft or other lawbreaking. For this reason, it is important to have an impeachment process in place. Critics of impeachments as a way of removing corrupt politicians note the expense both in terms of money and time that the process brings with it, but it is not clear to me that the recall process is any less expensive or faster. Regarding money, recall elections generally are not held in conjunction with other elections, which means that counties have to spend a significant amount of money to hold an additional election day (see Chapter 2). Plus, the elected official, political parties, and interest groups will no doubt spend a large amount of money trying to either defeat the recall or get it to pass. Regarding time, for a recall to be put on the ballot a certain number of signatures of registered voters must be obtained and then an election must be scheduled. This process, even when done quickly as was the case in California, can still take close to a year.

The effectiveness of the impeachment process can be best illustrated with the ouster of former Illinois Governor Rod Blagojevich in 2009. Among other things, Blagojevich was accused of soliciting bribes, accepting campaign contributions in return for government contracts, and, perhaps most oddly, using his power to appoint Barack Obama's successor to the U.S. Senate for personal gain. Blagojevich had been dogged by corruption charges during much of his time as governor. After he was arrested by federal agents in December of 2008, efforts began to amend the state's constitution to allow for elected statewide officials to be recalled. However, even if Illinois had a recall provision in its constitution, the process would have been slower (and likely more expensive) than the impeachment proceedings. Blagojevich was removed from office in January of 2009, a little more than a month after his arrest. There is no way that supporters of Blagojevich's recall would have been able to gain signatures to get the recall on the ballot and then have the recall election scheduled that quickly. In other words, the impeachment process, at least in this case, was more efficient in removing Blagojevich from office than a recall election.

If we are going to insist on having the ability to recall elected officials—and the public certainly seems to want this; one found that poll 74 percent of respondents said that it was a "good idea" for "people to be able to recall elected state governors solely on the basis of their performance in office"[85]—then we need to put certain rules in place to ensure a fairer process. First, the number of signatures needed to place a recall on the ballot should be high. One of the reasons why the Davis recall was successful was because recall supporters only had to obtain signatures equal in number to 12 percent of the last vote for the office;[86] most states require that the percentage of signatures be doubled (usually 25 percent). Second, politicians should be recalled only in cases where they have violated the law. Political recalls lead to an even more divisive political atmosphere than already exists. Finally, candidates who are facing a recall should be able to appear on the ballot to "replace themselves."

In the 2003 California gubernatorial recall, voters had to make two decisions: (1) Should Governor Gray Davis be recalled, and (2) who should replace him? Even if people voted "no" for the first question, they still had to vote on the second. The catch was that Davis could not appear as a candidate on the second question. Because of the large number of candidates who appeared on the ballot on the second question (134!), it was possible that more people could have voted to retain Davis than voted for his successor. For example, 48 percent of the public could have voted to retain Davis, in which case he would have been removed from office, but the winner to replace Davis may have received, say, only 35 percent of the vote. Just because this scenario did not occur in the 2003 Californian gubernatorial recall it does not mean it is something that cannot happen in the future.

The concept of direct democracy is an interesting one; it seems to be democracy at its purest. Because of the initiative and the recall, citizens have direct input into the types of laws that are passed and, in theory, are able to hold elected officials more accountable. Direct democracy can be problematic, however, as it may tie the hands of the legislature, undermine the courts, promote regressive policies, and makes compromise and deliberation difficult, in the case of the initiative, and creates a more divisive political climate, in the case of the recall. If states are going to continue to promote direct democracy, then they must ensure that rules regarding these two processes are in place to make both work more effectively.

Part II

Rethinking the Mechanics of Voting

Chapter 5

Ballot Laws

In the previous chapters, I covered topics that are seemingly obvious questions to consider regarding the quality of a country's electoral democracy. However, issues such as how easy it should be to vote and what offices people should elect affect voters before they step into the voting booth. Once in the booth, other questions arise that influence the quality of democracy. Who should be listed on the ballot? In what order should those people be listed? What information about the candidates should voters have available to them on the ballot? Should we know a candidate's partisan affiliation? What about whether this person is an incumbent? How about a candidate's occupation?

These questions do not receive nearly as much emphasis as those discussed in the preceding chapters, but they have a potentially dramatic influence on who gets elected and the quality of representation that constituents receive, perhaps as much so as the rules that guide voting. In this chapter we will examine several ballot laws, beginning with who should get on the ballot in the first place. Then we will discuss aspects of the actual ballot, including its design and the information that it provides to voters. I argue that we must always include a candidate's party affiliation on the ballot; in other words, we should eliminate nonpartisan elections. Furthermore, we must guarantee that candidates' names will be rotated so that one candidate is not always placed first, and we should strive for a consistent, simple ballot to cut down on voter confusion once in the booth. All of these reforms will make voting more democratic and allow citizens to vote more intelligently.

Getting on the Ballot

If you are a candidate who wants to win office, it is virtually impossible for you to do so if your name is not listed on the ballot.[1] The problem is that, in many states, getting on the ballot can be quite difficult. Because of federalism, each state and the District of Columbia have their own requirements for a party or individual to be placed on the ballot and, in the party's case, remain on the ballot. Even in federal elections, states determine the rules for ballot access. Generally, parties and candidates face some sort of filing fee or must obtain a certain number of signatures to appear on the ballot, and in some states they must do both. For example, in 2008 for an independent presidential candidate to get on the ballot in Arkansas, the candidate had to obtain 1,000 signatures. In states like Massachusetts, Missouri, and Virginia, the candidate needed 10,000 signatures. In others, such as California and Texas, the number of signatures required is much higher. In 2008, independent candidates needed 158, 372 signatures in California and 74,108 signatures in Texas to be placed on the ballot. Colorado and Louisiana have no signature requirement; the candidate must simply pay a filing fee of $500.

However, the laws are more complex than just paying a filing fee or getting a certain number of signatures. For example, some states allow only registered voters to sign petitions, while others allow anyone of voting age to sign. In some states, the party has to meet one criterion to qualify for all positions on the ballot; in other states, parties' candidates have to qualify for each individual office. In some states, petitions must be notarized; in other states they do not. Furthermore, the filing deadline is different in each state.

Ballot access laws generally work against third parties and independent candidates. It is quite difficult, for example, for a minor party presidential candidate to qualify for the ballot in all 50 states and the District of Columbia. There are 51 different requirements with 51 different closing dates. It is extremely expensive for candidates to obtain enough signatures. The costs of getting on the ballot are further exacerbated because minor party candidates are often forced to retain legal counsel. In some cases, the candidate might argue that a state ballot access law is too restrictive. Other times one of the two major parties will file lawsuits challenging the signatures on a minor party candidate's petitions, such as when the Democratic party filed lawsuits in numerous states in 2004 to keep Ralph Nader off the ballot.[2] Because of the complex requirements to get on each state's ballot in a presidential election, Nader only qualified for the ballot in 34 states and the District of Columbia.[3] Even when candidates qualify in all states, the process to get on the ballot drains an already small campaign chest. In 1980, independent John Anderson spent about half of his budget just getting on the ballot in all 50 states.[4] Since the two major parties always win enough votes to be retained on the ballot in the next election, they do not have to go through this unwieldy process.

There is debate over how much restrictive ballot access laws actually hinder the chances of minor party or independent candidates. Noted ballot access specialist Richard Winger writes, "Not surprisingly, minor parties are much more likely to win elections when such laws are lenient."[5] Still, it is unlikely that a third-party candidate will win an election, no matter what the ballot access law. Furthermore, not everyone is convinced that more stringent ballot access laws negatively affect third-party candidates. Political scientists Christian Collet and Martin Wattenberg find that "ballot access laws explain very little of the variance in either the number of minor party candidates or the vote for them."[6] They continue, "At best, lenient ballot access laws allow minor and independent candidates to preserve their limited resources for other activities."[7]

People in favor of more stringent ballot access requirements tend to make two arguments. First, they argue that it is in the best interest of the electorate to limit the number of candidates running in an election, otherwise elections become too complex and the costs of voting too high. Having to decide between 10 candidates is more difficult than having to decide between two. You do not want the situation to happen that occurred during the Californian gubernatorial recall, mentioned in the previous chapter, when 134 candidates appeared on the ballot. Candidates needed 65 signatures and a $3,500 filing fee or 10,000 signatures and no filing fee to get on the ballot. Yet, the Californian gubernatorial election was clearly a unique case; few races have more than three or four candidates on the ballot, even when requirements are not that steep. And, even in the recall case, the election was pared down quickly to three or four viable candidates. For all of the concern about the recall, it did not end up being much different from other elections. Furthermore, people often say that they do not vote because there are not enough choices. More candidates, then, may actually increase the likelihood of voting.

The second argument in favor of more stringent ballot access laws is that it protects the two-party system, which, as mentioned earlier, is exactly the problem that opponents of stringent ballot access laws have. If it is indeed more difficult for third parties to succeed when it is harder to gain access to the ballot, then the two-major parties' status as the two major parties is protected. There are few things on which Republicans and Democrats agree, but one is that they definitely like being the two major parties.

The pros and cons of a two-party system are beyond the scope of this book, although I do briefly discuss them in the concluding chapter, but it is not clear to me that less restrictive ballot-access laws threaten such a system. Ballot-access laws are only one factor that hinders the success of minor parties in the United States. Even when third-party or independent candidates get on the ballot, and they often do, they are unlikely to win. This is primarily because of the single-member district, winner-takes-all rules of most American elections. For the overwhelming majority of elections in the United States there is no prize for finishing in second place. The candidate who receives the most votes (a plurality) wins the election. As a result, a two-party system usually emerges.[8] Under proportional representation, the number of party candidates who win is proportional to the overall percentage of the vote won by the party slate. In other words, if there are 10 seats to fill and Party A wins 50 percent of the vote, Party B 30 percent, and Party C 20 percent, then the parties would receive five, three, and two seats, respectively. Under the American system, Parties B and C would be shut out. As a result, many people consider a vote for a third party to be wasted. To use an example from the 2000 presidential election, two candidates had a chance to win the election (Bush or Gore). Let us assume that Nader was your first choice, Gore your second, and Bush was unacceptable. It might make more sense to vote for Gore instead of Nader even though Nader was your most favored candidate, because it would help Gore, a candidate who was still acceptable, win and keep Bush, a candidate who was unacceptable, from winning. In the end, Nader loses votes that he otherwise might have won.

The single member district, winner-takes-all system is only one of several barriers to third-party success. Third-party candidates are regularly excluded from debates, they usually do not have the funds to run a competitive campaign, and they do not receive the same media coverage as the major party candidates. The point is that less restrictive ballot-access laws do not mean the end of America's two-party system. Conversely, restrictive ballot-access laws may weaken democracy and threaten electoral accountability. First, from a democratic standpoint, restrictive ballot-access laws limit the number of options from which voters may choose. To go back to the Nader example, there were still close to three million people who voted for Nader in 2000 even though he had no chance of winning. These people did so likely because they felt that neither Gore nor Bush was acceptable and they wanted their voices to be heard. If Nader was not on the ballot, then those voices would have been silenced.[9] Perhaps an even bigger concern about restrictive ballot-access laws is that there is evidence that such laws increase the frequency of uncontested House races.[10] According to a study by political scientists Stephen Ansolabehere and Alan Gerber, stringent filing fees and petition requirements actually discouraged one of the *two major parties* from running candidates in many House races. As the authors write:

> The usual justification states give for their restrictive ballot access laws is that they need to prevent cluttering the ballot, which would result if many frivolous candidates filed for office. The problem, though, is not that voters face too many choices, but too few. Our findings reveal that laws governing access to the ballot stunted competition in U.S. House races during the 1980s.[11]

If people do not have a choice when voting, then accountability suffers. Moreover, even a nominally contested race may raise the incumbent's awareness about issues that constituents are concerned about. Ansolabehere and Gerber continue:

> Elections are crude instruments with which constituents discipline their representatives. Absence of even a nominal challenger short-circuits the electoral connection. When an election is uncontested, an important opportunity for voters and their representatives is lost.[12]

The fact that the two-party system would not be affected by less restrictive ballot-access laws, that these laws do not usually lead to overly crowded ballots and even when they do, the election quickly is pared down to just a few serious challengers, and that electoral choice and accountability is hindered by restrictive ballot access laws are all reasons why states should make it easier for candidates to get on the ballot.

Candidate Information on the Ballot

Obviously, whether a candidate is placed on the ballot will influence whether a person votes for that candidate, but it is not the only ballot-related stimulus on vote choice. As discussed in Chapter 3, Americans vote for a large number of offices. Most of these elections receive virtually no media coverage, making information about the contests difficult to come by. As a result, for many of these "down ballot" contests—elections for offices that are listed at the bottom of the ballot—voters are starved for information about the candidates. They either choose not to participate in these races or they look for any cue that might give them at least some information about the candidates. For instance, in low-information elections voters often rely on a candidate's race or gender when determining their vote.[13]

Often, the ballot itself will provide the voters with cues. Perhaps the most useful cue—and the most recognized—that is sometimes available on the ballot is the candidates' partisan affiliations. While the candidates' party identifications are always listed on the ballot for federal offices,[14] the vast majority of local elections in the United States, and many elections for judge and state-wide office are nonpartisan; elections for the Nebraska state legislature are nonpartisan as well. In nonpartisan elections, the candidates' names are listed on the ballot without their party affiliations next to them.

As with many of the reforms mentioned in this book, the idea for nonpartisan elections originated with the progressive movement around the turn of the twentieth century. At the time, political machines controlled almost all aspects of government in many cities. The machine would determine the party's nominee, which was tantamount to determining who the elected official would be. Because of patronage, party bosses were able to demand loyalty from many of the cities' residents, especially the large immigrant populations who came to the United States with very little, only to be helped by the political machine in obtaining a job.

As a result of the powerful political machines, the progressives began advocating electoral reforms designed to cripple the machines' stranglehold on local government. For example, progressives pushed the Australian ballot to make voting private. Before the Australian ballot, a uniform ballot in a precinct did not exist. Instead, political parties would give color-coded ballots to their supporters who would then cast the ballots in the open. The machines often had "election officials" who watched to be sure that people voted the way they were supposed to. Progressives also introduced the party primary to limit the control of the political machine over the nomination process (see Chapter 8).

Another significant reform was the nonpartisan ballot. Progressives believed that if party politics were removed from the local level, then it would limit the power of the party machines and make government more responsive to the people. Not only would nonpartisan elections weaken the party machines, but they would also keep the divisive influence of national parties out of local government. After all, the old adage is that "there is no Democratic or Republican way to fill a pothole." Because most of municipal government was administrative in nature, progressives felt that people should choose the best leaders and managers to make government run effectively, not the person who was most political.

Removing party affiliation from the ballot, progressives argued, would force people to seek out information that was more relevant to the election than party affiliation.[15] The problem is that there is no empirical evidence that people actually do so. In fact, most of the research on nonpartisan elections indicates that people either skip the election altogether, rely on less reliable cues than partisanship, or simply guess when deciding for whom to vote.

In my work with Brian Schaffner and Gerald Wright, we find that voter roll-off—people who turn out to vote, but do not vote for a specific office—is generally higher in nonpartisan elections.[16] For example, the average roll-off in the Kansas state Senate elections between 1984 and 1990 was only 6 percent. However, in Nebraska, a state that is comparable to Kansas politically and demographically, but whose state legislative elections are nonpartisan, the average roll-off was 39 percent over the same time period, more than six times greater than the roll-off in Kansas. Other studies find similar results when comparing nonpartisan and partisan judicial elections.[17]

It is not simply the fact that, in some cases, millions of people who already made the effort to turn out to vote skip certain elections that is troublesome, but the fact that, in some cases, millions of people *are* voting in these elections with seemingly little information. Schaffner and I examined statewide elections in California, which include several partisan offices like insurance commissioner, attorney general, and treasurer, and one nonpartisan office, the superintendent of public instruction. We found that the more education a person had the more likely they were to provide an answer to a vote choice question for the superintendent race in a preelection survey.[18] Presumably, those with more education would then be more likely to vote. The problem is that those who provided an answer to the vote choice question were less likely to choose the candidate from their party in the nonpartisan election than in the partisan ones. For example, in the superintendent race that we studied, incumbent Delaine Eastin (a Democrat) ran against Gloria Matta Tuchman (a Republican). Each candidate took positions that were consistent with their parties' platforms. Eastin strongly opposed school vouchers and supported bilingual education; Tuchman supported school vouchers and was a cosponsor of an antibilingual education measure that California voters had approved. In other words, there should be no reason why Democrats would be less likely to support Eastin compared to Democratic candidates for other statewide partisan offices and vice versa for Republicans and Tuchman. Yet, that is exactly what we found. People appeared to either be guessing or using less reliable cues when making their vote choices.

Furthermore, nonpartisan elections have the potential to undermine representation. Schaffner, Wright, and I find that nonpartisan elections advantage the minority party in an area because they hide a reliable cue from voters.[19] "Consider a city council district where Democratic candidates tend to win 70 percent of the vote. In a partisan election, a Democratic candidate is likely to win, based solely on the normal Democratic vote he or she can expect to receive by being a Democrat. Likewise, a Republican in such a district faces an uphill battle once voters learn of his or her party affiliation. However, if party labels are removed from consideration, voters will rely on other cues or even vote randomly. Relative to a partisan contest, this situation favors the Republican because it is more likely to put him or her on an equal footing with the Democratic candidate. Of course, this situation can work against Republicans just as easily."[20] There is anecdotal evidence that the minority party advantage does allow minority party candidates to win elections that they otherwise would have lost had their party affiliations been listed on the ballot.[21]

In addition to questions about the quality of voting and representation, it is not obvious that we want partisanship to be removed from the local level. Sure, maybe issues such as abortion or the war in Afghanistan have no relevance for local government, but the notion that partisanship does not matter at the local level is shortsighted. There may not be a Democratic or Republican way to fill a pothole, but there are certainly differences of opinion between the two parties on how many and whose potholes are going to be filled. If partisanship did not matter at the local level, then people would not care about the party affiliation of the mayor or whether the city council was composed of Democrats, Republicans, Libertarians, or whatever. However, it is my experience that most people do care about such things. If you are a Republican, you would likely much rather have a Republican mayor than a Democratic one, and vice versa for Democrats. If this is the case, then partisanship must matter at the local level. For offices where it is less clear how partisanship plays a role, say the coroner or public weigher, as noted in Chapter 3, we should not be electing these positions anyway. The intentions of the progressives to cripple the party machines by instituting nonpartisan elections may have been noble, but the machines have either been destroyed or severely wounded, with no sign of returning to the power they had in their heyday, and we are left with a host of negative consequences. In other words, in this case the progressives' attempt to strengthen democracy only ended up weakening it.

A candidate's party affiliation is not the only information that is available (or not) on the ballot. California, for example, lists each candidate's occupation and whether he or she is an incumbent. Ohio does the same for judicial races. Other states, such as Massachusetts, Maine, and South Dakota, provide the candidates' hometowns. Again, these are low-cost cues that might help a voter decide when he or she has little or no information about the candidates in an election. Although they may not always be reliable cues, voters can still use them to make assumptions about who the best candidate might be. For instance, when voting for state treasurer, one might infer that a banker would be more qualified for the job than a college professor. Likewise, voters may perceive incumbents to be more qualified than challengers, since they have already held the post. "One way to gain the appropriate skills for a job, or at least give the impression of having gained such skills, is to have already held that job," writes political scientist Monika McDermott. "For voters with little actual information about the candidates, few people could seem more qualified than the person currently holding the office."[22]

Research indicates that voters do indeed use cues, such as the candidates' occupations or hometowns, or whether they are the incumbent.[23] First, in races when a candidate's occupation seems related to the office for which he or she is running or an incumbent is running, abstention decreases.[24] Second, the listing of occupations on the ballot not only influences whether people vote, but who they vote for as well. One study finds that in elections to the Board of Trustees for the Los Angeles Community College system, candidates in the field of education did better than opponents without any experience in this area.[25] Another study uncovers evidence that when candidates have a perceived qualification advantage based on their occupation or status as incumbents, voters are more likely to support those candidates.[26]

While occupation, incumbency, or hometown may be better than nothing, they are not necessarily reliable cues. As McDermott notes, "this does not mean that the incumbent candidate has actually performed well in their role— gaining requisite skills and exhibiting competence—merely that voters lacking real information may assume they have solely because they are the incumbent."[27] Including candidates' occupations, hometowns, or whether they are incumbents on the ballot makes little sense. As I argued earlier, we should not be electing officials to most of these low-information offices. However, if we are going to continue to do so, then these elections must be partisan because party identification is more likely to be an accurate cue than the others mentioned. Moreover, there is convincing evidence that when party affiliation is available as a cue, people use it.[28] Regarding other types of cues, why stop at hometown or occupation? Why not include a candidate's race or gender? These cues are likely to be as reliable as a person's hometown or occupation. How about endorsements from interest groups? Why not include statements from the candidates on the ballot or their positions on issues? This, too, would be useful information, perhaps more useful than even party affiliation. The problem is that if we do not limit the information available on the ballot, then ballots become too long and confusing, which, as I argue momentarily, has negative consequences regarding voting. There are rational reasons to only include a candidate's party identification on the ballot. First, it is the most beneficial shortcut for voters. Second, even if it is not the most reliable cue, parties nominate candidates to run for office; bankers, lawyers, and people from Peoria do not.

Incumbency status might be different from occupation, hometown, race, or some of the other cues just mentioned, because it allows voters to make retrospective evaluations. If people are pleased with the way government is currently running, then it makes sense to vote for the incumbent. However, the problem with including incumbency status on the ballot is that the significant advantage that incumbents have in elections will likely increase. Additionally, it is an assumption that people are voting for the incumbent because they are truly happy with the job the person is doing as opposed to simply recognizing the incumbent's name. The only candidate information that should be listed on the ballot is party identification.

The Order of Candidates' Names on the Ballot

It is not just the candidate information listed on the ballot that can influence the outcomes of elections, but the order in which the candidates' names appear as well. The next time you are asked to participate in a taste test for, say, Pepsi, I can almost guarantee which cup will contain Pepsi; it will be the first one you drink. How do I know? Because of what is called the "primacy effect." The primacy effect refers to the fact that people tend to choose the first choice offered, especially when they have little information about the decision they must make. Pollsters, for instance, want to constantly rotate the question stem when asking about a topic to alleviate the problem of the primacy effect. For example, you do not want to ask every person in your sample the question, "Do you support or oppose universal healthcare?" Instead, you want to make "support" the first option for half of the sample and "oppose" the first option for the other half to combat the primacy effect.

The primacy effect occurs in more than taste tests and public opinion surveys; it transpires in voting as well. Research finds that candidates who are listed on the ballot first do better than those who are not.[29] According to scholars, being listed first on the ballot has led to an advantage of anywhere from 2.5 percent to 25 percent.[30] Not surprisingly, the primacy effect is greater in races in which voters have little information about the candidates, such as nonpartisan elections. However, it is not simply in low-information elections where one sees the primacy effect. Political scientist Jon Krosnick and his colleagues find evidence of the effect, even in presidential elections.[31] According to Krosnick, when controlling for party registration, Bill Clinton's vote total was 4 percent higher in California Assembly districts in 1996 when his name was listed first as opposed to last. Similar results occurred in 2000, where George W. Bush did 9 percentage points better in California Assembly districts where he was listed first as opposed to last.[32] Krosnick and his colleagues even speculate that the primacy effect may have allowed Bush to win the 2000 presidential election since he was listed first on the ballot in the state of Florida where he beat Vice-President Al Gore by only 537 votes.

As with all aspects of the ballot, the order in which the candidates' names appear varies by state and sometimes locality. In fact, one study listed 33 different rules that states and localities employ regarding procedures for ordering names![33] Some states, such as Florida, require the candidate from the governor's party to be listed first. Since a Republican held the Florida governorship in 2000 (George Bush's brother Jeb), Bush was listed first on the ballot. In some jurisdictions, the candidate who files first is listed first; in others, names are simply put alphabetically. In some instances, the two major parties are listed first followed by minor party and independent candidates; in others, the Democratic candidate is always placed first. In some places, election officials are allowed to put the candidates in any order they please! The list goes on and on. The point is that in the overwhelming majority of elections, one candidate is always going to be advantaged by his or her place on the ballot.

The solution to this problem is simple: mandatory rotation of names. With the mandatory rotation of names the candidate listed first would vary by precinct or, potentially, county or assembly district. This would ensure that all candidates would have the same opportunity to appear first on the ballot. Amazingly, only 12 states have passed laws to rotate names in at least some of their elections.[34]

The major arguments against mandatory rotation of candidate names include voter confusion, cost, and difficulty counting ballots. Ballots that list the candidates alphabetically or always list the same party first are easier for voters to navigate. Furthermore, "states that require name rotation invest resources to print and distribute multiple different versions of ballots, and counting of ballots is a bit more complex when varying name orders are used," write Krosnick and his colleagues. "These resources are more substantial when different precincts use different voting methods (that is, some use paper ballots and others use punch cards)."[35]

This is another example of states and localities not investing the money to promote fair elections. Election costs could be cut numerous ways, most obviously by eliminating a number of the dates on which elections are held (see Chapter 2). If voter confusion is a problem, then sample ballots should be sent to registered voters in advance. Again, this idea will cost money, but as Krosnick writes, "When it comes to our ballots, and our elections, integrity has to come first on the list."[36] Some might question, from a cost-benefit analysis, whether name rotation is worth it. After all, the outcomes of most elections will not be influenced by the order the candidates' names appear on the ballot. Yet, there are many close elections and the outcomes of those, especially those that occur in low-information environments, may be in question. If the outcome of an election is 51 percent to 49 percent and the effect of appearing first gave the winning candidate a two-point boost, which would be at the low end of the advantage provided by the primacy effect, then the wrong candidate may have won. This scenario is not that unlikely.

A 2006 ruling by the New Hampshire Supreme Court provides some hope that the problem of the primacy effect is being taken seriously. The Court declared that New Hampshire's law mandating that candidates' names be listed in the order of whose party had received the most votes in the preceding election was unconstitutional. It also threw out the provision of the law that stated candidates whose party did not contest the previous election would be listed alphabetically. The Court based its decision on Part I, Article II of the state constitution, which states, "Every inhabitant of the state, having the proper qualifications, has an equal right to be elected into office."[37] However, not every court has ruled like New Hampshire's Supreme Court. In December 2006, a U.S. District court ruled that Maryland's law that puts candidates on the ballot alphabetically was constitutional.[38] In September 2007, the 4th Circuit Court upheld the lower court's ruling. In April 2008, the U.S. Supreme Court refused to hear the case.

Ballot Design

The order in which candidates' names appear on the ballot is a concern, but so is the design of the ballot itself. Once more, because of federalism, there are numerous formats of ballots. On the face of it, ballot design seems to be quite simple. After all, how complex can it be simply to list the candidates' names and have people check boxes indicating for whom they wish to vote? Quite complex, actually.[39] Confusing ballot designs can lead to frustration in the voting booth or worse, people's votes not being tallied correctly or at all.

If Americans were not familiar with the importance of ballot design before the 2000 election, they certainly should be after the election. The "butterfly ballot," where candidates names were alternated on opposite sides of the ballot, confused voters in Palm Beach County, Florida, many of whom believed they were voting for Al Gore when they actually voted for Pat Buchanan (see Figure 5.1). "The probable errors caused by the infamous 'butterfly ballot,'" write political scientists Richard Niemi and Paul Herrnson, "were enough to swing the outcome in the county, state, and Electoral College from one candidate to another."[40]

Certainly the effect of the butterfly ballot in Florida is an extreme example, but empirical studies find that complex ballot designs do lead to more unrecorded votes.[41] Directions on ballots can be confusing, especially when voters are asked to vote for more than one candidate for the same office. Furthermore, information that is designed to make it easier for people to vote can make voting more difficult. For example, according to Niemi and Herrnson, candidates' occupations or places of residence make the ballot unnecessarily complicated by causing too much "clutter."[42] Nevada and Rhode Island actually list the length of terms for the offices.[43] This makes absolutely no sense. At least with occupation or, to a lesser extent, a candidate's hometown, one could argue that these cues help a person decide how to vote; length of term is

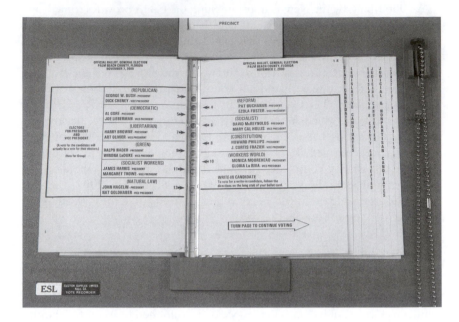

Figure 5.1 The "Butterfly Ballot" used in Palm Beach County, FL, during the 2000
Presidential Election

Source: Smithsonian National Museum of American History.

irrelevant when deciding how to vote.[44] The problem with clutter is another
reason why it makes sense only to include a candidate's party affiliation on the
ballot.

Several states give voters the option of casting a "straight-ticket" vote. In
these states, including Indiana and Iowa, voters can simply check one box to
vote for all Democratic (or Republican) candidates. The straight-ticket option
is an intriguing idea because it generally makes voting easier and reduces the
possibility of error. Furthermore, studies find that when a straight-ticket
option exists, voter roll-off decreases.[45] The problem is that straight-ticket
options can become confusing because of nonpartisan offices—yet another
reason to do away with nonpartisan elections. For example, in Iowa, voters
"who read only the instruction for straight-ticket voting would not even
realize that there were nonpartisan offices and propositions on the ballot."[46] It
is not just nonpartisan elections that create problems with the straight-ticket
option. In North Carolina, voters who choose to vote straight ticket still must
make a separate vote for president. And, in some states, like Pennsylvania,
voters have the option of voting "straight ticket with exception." In other
words, a person could check one box to vote for all Republican candidates, but
then still cast a vote for the Democratic candidate for controller. As Niemi and

Herrnson note, the "straight ticket with exception" option can be quite confusing.[47] The straight-ticket option is an interesting idea, but states must not make it unnecessarily complicated.

There is a concern that the straight-ticket option unfairly advantages the majority party in an area. If the majority of a state is Republican, then registered Republicans may simply vote a straight-ticket instead of considering a viable, attractive Democratic candidate. In fact, Illinois Republicans were so concerned about the advantages the majority party obtains from the straight-ticket option that one of the last acts they passed while in power in the mid-1990s was to remove the straight-ticket option from Illinois ballots. It is certainly understandable why minority parties would be concerned by the use of a straight-ticket voting option; their power and influence is at stake. Still, this concern is not a strong enough reason to eliminate a law that, if the ballot is designed correctly, makes voting easier.[48]

Who is on the ballot, the information available on the ballot, and the design of the ballot all have potentially significant effects on who wins elections, perhaps as much so as who gets to vote in those elections. Although the federal nature of the U.S. government will make this proposal unlikely to happen, voters in the United States would benefit from a consistent ballot and candidates would benefit from consistent ballot-access laws. To recap, ballot-access laws should not be too stringent to keep minor party or independent candidates from getting on the ballot, nonpartisan elections should be eliminated and party affiliation should be the only candidate information listed on the ballot, and states should enact laws that require the mandatory rotation of names on ballots.

The ballot design and ballot-access laws are not the only aspects of the mechanics of voting that vary dramatically state by state or locality by locality. In the next chapter, I turn to the actual voting machines that are used by people to cast votes. As with the topics discussed in this chapter, voting machines are not usually at the top of people's list when thinking about the quality of electoral democracy. As recent elections illustrate, however, they should be.

Chapter 6

Voting Machines

Here is a startling fact. In the 2000 presidential election, roughly 2 million people showed up on election day, but did not have a vote counted in the election.[1] Some of these people purposely did not vote in the presidential election, but a substantial number—an estimated 1.5 million people—believed that they had voted when in fact they had not.[2] Why were their votes not counted? Some may not have followed directions, but many people's votes were not counted because of problems with the voting machines they used to cast their ballots.

Before 2000, only a handful of political scientists and practitioners paid attention to the pros and cons of various voting machine systems. As Stephen Ansolabehere and Charles Stewart III, two political scientists who had studied this issue, write, "The methods used to cast and count ballots are surely one of the most mundane aspects of elections."[3] Few people would have considered the types of voting machines jurisdictions used to be an integral aspect of debates over fairness of elections and the quality of electoral democracy. The 2000 presidential election, particularly in Florida, proved otherwise. The country was captivated as election officials in several Florida counties counted and recounted people's ballots. Yet because of problems with the punch card ballots used in the counties, it was unclear on many ballots what the intentions of the voters actually were. In an election that was ultimately decided by 537 votes, it quickly became apparent that voting machines mattered. In the aftermath of that election emerged a new wave of studies examining the reliability of different systems, most notably the Caltech/MIT Voting Technology Project's *Voting: What Is, What Could Be* and the General Accounting Office's *Statistical Analysis of Factors That Affected Uncounted Votes in the 2000 Presidential Election.*[4]

As a result of the 2000 presidential election, states and localities were encouraged to replace archaic voting machines with state-of-the-art electronic voting machines. However, the push toward electronic voting raised new issues related to security and cost and questions regarding whether electronic voting machines were any more accurate than more traditional voting systems. As a result of the controversy over electronic voting, a movement emerged to encourage jurisdictions to return to election equipment that used paper ballots.

In this chapter, I analyze the current debate over the use of voting machines. One thing is for certain; all voting machines are not equal. Some are more accurate in determining people's vote intentions than others. Some may be more secure or get people out of the polling booth more quickly. And, the public has confidence in some systems more than in others. Based on the results of studies of voting machines, I believe that the movement away from two types of election equipment in particular—punch card and lever machines—is positive. However, the movement away from another kind of system—electronic voting—is disappointing. While optical scan machines may be the best option today, electronic voting is still an enticing possibility. Many of the arguments made against electronic voting are based on anecdotes rather than systematic evidence and focus solely on concerns over security without considering other issues such as accuracy of the system (or, for that matter, the security of other election equipment). Selective media coverage highlighting the negatives of electronic voting but often ignoring the negatives of other systems has only exacerbated the concern over electronic voting.[5] As important, I argue that decisions about voting machines, whichever type is employed, should be made by states, not localities, to eliminate equal protection concerns raised by precincts using different voting machines. Finally, states should require random audits of elections to discover attacks or failures in the voting machines.

Different Types of Voting Equipment

Before getting into the strengths and weaknesses of various voting equipment, it is essential to define a few terms that are needed to understand how well the systems perform. One also needs to be aware of the different types of voting systems that exist. In the past, localities have used one of five voting systems or a combination of them. However, three of the systems are on the verge of extinction.

1   **Hand-counted paper ballot**—This is the simplest and oldest voting system. Candidates' names are simply listed on a piece of paper and voters make their marks on the ballots, which are then counted manually. The number of counties using hand-counted paper ballots has declined from 32.7 percent in 1988 to 1.8 percent in 2008.[6] By 2008, hand-counted paper ballots were used in counties comprising only 0.17 percent of registered voters.[7] It is important to note that some people refer to the optical scan ballots discussed below as paper ballots because, unlike with some electronic voting systems, voters turn in an actual ballot once they are finished voting. However, the optical scan ballots are generally counted by machine, not manually. The paper ballots I am referring to here are essentially no different than what students may use when voting in a student government election.

2   **Mechanical lever machine**—Around since the late 1800s, voters walk into a large steel booth, make their choices, and then pull a lever to cast their votes. The machine then tabulates the votes. Although roughly 30 percent of counties used lever machines in 1988, today they have been virtually eliminated.[8] In recent elections, New York was the only state to use lever machines. However, in 2005 the state passed the Election Reform and Modernization Act, which mandated that the machines be replaced in time for the New York's 2010 primary. Election officials in Nassau County filed a lawsuit challenging the constitutionality of the act, claiming that it forces counties to use voting equipment that is inaccurate and subject to tampering. At the time of this writing, the case had not been decided.

3   **Punch cards**—With punch cards, voters remove a small circle, known as a "chad," when voting. Voters use a stylus that, in theory, should cleanly remove the chad. There are slightly different versions of punch card ballots, including Votomatic, Pollstar, and Datavote. Votomatic punch card ballots, for example, do not have the names of the candidates listed on the ballot, while Datavote punch card ballots do. Once the chads are removed, the ballot is then placed into a computer that reads the votes. In the 2000 presidential election, the largest percentage of the voting population used some form of a punch card.[9] Because of the controversy in Florida, like traditional paper ballots and the mechanical lever machines, punch card ballots have become virtually nonexistent. In fact, in 2008, only eleven counties, all in Idaho, used punch card ballots.[10]

4   **Optical scan**—Students who have taken a multiple-choice test are familiar with optical scan technology. With optical scan ballots, voters fill in an oval with machine-readable ink (or they must connect lines). Votes are then tabulated in optical scanning machines either at the precinct or in a central location. Today, optical scan equipment is the most commonly used voting system and is generally the machine that most election practitioners prefer. In 2008, counties representing more than 56 percent of the nation's registered voters used optical scan equipment. Optical scan machines are used in 41 states, including 17 on a statewide basis. All 86 counties that changed voting systems between 2006 and 2008 chose to use a version of the optical scan machine.[11]

5   **Electronic voting machines**—With direct recording electronic (DRE) machines, people cast their ballots in a similar manner as they would if they were taking money out of an ATM. They may press a button to vote for a candidate, or some machines allow the person to simply touch the candidate's name on the screen. Votes are tabulated electronically, although some systems create what is essentially a receipt to keep a paper trail of votes in case a recount is needed or there is concern about fraud. In 1988, only 1.9 percent of the counties used DRE machines.[12] Between 1988 and 2004, the number of counties using DRE machines grew

substantially.[13] However, the 2008 election was the first time that the number of counties using electronic voting systems declined. In that election, counties representing 32.6 percent of registered voters used electronic systems, down from 37.6 percent in 2006.[14]

6   **Mixed voting systems**—Some jurisdictions use a combination of the five voting systems just mentioned.

When evaluating voting machines, a person should know the residual vote rate, which is simply the percentage of all ballots cast in a geographical unit that did not record a vote for a certain elected office or initiative.[15] For example, if 10 people showed up to vote, but only eight cast votes that were tallied, the residual vote rate would be 20 percent. A vote may not be recorded because of "overvotes," when people cast more votes for an office than they should have—for instance, they voted for both Barack Obama and Ralph Nader for president—or "undervotes," when there is no vote apparent on an individual's ballot. Although overvotes almost always indicate voter error, the same cannot be said for undervotes. Certainly some undervotes occur because the machine did not tabulate the vote correctly, like if the chad was not completely removed from the ballot or because voters did not follow directions, but often people skip an elected office or initiative either because they do not know enough about the candidate or initiative, or because they do not care enough about either.[16] This latter type of undervote does not indicate a problem with the voting machine. Perhaps the best way to measure the residual vote rate is to examine presidential elections because, although certainly some people purposely do not vote in presidential elections, voter roll-off is usually lowest in these elections, providing a better indication of the number of votes that were not counted either because of human or machine error.

The Problem with Punch Card Ballots

As I will show over the next few pages, there is great debate and often conflicting results over what is the most reliable voting machine. However, one result is remarkably clear: punch card ballots are consistently the least reliable of the five different kinds of voting technology when it comes to residual votes.

Punch card ballots became notorious after the 2000 presidential election because of the problems with recounts in several Florida counties. Terms like "hanging," "pregnant," or "dimpled" chads became common jargon. The problems with punch card ballots should not have been surprising since several academic studies of voting machines find them to regularly have the highest percentage of residual votes. Analyzing residual vote rates as a percent of all ballots cast from 1988 to 2000, the Caltech/MIT Voting Technology Project found that the residual vote rate for punch cards in presidential elections was 2.5 percent, compared to 2.3 percent for DRE, 1.8 percent for paper ballot, and 1.5 percent for optical scan and lever machines, respectively.[17] The Caltech/MIT study is just one of several studies that discovered that punch cards are least reliable.[18] Ansolabehere and Stewart estimate that had all the jurisdictions who voted with punch cards in 2000 used optical scanners instead, roughly 500,000 additional presidential votes would have been recorded.[19]

Another concern with punch card ballots is that while, contrary to conventional wisdom, there is little evidence that they are used predominantly in poorer counties,[20] some people are more likely to commit errors using punch card ballots than others. In their examination of voting in the 2000 elections in Los Angeles County where all voters used punch card ballots, D.E. "Betsy" Sinclair and R. Michael Alvarez find that minorities and women are more likely to cast under or over votes than whites and males.[21] Studying elections in South Carolina and Louisiana in 2000, Michael Tomz and Robert Van Houweling come to a similar conclusion.[22]

Because of worries about the accuracy of punch cards after the 2000 election, Florida, as well as several other states and localities, moved to other voting systems. In 2002, Congress passed the Help America Vote Act (HAVA), a central component of which was subsidizing the replacement of punch card systems and lever machines in favor of more modern equipment. In his study of residual rates in the 2004 election, Stewart finds that the replacement of such equipment led to fewer voter errors. Overall, the residual rate fell from 1.9 percent in 2000 to 1.06 percent in 2004, the equivalent of about 1 million votes. Much of the decline in the residual rate is attributed to localities changing from punch cards to either DRE or optical scan technology.[23]

The Pros and Cons of the Remaining Contenders

It is clear that punch card ballots are the most prone to voter error, and, as noted, this fact has resulted in the virtual elimination of them. Another older technology, the lever machine, actually does relatively well regarding residual vote rates. Although performing poorly in races for governor or senator between 1988 and 2000, lever machines, along with the optical scan technology, had the lowest residual rate in races for president.[24] Another study uncovers evidence that lever machines had the smallest percentage of voided ballots during the 1996 presidential election.[25] Furthermore, Tomz and Van Houweling find that lever machines lessen the racial gap in voided ballots that is common with punch card ballots.[26] The supposed accuracy of lever machines is one reason why some jurisdictions in New York have fought against their elimination. Even so, while they perform reasonably well on one measure of success for voting machines— residual rate—they do not perform as well on another measure—getting people through the polls quickly. Moreover, it is impossible to determine if votes are recorded correctly and election officials cannot perform audits. As a result, lever machines are no longer produced making them an unviable option as well. This leaves three possible alternatives: paper ballots, optical scan, and DRE. Here are some of the strengths and weaknesses of all three.

Hand-Counted Paper Ballots

Paper ballots are by far the least technologically advanced of any of the voting systems. Indeed, there is no technology involved at all. People simply make their marks on a ballot, which are then hand-counted by an election official. It is a system that has been in use longer than any other voting system. Perhaps it is most surprising, then, that, according to the Caltech/MIT study, paper ballots had the lowest percentage of residual votes in races for governor and senator from 1988 to 2000 and performed quite competitively with other types of equipment in presidential elections.[27] Still, even with the success of paper ballots when it comes to residual votes, a very small percentage of counties use them.

Since paper ballots must be counted by hand, they put a large burden on local election officials. For some people, a goal of voting technology is to determine a winner quickly. Paper ballots perform less well on this criterion than do either the optical scan or electronic voting machines. More importantly, ballot security is a worry. During the height of the party machines, stories about "stuffing the ballot box" were common. Additionally, paper ballots could be stolen or misplaced. There have been anecdotes of election officials accidentally bringing ballots home with them. In a country that is obsessed with technology, paper ballots are on their way to extinction.

Optical Scan

Another voting equipment that has fared well when it comes to residual votes is the optical scan ballots, first introduced in the 1970s. According to the Caltech/MIT report, optical scan ballots had the lowest residual rates along with lever machines in presidential elections (1.5 percent) and trailed only paper ballots in races for governor and the Senate.[28] A later study by Ansolabehere and Stewart finds optical scanned ballots to have the lowest average residual rates in elections for president, governor, and Senate when counties are weighted by turnout.[29] These results are especially positive given the fact that a majority of counties use optical scan equipment.

However, optical scan equipment is not perfect. Many of the same flaws with hand-counted paper ballots exist for optical scan ballots as well. The ballots may be difficult for people to use if they are visually impaired or have a disability. If there are many offices up for election in a jurisdiction, the ballot can become unwieldy. Election administration can be difficult because of the number of ballots that must be secured.

Additionally, machines may still have difficulty reading a ballot if, say, an oval is not perfectly filled in (a reason that students should always check their scantron sheets with the correct answers on a test!). People often put an "X" in the oval next to the candidate for whom they want to vote or circle a candidate's name; neither of these would be counted by the optical scan equipment. Moreover, voters cannot be sure that their ballots were counted accurately, because they do not receive a "receipt" from voting. Furthermore, optical scan equipment is easier to use for some groups of people than others. For example, Tomz and Van Houweling find that optical scan equipment widens the racial gap in voided ballots.[30] Finally, optical scan machines are not immune from fraud. One study of Florida's optical scan voting machines finds that "someone with only brief access to a machine could replace a memory card with one preprogrammed to read one candidate's vote as counting for another, essentially switching the candidates and showing the loser winning in that precinct."[31]

DRE

The newest voting technology used on a wide basis—and the most controversial today—is the DRE machine. Because of its ability to record and tabulate votes quickly, DRE machines became a popular choice of localities after the problems in the 2000 presidential election. However, because of concerns that I will discuss momentarily, a number of states and localities moved away from DRE machines for the 2008 election. In fact, Representative Rush Holt (D-NJ) introduced a bill in the 111th Congress that would eliminate the use of electronic voting in federal elections.[32]

Although controversial, there are several positive aspects of electronic voting. In addition to recording and tabulating votes quickly, it is easy to present ballots in several different languages. Furthermore, because the font size can change, elderly votes and the visually impaired may have less difficulty voting than they would on the much smaller optical scan ballots. Moreover, the primacy effect (discussed in Chapter 5) can be combated because candidates' names can be randomly rotated. Perhaps the most positive aspect of DRE machines is that, like the lever machines, they keep people from overvoting by not allowing a person to select more candidates than are allowed. In fact, two empirical studies find that electronic machines can eliminate the racial gap in voided ballots because they do not allow overvotes.[33] Another plus of DRE machines is that some flash red lights above each contest and continue flashing until a person casts a vote for that office or initiative, so it can lessen undervoting.[34] Yet, even with these advantages, DRE machines initially performed poorly with regard to residual votes. In the Caltech/MIT study, only punch cards had a greater residual vote percentage.[35]

What led to the high residual vote percentages for electronic machines? The problem seemed to be a confusing interface that made it difficult to vote. According to the Caltech/MIT study:

The mechanics of voting on [DREs] are often confusing. It is often not obvious how to undo a selection, how to check that all races have been voted, how to distinguish between the offices, and how to register the votes. Some interfaces are "too responsive": a voter can push a button for the next page and more than one page will pass by without the voter seeing it. The formatting of the "ballot"—the presentation of choices—is often confusing as well. It is sometimes unclear where one office (a set of candidates to choose among) ends and the next one begins.[36]

However, improvements have been made to the interface, which has lessened residual vote rates for DREs. In his study of residual vote rates in the 2004 election, Charles Stewart finds that DRE machines performed quite well, and that "the adoption of DREs turned out to produce the greatest drop in the residual vote rate."[37] Alvarez and Hall note that residual vote rates for DREs declined from 3.6 percent in 1988 to 1.6 percent in 2004.[38] Residual rates for DREs now look similar to or are better than those for other voting systems.[39]

Another criticism of DREs is that they will make voting take longer and people, especially the elderly, will be frustrated by using them. However, studies regularly find that voters report a positive experience with electronic voting. In their study of the Diebold Accu VoteTS voting system, a specific kind of electronic voting machine, Paul Herrnson and his colleagues note that voters were generally pleased with their experience using the machine. In a survey of 365 respondents, 81 percent said that their overall assessment of DRE was positive; only 9 percent reported a negative experience. More than 80 percent of respondents gave positive responses to questions regarding comfort using the system, the readability of characters, understanding terminology on the screen, the ease of correcting mistakes, and trusting that their vote was recorded. In a 2002 exit poll conducted in 23 precincts located in Prince George's County and Montgomery County, Maryland, respondents were even more upbeat. In this instance, 91 percent of respondents reported having a positive experience while only 5 percent said that their experience was negative.[40] In a different study, Herrnson and his colleagues find that satisfaction with electronic voting was consistent across various groups, including the elderly and those who do not regularly use computers.[41] Additionally, Stein and his colleagues find that, when given the option of choosing between voting with a DRE or optical scan machine, voters overwhelming chose the former. Perhaps most interestingly, DREs were uniformly preferred by almost every demographic of voter including age. They also uncover no evidence that it took people longer to vote using DREs (in fact, voters actually rated the DREs higher on "usability" than optical scan ballots) or that voters were less confident that their votes would be counted accurately.[42] Similar to other studies, they conclude that election administration (for example, helpful poll workers, easily accessible precincts) is what drives a person's feelings about their voting experience, not the machine on which they voted.[43]

Residual vote rates and the usability of the machines are not the biggest concern with the use of DREs, however, but the security of such machines instead. "In a paper-based election, one might observe the ballots being counted," writes computer scientist Earl Barr and colleagues. "But many electronic voting systems being used today record votes and ballot images as bits on flash card and in memory. They tally them and report totals. An observer cannot look inside a computer's memory to verify that the ballots are recorded correctly or the votes tallied correctly because the bits are not visible."[44] After an initial push for jurisdictions to adopt DRE machines because of the 2000 presidential election, states and localities have moved away from electronic voting because of the concern over security.

Likewise, DRE machines may be susceptible to software attack programs, such as Trojan horses, that take over a voting machine and switch votes from one candidate to the other. Recently, computer scientists from California universities were able to hack into three electronic voting systems used in California and several other places in the country. Some DREs have wireless components, which make them more prone to fraud.[45] Furthermore, there is no paper trail of votes with some electronic systems, and even those machines with a paper trail may be subject to manipulation.[46] And, although they may not have been caused because of fraud, there are numerous examples of vote tallying errors with electronic machines, specifically those provided by Diebold Election Systems.[47]

In addition to fraud and errors, opponents of electronic voting argue that, with DRE machines, longer lines at the polls are likely since fewer machines can be purchased because of the cost. In his study of the 2008 presidential election, Stewart found that those who voted on DREs waited in line almost twice as long as those who voted using optical scan ballots.[48] It is true that DRE machines are more expensive to purchase than optical scanners, but they are less expensive to operate. Over a 20-year period, the difference in cost between DRE machines and optical scan machines is a wash,[49] although this assumes that the DRE machines will last the duration of the 20 years. Nevertheless, the startup costs of implementing DRE machines can be daunting for localities. Besides cost, the use of electronic machines requires even greater training of poll workers, most of whom are elderly and less likely to feel comfortable with the equipment. Finally, the machines could break, keeping some people from voting and creating chaos at the polls.

The problems with electronic voting machines might be best documented in the 2006 congressional race for Florida's 13th District, a race that caused the state to reconsider its use of DREs. In that race, in which voters used electronic machines, Republican Vern Buchanan narrowly defeated Democrat Christine Jennings by 369 votes. However, there were roughly 18,000 undervotes in Sarasota County, a number that seemed unusually high. Jennings alleged that the undervotes resulted from machine malfunction, but a panel of computer scientists appointed to study the voting software used in the race concluded that it was not a problem with the machines that led to the large number of undervotes, but voter error instead. According to the report, the machines' interface was confusing and likely led to a number of people accidentally skipping the race. Also, the machines did not have a paper trail, making it difficult for voters to notice any errors.

Even with the problems associated today with DREs and the recent movement away from them, given the United States' obsession with technology it is still likely that electronic voting machines will be prominent in the future. That might not be a bad thing. As the authors of the Caltech/MIT Voting Technology Project report write, "We see electronic voting as an improving technology. It has great potential."[50] As noted, residual rates of DRE machines are lessening and people seem to be comfortable voting electronically. As people have more experience with electronic voting, residual rates and user comfort will likely continue to improve.

The adequate training of polling workers is a concern. Indeed, during the 2006 midterm elections, a judge ordered several precincts in Kane County, IL, to remain open past the poll closing time because precinct workers had difficulty powering up electronic voting machines. One can find numerous similar examples around the country. There is no doubt that precinct workers need to better familiarize themselves with the electronic machines, but this problem is correctable. With time, precinct workers will become more familiar with electronic voting.

The most persuasive argument against electronic voting, then, remains security. It amazes me that we have not been able to do better as of yet on this account. Americans regularly do their banking, make purchases, file their taxes, and view their retirement and stock portfolios via the Internet. Certainly there have been high-profile cases of websites being hacked or people's personal information being stolen on the Internet, but these instances are surprisingly rare, and I have to believe that there are more people out there who would try to steal a credit card or bank account number than there are people who would try to rig an election. Perhaps I have too much faith in the security of the Internet, but it seems to me that if we can create programs that keep your bank account or credit card information secure, we certainly should be able to create a program that will make your vote secure.

However, perhaps the concern about voter fraud and electronic voting is exaggerated. Some people, far more knowledgeable than I on such matters, think so. "Hackers can do anything only in books and movies," says computer scientist Michael Shamos, who served as Pennyslvania's examiner of electronic voting systems for 20 years. "The prospect that a hacker could not only manipulate an election but do it without employing a detectable bug is so farfetched an idea no one has come close to showing how it might be done."[51]Former chairman of the Democratic National Committee, Joe Andrew, concurred. According to Andrew, "[I]t is not possible to move a constant fraction of votes from one party to another in each jurisdiction without it being obvious that something is going on."[52] Referring back to the ability of computer scientists to hack into voting machines in California, many criticized the exercise as being unrealistic because the computer scientists did not face the safeguards that voting machine vendors or counties use. The testers were provided with encrypted source codes by the companies that government employees would not have.[53]

It seems to me that asking whether electronic voting is secure is the wrong question. DRE machines may not be completely secure, but neither are any of the other voting systems mentioned previously. It is not as if paper ballots or optical scans are totally safe. In fact, examples of "hackers" stealing ballots or stuffing ballot boxes have been commonplace for more than one hundred years. As Charles Stewart writes:

> On the one side, we have over a century's experience with stealing elections using paper. A large fraction of contemporary election fraud cases involve compromising absentee voting, which is all conducted on paper. On the other side, we have no confirmed cases of elections stolen by hacking DREs, and a surprisingly small number of cases in which inherent features of DREs caused lost votes, though such examples do exist.[54]

The criteria for evaluating security should be which voting system is the *most* secure, not which is completely secure. If the latter was the standard for voting machines, then no voting would ever take place. Surprisingly, I have seen no research that tests the security of electronic voting versus other types of voting machines. I do not mean to discount completely the concern over security and fraud, but the bigger problem with electronic voting seems to be user error or system error, rather than any malicious attempt to influence the outcomes of elections.

However, if jurisdictions are going to use electronic voting machines, then it is important that the machines contain a Voter-Verified Paper Trail (VVPT) that essentially gives the voter a receipt of the votes they cast. Since voting on electronic machines is done within a "black box," VVPT allows voters to check that their ballots were counted accurately. There are some issues with VVPT as well. The machines are more expensive to purchase and there are more parts that could potentially break. Some VVPT receipts are too flimsy, making paper jams common. Also, since ballots are often quite long, the receipt is not as succinct as one a person might receive from an ATM. Finally, some people are not convinced that VVPT is immune to fraud or manipulation as well.[55]

Still, VVPT on electronic machines is essential because it gives election officials a nonelectronic ballot should a recount be needed. As important, without a paper trail it is much more difficult for governments to conduct audits of elections. Random audits of election results are imperative for a few reasons. First, audits will be likely to discover fraud should it exist, or prevent it from occurring in the first place. Second, audits will likely improve voter confidence that their votes have been counted accurately and that the election results are legitimate. It is imperative, however, that any audit of election results be transparent. Lawrence Norden and his colleagues argue that the whole process of the audit should be publicly observable and "ideally video-taped and archived."[56] Currently, only 21 states require VVPT and statewide audits, while another 11 require VVPT without statewide audits. Eight states still require neither VVPT nor statewide audits.[57]

A Word on Internet Voting

It is necessary in a chapter on voting machines to make some brief comments about an even newer voting technology than DRE machines: Internet voting. The Internet is increasingly essential to the lives of millions of Americans. When I graduated as an undergraduate in 1996, I had never used the Internet for my research papers. Today, many students do not know how to research papers without the help of the Internet! Americans are increasingly going online to get their news. We regularly buy all sorts of products via the Internet. Many people have found their significant others via the Internet. With the advent of such sites as Facebook, MySpace, and Twitter people post their every move over the Internet. It only makes sense, then, that we will eventually do all of our voting via the Internet as well. "It seems to us inevitable," write Michael Alvarez and Thad Hall. "Internet voting is the future of voting in the United States."[58]

Although it is understandable why Internet voting may seem "inevitable," advances in Internet voting have stalled in the United States. In 2000, voters in the Arizona Democratic presidential primary had the option of remote Internet voting, while, in 2004, Democrats in the Michigan caucuses had the opportunity to do so. However, no Internet voting took place during the 2008 election season. Again, concerns over security have thwarted a movement toward Internet voting. Although Internet voting has, to this point anyway, failed to catch on in the United States, Internet voting trials have been conducted in other countries, including the United Kingdom, France, and Switzerland.[59]

There are definite advantages of Internet voting. Internet voting significantly reduces the costs of voting (see Chapter 2) because voters no longer have to leave their residences. In fact, they could vote from anywhere that had Internet access. Internet voting might be especially helpful for those people overseas, the disabled, frequent business travelers, and students—a group that does not regularly show up at the polls. Also, because people would be voting online, they would have access to a plethora of information that would not be available in a traditional voting booth, which could increase the quality of voting. People could compare the information on the websites of candidates, browse the websites of interest groups for endorsements, or read articles about the candidates. Like electronic voting, overvotes could be prohibited and undervotes caused by error could be lessened significantly. Finally, if used on a wide-scale basis Internet voting could impose uniformity regarding voting, eliminating the equal protection concern raised by the fact that people in a state or locality are often voting on different machines. While the interface might be different for voters in various states or localities, everyone would be using the same "voting machine." These advantages make Internet voting especially attractive.

However, there are many arguments against Internet voting. First, similar to the claims made against no-excuse absentee voting and early voting discussed in Chapter 2, Internet voting may "further the disintegration of civic life in the United States."[60] There are few things we do together as Americans, the argument goes, but going to the polls on the same day to vote is one of them. As I stated in Chapter 2, there is a trade-off between making voting easier and protecting a cherished civic rite. I sympathize with the view of protecting the sanctity of election day, but with the increase in the number of states moving to no-excuse-absentee voting and early voting, the train has left the station; we are already headed away from the concept of "one election day." Internet voting, then, only seems to be a logical next step.

Second, as with electronic voting, many researchers question the security of voting over the Internet. In fact, the two major reports on Internet voting— the California Internet Voting Task Force and the Report of the National Workshop on Internet Voting—both argued against Internet voting because of security reasons.[61] More recently, the Brennan Center for Justice has also questioned the security of Internet voting.[62] In response to the argument that Internet voting is not safe, Alvarez and Hall, two of the most vocal supporters of Internet voting and the authors of the book *Point, Click, & Vote*, make a similar argument as the one I made earlier regarding security and electronic voting. "It is impossible to create a perfectly secure voting system; the current system of paper ballots is not completely secure, and neither would an Internet voting system be," write Alvarez and Hall. "However, tools exist today to overcome the security challenges posed by Internet voting—something that opponents of Internet voting often fail to note."[63] They continue:

> Before concluding that [threats to Internet voting security are] too much to handle, one should remember that the common threats to any Internet voting system . . . are known threats, with known solutions and mitigation strategies. There is no reason to think that Internet voting websites will be any different from commercial websites—they will come under attack, and they must be designed to eliminate or mitigate each threat. Well-designed networks mitigate the risk of attacks, and a well-designed Internet voting site should do the same.[64]

As I argued earlier, we need to take security risks seriously, whether it is related to Internet or electronic voting, but these are problems that, with a little ingenuity, can be overcome.

Although I am less concerned with the security of Internet voting or the fact that it undermines election day, I do worry about two other issues that should keep Internet voting from being enacted on a widespread basis anytime soon. First, voters could become extremely frustrated by Internet voting if the system was fraught with errors. I cannot tell you the number of times that I have tried to buy an airplane ticket or make a hotel reservation online only to have an error occur and then have to start the process over. Anyone who regularly makes purchases on the Internet probably has similar experiences. Also, there may be issues with browser compatibilities or certain operating systems making errors more likely. Indeed, these problems plagued Internet voters in the Arizona Democratic primary in 2000.[65]

If people trying to vote received an error, then there is little they could do. If they were voting early enough before the election they might try again later, but no doubt many would give up and, if they were voting at the last minute, there seems to be little that could be done. In a precinct, when people receive an error message or have a question, they can go to a precinct worker for help. The same cannot be done with Internet voting. A help desk could be established, similar to those on college campuses when students or faculty have computer problems, but this would be extremely expensive, as it would have to be staffed regularly by numerous technicians. Additionally, while help desk technicians may be able to answer questions, it is not clear that they would be able to fix problems immediately.

The second difficulty with implementing Internet voting today is the trouble of the digital divide: some people have easier access to the Internet than others. The people who are less likely to be able to access the Internet are more likely to be poor, less educated, and nonwhite.[66] Because of this fact, it is likely that Internet voting on a widespread basis would not survive a court challenge. The Voting Rights Act clearly states that any system that makes it more difficult for nonwhites to participate in the political process than whites is illegal. Even Alvarez and Hall concede this point. "Internet voting can be implemented throughout the nation for a federal election only after the problem of unequal Internet access is addressed," they write.[67]

Internet voting may not be ready for prime time today, but its time is on the horizon. Eventually, the digital divide will lessen, making Internet voting a real possibility. The only way to eliminate the bugs in such a system is to experiment with Internet voting. Ultimately, I agree with the conclusion of Alvarez and Hall regarding Internet voting and its future. "There is no way to know whether any argument regarding Internet voting is accurate unless real Internet voting systems are tested," the authors write, "and they should be tested in small-scale, scientific trials so that their successes and failures can be evaluated."[68] "Internet voting can be implemented and studied *now*," they continue, "in meaningful, although limited and controlled, efforts before it is used in major statewide or national elections."[69]

So, What's the Solution?

There is no perfect voting machine; every system discussed in this chapter is susceptible to residual votes, every one not completely secure. One thing is clear: punch card ballots seem to be least reliable in accurately recording people's votes. As a result, they are moving toward extinction. Two other voting systems—the lever machine and paper ballots—also seem to be on their way out because of the lack of technology that each provides. As a result, if states or localities are considering new voting machines, there appears to be only two viable options: optical scan or DRE.[70]

The superior of these two options *today* looks to be the optical scan machines. They have generally performed better regarding lessening the number of residual votes and, while it is difficult to know because of the lack of studies on the subject, likely do at least as well if not better than DRE machines regarding security. If localities use optical scanners, however, then they should use ballots where voters must fill in an oval instead of ballots where voters must connect the lines because the former is likely to be less confusing than the latter. Moreover, optical scan ballots should be tabulated at the precinct rather than in a centralized location because doing so reduces residual rates.[71] Tabulating ballots at the precinct gives workers the opportunity to question a voter if there is a problem with their ballot and the voter has the chance to fix a mistake. That cannot be done when ballots are counted in a central location.

Yet, the recommendation in favor of optical scan machines is not an argument against localities implementing electronic voting machines. DRE machines made significant improvements in lowering residual vote rates in 2004.[72] As voters become more familiar with electronic voting, we can expect the percentage of residual votes to continue to decline. DRE machines are certainly far from perfect, but they have a potentially great upside. We need to continue to work to make DRE machines more secure, but the only way to hone electronic voting is to continue using it. Again, if localities do use electronic voting, then it is imperative that the machines have a VVPT and that a regular audit of paper records occur. These actions will make the administration of elections more transparent and alert election officials to any fraud or machine malfunctions that might have occurred as well as improve citizens' confidence in the electoral process.

Finally, while I am less concerned about whether optical scan or DRE machines should be used, it is imperative that every precinct in a state use the same voting machine. It is unfair for voters in one precinct or county to use one voting machine and voters in a different precinct or county to use another. Different voting machines have different success rates at accurately recording a person's vote. A central tenet of democracy is that every vote should count equally. If different voting systems are used for statewide elections, then some people have a greater probability of their voting counting than others. Holding the voting machine constant helps to alleviate this problem.

Part III

Rethinking National Elections

Chapter 7

The Redistricting Process

In the 1990s, California's 36th congressional district was one of the most competitive in the country. The district spread from funky Venice in the north down through the beach communities of Marina Del Rey, Manhattan Beach, Hermosa Beach, Redondo Beach, the South Bay, and San Pedro. The district was split almost equally among Democratic and Republican identifiers. It was a fiscally conservative district, "leery of taxes,"[1] but liberal on cultural issues, such as abortion and gay rights. Jane Harman, a Democrat, who is an ardent supporter of the defense industry—an important constituency within her district—represented the district throughout most of the 1990s. Harman regularly faced competitive elections, defeating one opponent by only 812 votes even though she outspent her by more than two to one. When Harman decided not to run for reelection in 1998 to pursue California's governorship, Republican Steve Kuykendall, another moderate politician, was elected with only 49 percent of the vote. After her failed gubernatorial campaign, Harman returned to barely defeat Kuykendall in 2000.

As the representative of one of the most politically competitive districts in the country, Harman would always likely be a vulnerable incumbent and, as a result, hold a spot at the top of the "Republican Hit List." That was, until the new district lines were drawn in time for the 2002 midterm elections. Democrats in the state legislature moved to protect Harman by removing some of the most heavily Republican areas from the district. In 2002, Harman defeated her Republican opponent by more than 25 percent of the vote and she has not been challenged seriously since.

As the Harman example illustrates, politicians are often electorally safe or vulnerable depending on the demographic makeup of the district, which changes every 10 years when new district lines are drawn.[2] Because of the importance of drawing district lines and the fact that, in most states, politicians conduct the redistricting process, redistricting is an extremely political process. It can be used to make incumbents safe, as was done in the case of Harman, or vulnerable. It can be used to increase minority representation or divide heavily populated minority areas making the election of a racial or ethnic minority more difficult. It can be used to the advantages of one political party at the expense of the other.

Critics of the redistricting process assert that it leads to oddly drawn districts that are spread throughout the state, which makes it more difficult for representatives to listen to the wishes of their constituents. More important, critics allege, is the fact that the protection of incumbents, political parties, or racial or ethnic politicians has led to increasingly uncompetitive elections, even more so than usual. The lack of competition in elections can have dire consequences. Political efficacy and trust may decline; voters may be less likely to participate in the electoral process; and Congress may become increasingly polarized and ideological, making the policy it produces less likely to reflect the wishes of the public it represents.

Creating an optimal redistricting process is nearly impossible, given several worthwhile, but usually competing goals. While not a panacea for the ills of the redistricting process, I believe that independent commissions, not state legislatures, should be given the authority to draw and implement new district maps. Such commissions will lessen the conflict of interest that drives the current redistricting method in the majority of states and be the most apt to balance successfully the competing goals that face mapmakers. Before turning to the goals of redistricting and how such a commission would work, it is essential to understand the current redistricting practices in the states.

How Does the Process Work?

The U.S. Constitution requires that a census be taken every 10 years to determine the population of each state (and the country as a whole). Because state populations are constantly changing and the populations of congressional districts should be roughly equal, the reapportionment of seats becomes an issue in the House of Representatives, as well as in state legislatures. Also, in 1929, Congress passed a law limiting the size of the House of Representatives at 435, meaning that as some states gained seats because of population increases, others would lose seats.[3] For example, it is projected that, after the 2010 census, Texas will pick up four seats and Florida will gain two, while Ohio and New York will each lose two.[4]

Once the census is completed and the 435 seats are divided between the states, then the question becomes: How will the districts within the states be drawn? For states such as Wyoming or Delaware, which only have one representative in the House, the redistricting process is not usually a concern.[5] For the vast majority of states, however, district lines must be determined. In all but seven states, the congressional redistricting process is quite similar to the procedure for passing any piece of legislation: the state legislature must pass a bill that the governor either signs into law or vetoes. If the governor vetoes the plan, then the legislature can override the veto.[6] In all states, if no agreement can be met between the governor and the state legislature, then the process is turned over to the courts.

That is generally how the practice works, but there are a few variations. For example, in North Carolina the governor does not have veto power over a redistricting plan. Some states, like Maine and Connecticut, require that the legislature adopt a plan with two-thirds vote. In Maryland, the governor proposes a districting plan to the legislature, who then can approve it with a majority vote. If the legislature decides to use its own proposal instead, then the plan must pass with a two-thirds vote. If the legislature cannot obtain a two-thirds vote, then the governor's plan becomes law.[7]

The involvement of the state legislatures and governors makes redistricting a contentious, political process. "[L]egislative redistricting is one of the conflictual forms of regular politics in the United States short of violence," write political scientists Andrew Gelman and Gary King.[8] Incumbent House members may want to make their seats as safe as possible by putting pressure on state representatives to draw favorable districts. State representatives may have their eyes set on running for the House and want to create a district that would be most beneficial to their candidacies. National parties may coerce certain states' legislatures in hopes of maximizing the party's influence nationally. Organizations representing racial and ethnic minorities will argue for districts that maximize the representation of their groups. In short, nothing that government does illustrates politics better than the redistricting process.

Because of the contentious and political nature of the redistricting process, seven states (Arizona, California, Hawaii, Idaho, Montana, New Jersey, and Washington) have created redistricting commissions comprising between five and 13 people to draw district lines instead of allowing the state legislatures to do so. For example, in Montana, where the commission has five members, majority and minority party leaders of both houses of the legislature each selects one member who then selects a fifth person to serve as chair. To lessen the likelihood of a conflict of interest, members cannot be public officials and may not run for public office for at least two years after serving on the commission. Washington and Hawaii have essentially the same system, although Hawaii allows legislative leaders to each appoint two people instead of one. Several states, including Maine and Vermont, use commissions in an advisory capacity, and Iowa delegates the districting process to a nonpartisan agency. In all three states, however, the state legislature is the final authority on enacting a redistricting proposal. As I will argue, placing the power of redistricting in the hands of redistricting commissions is more preferential than allowing state politicians to determine district lines. However, before discussing why redistricting commissions are advantageous, it is first essential to understand the conflicting goals that mapmakers face when drawing districts.

The Goals of Redistricting

When new districts are created, map drawers consider several criteria, some of which are mandated by the courts, others of which are stated in state constitutions or statutes, and still others of which are merely to protect political interests. The goals of redistricting are to:

1   establish a roughly equal number of people living within a district in a state;
2   develop compact and contiguous districts;
3   protect minority representation;
4   create a partisan advantage;
5   protect incumbents;
6   keep communities of interest and political subdivisions intact;
7   promote electoral competition.

Roughly Equal Numbers of People in a District

This requirement has not always been in place. In fact, malapportionment—when state district populations are not equal—was quite common before the 1960s, especially in the South. Often, states would simply refuse to redraw district lines, which led to problems regarding representation. As the cities in southern states began to grow, those districts had far more people than the surrounding rural areas. This meant that a person living in, say, Atlanta, GA, had less political influence than a person living in Albany, GA, because the representative in Atlanta had many more constituents than the representative in Albany.[9] The courts were initially hesitant to get involved in battles over redistricting, claiming that it was a political, not a constitutional issue.[10] That view changed in 1962 when the Supreme Court ruled in *Baker v. Carr* that the Equal Protection Clause of the Fourteenth Amendment guaranteed the right of citizens to have votes given approximately the same weight regardless of where they lived.[11] In other words, *Baker* was the first case to establish the idea of "one person, one vote" as a constitutional right. Yet, *Baker* only applied to state legislative assemblies;[12] it was not until *Wesberry v. Sanders* that the idea of "one person, one vote" pertained to the House of Representatives.[13]

Since *Wesberry*, the courts have been quite strict regarding acceptable population deviations for congressional districts.[14] In *Karcher v. Daggett*, the Court threw out a New Jersey redistricting plan where the districts varied by no more than one-seventh of one percent.[15] In 2002, a federal court rejected a Pennsylvania plan with a deviation of 19 people.[16] Fortunately, advances in technology have made it easy to draw numerous potential plans quickly in which the maximum population range is no more than a single person.

Compactness and Contiguity

Contiguity is relatively straightforward. District lines should be touching, although some state constitutions allow the district lines to be separated by a body of water. There have been some districts that have pushed the "spirit" of the contiguity requirement, such as the Illinois 17th congressional district from 2002 to 2010 that at one point was held together by a single block in Springfield in which no one lives (see Figure 7.1), but the criteria here is clear. Compactness is an entirely different story. District lines should not be spread throughout the state, as was the case with the old Louisiana 4th congressional district, known as the Zorro district, because the district started in the northwest corner of the state moving east to the state line, jetted south to the middle of the state, and then moved east again making a "Z" similar to the mark made by the fictional hero (see Figure 7.2). Altogether, the district covered more than 600 miles and included parts of every urban area in the state except for New Orleans and Lake Charles. The problem with judging whether a district is compact, however, is that there is no agreed-upon definition of what compactness entails, therefore there is no generally accepted

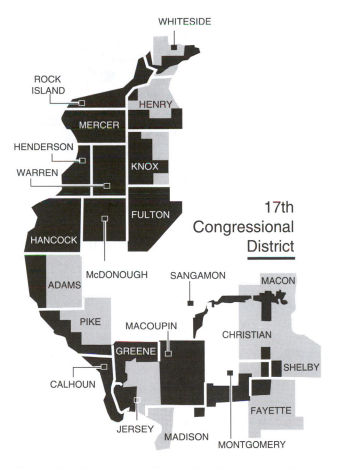

Figure 7.1 District Map of the Current Illinois 17th Congressional District

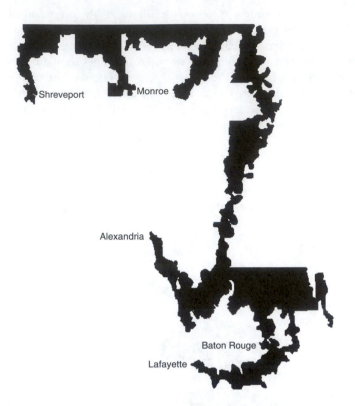

Figure 7.2 District Map of Louisiana's Former 4th Congressional District (shaded)

measure of it.[17] It is akin to Justice Stewart's well-known definition of pornography: "I can't define it, but I know it when I see it." Likewise, some justices, such as John Paul Stevens, have questioned whether there is any constitutional basis for compactness.[18]

Protect Minority Representation

Of all the goals of redistricting, perhaps none have caused as much controversy as this one. Throughout much of American history, states, particularly those in the South, drew districts lines in ways that would purposely dilute minority representation. This process is known as "gerrymandering"—named after a former governor of Massachusetts, Elbridge Gerry, who pushed for oddly shaped districts to help members of his party get elected. With single-member districts, there are two gerrymandering techniques: cracking and packing. African American populations were being "cracked" purposely—in other words, split up—to prevent African American representation in Congress, the state legislatures, or city councils. Instead of allowing the African American population to be a majority in a district, African American communities were divided. In addition, voter disenfranchise techniques, like literacy tests and polls taxes, made it virtually impossible for a minority candidate to be elected.

The Voting Rights Act of 1965 was designed to eliminate the dilution of African American political power. Under Section 5 of the Act, states targeted under the Act had to seek preclearance to get new district lines or any changes in voting laws approved. States could seek preclearance in one of two ways: the plan could be permitted by the U.S. Attorney General or by the U.S. District Court of the District of Columbia. Initially, only state districting plans that threatened minority representation—those that purposely cracked racial and ethnic minority populations—were not accepted. However, the state did not have to draw districts designed to *increase* minority representation.[19] In other words, states only had to show that their redistricting plans were not discriminatory; they did not have to be constructed to improve minority representation. That changed when the Voting Rights Act was extended in 1982, sparking what redistricting scholar Bruce Cain and his colleagues call the "vote dilution period" of redistricting.[20] No longer did states have to simply show that they were not weakening representation by intentionally cracking minority populations; now they were encouraged to increase minority representation by "packing" minority populations.[21] Instead of districts where African Americans would comprise roughly 30 percent of the district population consistently, African Americans might make up 70 percent or more of one or two districts' populations, but be virtually nonexistent in the other districts. So-called majority-minority districts, the number of which increased dramatically after the 1990 census, would likely elect racial and ethnic minority candidates, thereby enhancing minority representation in Congress.[22] The Supreme Court has since taken a step back regarding the drawing of majority-minority districts. The Court has still generally held the view that purposely diluting minority populations is unacceptable,[23] but also that race cannot be the predominant factor in drawing district lines.[24] As Dennis Thompson writes, "States must use race, but not too much."[25]

Create a Partisan Advantage

The courts have mandated the previous three goals because of constitutional issues. Still, redistricting is an inherently political process and political parties and politicians often have other goals in mind. The majority party in a state's legislature may draw district lines in a way that they believe will benefit their party. Partisan redistricting plans are most likely to be created when a party holds control of both houses of the state legislature and the governor's mansion. The most notorious example of partisan redistricting is the mid-decade redistricting conducted by Republicans in the Texas state legislature in 2003. This case was downright bizarre, as several Democrats in the legislature initially fled the state to keep a vote from going forth on the new redistricting plan.[26] What led to such strange actions by the Democrats? Republicans, who won both state houses in 2002 and held the governor's seat, took the unprecedented step of redrawing congressional and state legislative districts after new district lines had already been approved, as is usually the case, after the most recent census.[27] However, Republicans, led by the majority leader in the U.S. House of Representatives at the time, Tom Delay, believed they could gain several additional congressional and state legislative seats by creating new districts. The new plan forced a few incumbent Democratic representatives to run against each other and created several other districts that would benefit Republican incumbents or challengers.

While the courts had ruled that a few racial gerrymanders were unconstitutional, they had never done so regarding a partisan gerrymander in a congressional district. In *Davis v. Bandemer* (1986), the Court held that partisan gerrymandering was a justiciable issue—in other words, it can be raised in court—but it has never found a partisan gerrymander to be so egregious that it was unconstitutional.[28] The Court ruled no differently in the Texas case. While the Court forced one district to be redrawn because it believed the district violated the Voting Rights Act by diluting the voting power of Latinos, it did not find that the partisan gerrymander was unconstitutional. Perhaps more importantly, the Court ruled that mid-decade redistricting was not unconstitutional. Many redistricting scholars worried that the Court's ruling would open the floodgates by encouraging more mid-decade redistricting when a party believes that new district lines can be drawn to their advantage. Sure enough, Georgia redistricted in 2005 after Republicans took control of the state legislature. However, attempts at mid-decade partisan redistricting were not abundant. Yet, it is possible that mid-decade partisan redistricting will be frequent in the future. While a few states have explicit laws on the books that prevent mid-decade redistricting for congressional districts, others allow the process to occur at any time. Most states do not have any laws on the books that address the issue.

Protect Incumbents

When a party controls both houses of the state legislature and the governor's mansion, as was the case in Texas, it is likely to engage in a partisan gerrymander. However, when the state government is divided where one party controls the legislature and the other party controls the governorship or the state legislature is divided, politicians might engage in bipartisan, or "sweetheart," gerrymandering that is designed to protect incumbents. Parties often view incumbent gerrymandering as an acceptable compromise to maintain their party's strength. However, incumbent gerrymandering does not only occur under divided government. The California example mentioned at the beginning of this chapter was actually a bipartisan, not a partisan, gerrymander. Even though Democrats held majorities in both houses of the state legislature and the governorship, they worked to make some of their incumbents, like Harman, safer in exchange for doing the same for some vulnerable Republican incumbents. California was not alone in protecting incumbents. According to redistricting expert Michael McDonald, after the 2000 census incumbency protection maps were adopted in 20 states, which affected 231 districts.[29] While bipartisan gerrymanders are controversial, because many scholars believe that they entrench incumbents, in several redistricting cases the Supreme Court has named incumbent protection as a legitimate state interest.[30]

Keep Communities of Interest Intact

Nineteen states require or encourage the protection of communities of interest in congressional or state legislative redistricting. What exactly constitutes a community of interest, however, is generally unclear and only six states have attempted to define the term. The concept might imply that a neighborhood not be divided or that certain economic or cultural areas be held together. After the Supreme Court ruled in *Shaw v. Reno* and its progeny that race cannot be the predominant factor in redistricting, protecting communities of interest became a "particularly attractive neutral criterion, especially in states with large minority populations, since the vagueness and lack of a commonly accepted definition allowed creative arguments on what could and should constitute a community of interest."[31]

Promote Electoral Competition

There is a seventh goal of redistricting that is popular with reformers and democratic theorists, but is definitely not a concern of the political parties and even many of the commissions drawing the districts or the courts ruling on the constitutionality of them. That is, districts should be drawn in a way to promote electoral competition.[32] "A competitive struggle for the people's vote," writes political philosopher Dennis Thompson, "is for many political scientists and political theorists the very definition of democracy."[33]

As I note in Chapter 1, electoral competition is an essential aspect of a democracy for a few reasons. First, a significant amount of research finds that voter turnout is higher in competitive elections for offices at all levels of government.[34] From a rational choice perspective, this result makes sense. When elections are close, the outcome of the election may be in doubt, leading more people to cast their ballots.[35] More importantly, close elections receive more media coverage,[36] which can significantly lessen the costs of voting. Additionally, political parties are more likely to engage in voter mobilization efforts when races are close, which can lead to greater voter turnout.[37]

Second, electoral competition is important for translating the wishes of the people into public policy. Competition may require incumbents to moderate their positions on issues to appeal to the median voter. If a congressperson has just emerged from a close election, she might think twice about taking positions on issues that are more ideologically extreme than her constituents. If that congressperson knows that she will not have a competitive upcoming race, she may be more willing to take positions that are ideologically to the left or right of her constituents. Literature on the decline of competition in the U.S. House has raised red flags regarding the ability of citizens to keep their representatives in check. For example, Monica Bauer and John Hibbing write, "The level of competition in congressional elections *has* declined and should be a source of concern to those who value electoral accountability."[38]

Third, electoral competition will minimize the amount of corruption in Congress by holding corrupt members accountable. Because they are virtually guaranteed reelection given the way the district lines are drawn, some members of Congress become too comfortable in office and, as a result, bend the rules or engage in activities that they otherwise would not if they had the potential to face a legitimate challenge. President Barack Obama's former Chief of Staff, Rahm Emanuel, believes that "competition is the best disinfectant" for corruption.[39]

To say that there has been little electoral competition in recent races for the House of Representatives would be an understatement. As Alan Abramowitz and his colleagues note, "In the 2004 U.S. House elections, only five challengers in the entire nation succeeded in defeating an incumbent. Of the 435 seats in the House, only 22 were decided by a margin of less than 10 percentage points."[40] The 2006 and 2008 congressional elections were more competitive than 2004. In 2006, 63 seats were decided by a margin of less than 10 percentage points and 21 incumbents were defeated in the general election. In 2008, 51 seats were decided by a margin of 10 percentage points or less and 19 incumbents were defeated in the general election. Still, less than 15 percent of House races were decided by less than 10 percent of the vote. The 2010 midterm elections saw a surprising 51 incumbents lose. This election was clearly an outlier, however. Congressional scholar Gary Jacobson documents a decline in the number of competitive House elections over a 50-year period.[41]

The question is: What is responsible for the lack of competitive House elections? The popular choice today, especially in the media, is the partisan redistricting process. Respected columnists David Broder of the *Washington Post* and Ronald Brownstein of the *Los Angeles Times* are just two of many who blame the lack of competitive House elections at least partially on the redistricting process.[42] As Brownstein writes, "[The lack of uncompetitive seats as a result of redistricting] will make governing tough. Governing will get even tougher as more House members represent seats so safe that they don't have to consider the views of voters outside their own base. That allows—indeed encourages—them to embrace purist ideological positions, which impedes compromise."[43] Election reform groups, such as Common Cause, Demos, and the League of Women Voters, believe that redistricting is the culprit for uncompetitive House elections as well. Additionally, some empirical studies provide evidence for this claim.[44] It is easy to see why redistricting bears so much of the blame for the scarcity of competitive elections. While members of Congress do not have a direct say in the drawing of district lines, they do have an indirect influence by lobbying members of the legislature and, in some cases, they actually create their own district plans. Certainly they do not have an incentive to draw competitive districts!

However, it would be a mistake to place too much of the blame for the lack of competitive elections on redistricting, and some people argue that it is not responsible at all. First, while some empirical works find that redistricting decreases electoral competition, other research determines that it has no effect.[45] For example, Abramowitz and his colleagues find that the growing financial advantage enjoyed by incumbents as well as the fact that Americans are increasingly living in homogenous communities are responsible for the decrease in electoral competition, not redistricting.[46] Even if one wanted to, it is often not possible to draw competitive districts because of the homogeneity of many communities. Second, most Senate elections are also uncompetitive and redistricting cannot be blamed for that fact. Similarly, while there is no doubt that Democrats and Republicans in the House of Representatives have become increasingly polarized, the same trend has occurred in the Senate, indicating that redistricting cannot be the main culprit.

Regarding partisan gerrymandering in relation to electoral responsiveness, not everyone is convinced that outright partisan gerrymandering has negative consequences for democracy. In their often-cited article on redistricting, Gelman and King find that partisan or bipartisan redistricting actually *increases* electoral responsiveness, which they define as "the degree to which the partisan composition of the legislature responds to changes in voter preferences."[47] If a party is trying to draw district lines to its advantage, the two scholars argue, then the party is going to have to remove some partisans from safe districts and place them in districts that are currently competitive. In other words, "incumbents are often forced to give up votes (hence electoral safety) in order to increase the number of legislative seats their party is likely to capture."[48] Although partisan gerrymandering may lead to more competitive districts, the number of incumbents who actually lose may decrease. Instead of having two districts where incumbent A wins 80 percent to 20 percent and incumbent B loses 60 percent to 40 percent, the outcomes under the new district plans might be incumbent A winning 60 percent to 40 percent and incumbent B winning by the same margin. Under the new districts, both elections are more competitive, but neither incumbent loses.

Redistricting scholar Thomas Brunell argues that packing partisans in a district should be encouraged to purposely *decrease* electoral competition because a greater number of people will be satisfied with the outcome of the election. In a congressional district whose winner barely captures 50 percent of the vote, roughly half of the district will be upset by the outcome. Conversely, if a candidate wins with, say, 80 percent of the vote, then only

20 percent of the district will be upset by the outcome. Brunell writes that "map makers ought to 'pack' districts with as many like-minded partisans as possible. Trying to draw 'competitive' districts effectively cracks ideologically congruent voters into separate districts, which has the effect of increasing the absolute number of voters who will be unhappy with the outcome and dissatisfied with their representative."[49] Indeed, my research with Matt Barreto finds that, while the opposite was once true, today, people who vote in competitive House elections are actually less efficacious and trusting of government than those who live in safe districts.[50]

Not only does Brunell question whether drawing competitive districts makes sense because of voter attitudes, he questions whether competitive districts improve representation. If districts are perfectly competitive, Brunell notes, then small changes in citizen voting could lead to enormous changes in the electoral system. "The goal of redistricting is not to maximize the number of seats that switch from one party to the other every two years," Brunell writes, "rather the goal of redistricting is for the House to pass legislation in such a way that policy preferences among the electorate are reflected in policy outputs. Drawing districts on the basis of ideology satisfies this goal, while drawing competitive districts does not."[51] He continues, "The implied threat of competition, especially at the primary level, is sufficient to keep our elected officials faithful to our opinions."[52]

Whether electoral competition is a criterion that mapmakers should concern themselves with is a subject I return to momentarily. What is important for the time being is that the courts have not considered the promotion of competition to be an essential goal of redistricting, and in fact have made rulings that actually would decrease competition in a district. Moreover, state constitutions and statutes virtually ignore competition as a goal as well. Only Arizona's constitution and Washington state's statute require electoral competition, and, as Cain and his colleagues note, Washington's statute is essentially unenforceable because a bipartisan commission draws the districts and bipartisan plans are generally not challenged in court.[53]

What *Should* be the Goals of Redistricting?

Clearly, the goals of redistricting can conflict. The courts have made clear that districts must be equally populated, but that can come at the expense of many of the other goals, such as protecting communities of interest. Gerrymandered districts, whether to benefit racial or ethnic minorities, political parties, or incumbents, are often spread out for hundreds of miles in all sorts of strange geographical shapes. Likewise, gerrymandered districts rarely are competitive. Protecting communities of interest that are homogenous will not likely promote competition, which requires diversity of opinion. "In order to draw competitive districts," write Cain and his colleagues, "large communities of interest must be split and diametrically opposed communities must be grouped together."[54] If an incumbent is a member of the opposing party, then it is difficult to protect the incumbent *and* draw districts that will benefit your party. Conversely, an incumbent may have to give up votes for the good of the party. Drawing districts to benefit a party may keep minority representatives from being elected since the party may benefit more by spreading out minority voters.

The trade-offs that must be made when drawing districts require a person to be clear regarding which of the goals previously listed should be emphasized most, and whether some should be ignored. The goals of greatest importance will also help determine the best procedure for redistricting.

In my mind, the first criterion that mapmakers must consider when drawing districts is equal population, or as close to equal as possible. Equally populated districts are most consistent with the notion of one person, one vote, although this is not perfect, because districts with equal populations will have different voting age populations or numbers of eligible or registered voters.[55] Studies find that representation is enhanced when district populations are equal. For instance, Stephen Ansolabehere and his colleagues find that the elimination of malapportionment has resulted in the redistribution of roughly $7 billion to more populous counties.[56] When districts were malapportioned, less populated communities often had more representatives than more populated communities, which gave the representatives in less populated communities great power to bring back more pork barrel projects than they otherwise should have.[57] Since the 1960s, the courts have ruled that one person, one vote is not negotiable, and rightly so.

Second, consistent with the Voting Rights Act and its extensions, racial and ethnic minority representation should not be diluted since these groups were historically disenfranchised. However, this does not mean that mapmakers must draw majority-minority districts, which have the potential of reinforcing racial stereotypes as the Court noted in *Shaw*. Here is an area where the Court's rulings have improved over time. No longer does the Court require that district plans maximize the number of majority-minority districts or the percentage of racial or ethnic minorities living in those districts. Instead, in the 2003 case of *Georgia v. Ashcroft*, the Court ruled that districts in which minorities did not necessarily control the outcome but where they had significant influence were permitted, although admittedly there does not seem to be a consensus on what illustrates "significant influence."[58] While the ruling did not receive universal support, 44 of the 45 black Georgia state legislators and civil rights activist and congressman John Lewis supported the Georgia districting plan as protecting African American interests. This ruling will ultimately prove to increase both the descriptive representation—the idea that an elected body should mirror demographically the population it represents—and substantive representation—when a legislator consciously acts for people and their interests, whether or not the person is a member of that group—of African Americans.[59] Minority representation in Congress has not lessened with the dismantling of majority-minority districts.[60] Minority representatives reap the advantages of incumbency just like white representatives, which has allowed them to retain their seats. Lessening the number of majority-minority districts will also improve the substantive representation of racial or ethnic minorities. Moreover, non-majority-minority districts will be more compatible with the goals of creating competitive districts as well as compact districts since majority-minority districts historically have been geographically large.

After the goals of equal population and the nondilution of racial and ethnic minorities, things get a little dicey because the drawing of competitive districts, the drawing of compact districts, and keeping communities of interest intact are all worthwhile but competing goals. It is likely, although not a certainty, that districts drawn around communities of interest will be compact. It does depend on how one defines a community of interest. If by community of interest one means specific neighborhoods, then district lines will look less strange. If by community of interest one means, say, blue-collar workers, then compactness is not guaranteed. In Illinois, for example, such a district might comprise parts of Springfield, Peoria, the Quad Cities, and Rockford, making it far from compact. My general feeling is that communities of interest should be defined by geography (for example, housing developments, neighborhoods, small towns) rather than by demographics (for example, blue-collar workers, farmers). It is important that, when possible, communities and neighborhoods not be divided because they do share common interests. It would make absolutely no sense for my hometown of Malta, IL (population of roughly 1,000), to be split into two or more congressional districts. Whatever the case, it is important that state constitutions or statutes clearly and, in my opinion, narrowly define "community of interest," otherwise the term could be used to justify any districting plan.

Compact congressional districts that protect communities of interest seemed to be a priority of many of the founding fathers, who wanted representatives to be close to their constituents. In fact, of all the goals of redistricting, one could make an argument that compact districts were most consistent with the founders' views. Some might claim that compactness is a goal that is less important today than at the time of the founding, because of advances in technology like phones, fax machines, and email. It is true that it is easier to contact a member of Congress today than it was 100 years ago, but there is still something to be said for having a community or a few communities comprise a congressional district. If compactness is not important today, then it is not clear why we even need districts. States might as well eliminate congressional districts and simply have all of its members of Congress represent the entire state. To most, that idea sounds absurd. And, it should. The purpose of the House of Representatives is to have *local* representation in Congress. That cannot happen as effectively if a member of Congress is representing a district that is several hundred miles long. In reality, there will be several large districts because of sparse populations in some areas; no matter how hard one tries, creating compact districts will be difficult in a state like Idaho. Even heavily populated states like California and Texas have areas that are sparsely populated and require larger districts. However, whenever mapmakers can draw districts that keep communities together and are not spread over most of the state, they should do so. Districts whose borders are connected at points by a few blocks, as the Illinois 17th congressional district mentioned previously is, or by a lane on a highway, as the old North Carolina 12th congressional district was, in order to protect an incumbent or political party should not be permitted.

Of course, creating compact districts and protecting communities undermines another worthwhile goal of redistricting: promoting electoral competition. Competitive electoral districts are more likely to produce more moderate candidates,[61] which could reduce polarization in Congress and create conditions for compromise. Moreover, competitive elections make it easier for constituents to hold their representatives accountable and increase policy responsiveness.[62] Earlier, I mentioned Brunell's argument that we should eliminate competitive districts in favor of plans that pack as many partisans into one district as possible. Brunell believes that his proposal would not undermine accountability because candidates must still be nominated in a primary. Members of Congress might face token opposition in the general election, but, according to Brunell, they could not get too out of line with district opinion because of the threat of a primary challenge. The problem with this argument is that there is little evidence that the primary process works the way Brunell says it does. Few incumbents are challenged in the primary and those who are normally win with ease.[63] And, it is unclear exactly how independents fit into a plan that purposely packs partisans and relies so heavily on primaries. What about states that hold closed primaries where only registered partisans can participate? Independents are effectively disenfranchised. Some might argue that independents could register with the dominant party to participate in the primary, but why should they have to affiliate with a political party that does not reflect their wishes?[64]

The results of my research with Matt Barreto indicate potential negative aspects of competition and might comport with Brunell's argument regarding people being more satisfied with government in less competitive districts. Again, we find that competitive districts lead to less trust in government and lower levels of political efficacy. Yet, I am not sure that these are necessarily negative findings. First, a healthy dose of distrust in government is probably a good thing. Too much satisfaction with government can make the people complacent. Second, while low levels of political efficacy are not necessarily positive, it does not seem to keep people from participating in the political process. As noted, a long line of research finds that the more competitive the district, the higher the voter turnout.

This is not to say that drawing competitive districts should trump all other goals. In fact, too many competitive districts could have negative consequences as well. As Dennis Thompson aptly writes:

Too little competition may make legislators less accountable than they should be. Too little turnover may block necessary and desirable change. But too much competition may distract legislators from the business of government. Too much turnover in office may deprive government of the benefits of experience, and discourage leaders from pursuing just but unpopular causes. The goal should be not to maximize competition, but to find the optimal level for sustaining a just democratic process.[65]

Finding that "optimal level" may not be easy, in fact it is not entirely clear how competitiveness should be measured, but it is a sensible goal. Indeed, one of the criteria that the Arizona redistricting commission must follow is "[t]o the extent practicable, competitive districts should be favored where to do so would create no significant detriment to the other goals."[66] Meeting this goal is not simple, but it is certainly a worthwhile aspiration.

That leaves us with two remaining goals, neither of which I have much sympathy for. First, the objective of redistricting should not be to create a partisan advantage, but to devise the best set of districts that promote account-ability and effective representation. This is not to say that a heavily partisan area should be purposely divided. In fact, drawing districts to maintain communities of interest will often keep heavily partisan areas together. But redistricting plans designed solely to benefit a party, such as the mid-decade Texas redistricting, should not be approved.

Some people might argue that partisan politics in the redistricting process is no different than partisan politics in other aspects of government. As Thompson asks, "What is wrong with partisan gerrymandering? In some circumstances, arguably nothing. Control over redistricting is one of the fruits of political victory, and a party's using the control to its advantage is no more objectionable than its using majority power to appoint permanent judges, enact laws with long-term effects, or commit the government to binding contracts."[67] But Thompson argues that partisan redistricting has to be done in a way in which the out-of-power party has the ability to become the party in power. This is exactly the problem. While admittedly partisan gerrymanders do not always lead to the intended outcomes, the goal is to permanently weaken the other party. Furthermore, there is no reason that redistricting should be one of the "fruits of political victory." The Constitution requires that the Senate confirm judges and that Congress pass laws making these inherently political processes. There are few other alternatives here. That is not the case with redistricting. As I argue momentarily, there are options that severely constrain partisan posturing in the redistricting process. Finally, partisan gerrymandering only further exacerbates the public's belief that politicians are self-interested actors who are out to protect their own interests, instead of working for the best interests of the country.

Incumbency gerrymanders are just as bad as partisan ones. Here is a case where bipartisan is not a positive. Protecting incumbents severely undermines electoral competition—an essential component of a sound democracy. The Supreme Court has actually held that protecting incumbents may be in a state's best interest. A representative who has been in Congress for an eternity has likely gained positions on powerful committees that may benefit the district or state. However, it is hard to fathom that protecting incumbents is a more compelling interest than promoting competitive elections. Certainly, a Congress that constantly turned over all of its members every two years would be problematic, but even with the drawing of more competitive districts it is unlikely that more than about one-quarter of incumbents will be defeated. Furthermore, incumbents already have several advantages over challengers, whether it is name recognition, fundraising, the ability to bring home pork or perform casework, the franking privilege; the list goes on and on. Even without favorable gerrymanders, most incumbents would still win easily.

What Process Best Achieves the Goals of Redistricting?

Given where I stand on the goals of promoting partisan or incumbent gerrymanders, it is obvious that the job of drawing district maps should not rest with the state legislatures. An unnecessary conflict of interest exists that promotes the welfare of the party or the politician above that of the district, state, or country. It seems clear to me that the best solution is to take the politics out of the redistricting process as much as possible by putting the authority to draw districts in the hands of a redistricting commission.

However, not just any commission will do. Several of the state redistricting commissions that are in place are nonpartisan in name only, not in spirit. Legislative leaders who have partisan interests to protect choose commission members. Some commissions require supermajorities to pass a redistricting plan, which often simply leads to bipartisan gerrymanders so all sides will be happy. Yet, Arizona has enacted a model for redistricting commissions that, while perhaps not ideal, has substantial upside. Worthy of noting, the commission was enacted through the initiative process—one example of the potential advantages of the initiative (see Chapter 4). The Arizona plan will not solve all of the problems with the redistricting process and because it is on the verge of only going through its second redistricting it is still unclear how successful the model will be, but initial results are encouraging and there is certainly no reason to believe that this model will lead to any worse results than the process in place in the majority of the states.

In Arizona, "the commission on appellate court nominees creates a pool of 25 nominees, ten from each of the two largest parties and five not from either of the two largest parties. The highest ranking officer of the house appoints one from the pool, then the minority leader of the house appoints one, then the highest ranking officer of the Senate appoints one, then the minority leader of the Senate appoints one. These four appoint a fifth from the pool, not a member of any party already represented on the commission, as chair. If the four deadlock, the commission on appellate court appointments appoints the chair."[68] Democrats and Republicans still sit on the commission, and there is no reason to argue that they should not, but an impartial body puts the list of possible candidates together. Unlike with some of the other redistricting commissions, it is harder in Arizona for legislative leaders to simply appoint their friends.

What's more, the commission is guided by explicit standards and procedures spelled out in the state's constitution:

> The independent redistricting commission shall establish congressional and legislative districts. The commencement of the mapping process for both the congressional and legislative districts shall be the creation of districts of equal population in a grid-like pattern across the state. Adjustments to the grid shall then be made as necessary to accommodate the goals as set forth below:
>
> A. Districts shall comply with the United States Constitution and the United States Voting Rights Act;
> B. Congressional districts shall have equal population to the extent practicable, and state legislative districts shall have equal population to the extent practicable;
> C. Districts shall be geographically compact and contiguous to the extent practicable;
> D. District boundaries shall respect communities of interest to the extent practicable;
> E. To the extent practicable, district lines shall use visible geographic features, city, town, and county boundaries, and undivided census tracts;
> F.   To the extent practicable, competitive districts should be favored where to do so would create no significant detriment to the other goals.
> (15) Party registration and voting history data shall be excluded from the initial phase of the mapping process but may be used to test maps for compliance with the above goals. The places of residence of incumbents or candidates shall not be identified or considered.[69]

Surely, the criteria do not eliminate the conflict over the goals—and "communities of interest," is not defined, which is problematic—but they do provide a starting point for drawing maps. More importantly, they make it clear that partisan or incumbent gerrymanders are not acceptable. The use of party registration and voting history data is allowed, but such information is crucial if the commission is to draw competitive districts. Additionally, the process is transparent. Not only are plans not concocted behind closed doors, but public input is encouraged. Finally, support of only a majority of the commission is required, which lessens the likelihood of a bipartisan gerrymander.

I do not want to overstate the effects of the Arizona redistricting commission. As noted, it is still too early to really evaluate the system and it is possible that what works in Arizona may not in a state with a different demographic makeup; in other words, one size might not fit all when it comes to the rules of redistricting commissions.[70] Also, it would be naïve to believe that, if all states adopted the Arizona system tomorrow, competitive congressional elections would be the norm and party polarization in the House of Representatives would disappear. As I argued earlier, redistricting may have contributed to fewer competitive districts, but it is not the main culprit. In Chapter 10, I argue that the current system of campaign finance shoulders far more of the blame. But the Arizona commission seems to be a marked improvement over the process used in other states and appears to be the best system for promoting electoral accountability and effective representation.

Chapter 8

Presidential Primaries

One of the great spectacles of American politics is the presidential election process. Every four years people who pay only minimal attention to politics find themselves glued in front of a television watching states on electoral maps turn blue or red. It is the political equivalent of the Super Bowl. Yet, as shown in the next two chapters, the presidential election process is unique to say the least. In the next chapter, I discuss the Electoral College and its problems. However, the Electoral College may not be the strangest aspect of presidential elections. The process to choose the major parties' nominees is severely flawed, leading to an unnecessarily long and complicated election season. "Hardly anyone is a fan of the current presidential nominating process," writes noted scholar and journalist Rhodes Cook. "The feedback one hears is sometimes colorful, nearly always critical, and ranges from a sense of exasperation to hopelessness that the process can ever be changed for the better."[1]

The presidential nomination process is vastly different than the nomination process for other offices. If a candidate is running in a gubernatorial or congressional primary, all voters in the state or district go to the polls on the same day; at the end of the day the party's nominee will be apparent.[2] In the presidential nomination process, on the other hand, it can take weeks—or in the case of the Democrats in 2008, months—before the party's candidate is known.[3] Unlike in other primaries, voters in presidential primaries or caucuses—a gathering of party members who debate the pros and cons of each candidate and then often vote in the open—do not directly vote for a candidate. Instead, they vote for delegates, usually local political activists, who pledge to that candidate. The elected delegates then convene at the party's national convention in the summer to formally nominate the party's candidate.[4] A candidate must receive a majority of the delegates to win the party's nomination.

In this chapter, I argue that major reforms are needed in presidential primaries, specifically all party primaries should be open, delegates should be allocated proportionally, and, most importantly, a national primary should be instituted that would significantly shorten the nomination season. First, a brief history of the presidential nomination process is needed to better understand how we have ended up with the system in place today.

King Caucus and the Smoke-Filled Rooms

The presidential nomination process of today is quite different than the process at the time of the country's founding. Initially, nominating party candidates was not a concern because there were no parties. It was clear that George Washington would be the first president; in fact, the founders conceived the position specifically for him. However, almost immediately the country split into two parties: the Federalists, led by Alexander Hamilton and John Adams, and the Democratic–Republicans, led by Thomas Jefferson and James Madison. All of a sudden, how parties should nominate candidates became an issue.

Initially, the nomination process was undemocratic—rank-and-file members of the party had no say over who the party's candidate would be. Instead, congressional leaders chose party nominees; this period is sometimes referred to as "King Caucus." As the Federalists collapsed in the early 1800s and the Democratic–Republicans became the party of power in the country, people began to feel that the nomination of presidential candidates by political parties was too elitist. Rhodes Cook writes, "To its critics, the caucus was too small in number, too elitist in character, and often too secretive in its deliberations."[5]

With the increasing democratic sentiment in the country and the controversy surrounding the election of 1824 where Andrew Jackson won both a plurality of the popular and electoral vote but ultimately lost to John Quincy Adams, King Caucus gave way to the infamous "smoke-filled room" nominating conventions in which delegates from each state, chosen generally by state party leaders, determined the party's nominee. The convention process was slightly more democratic than under King Caucus, but critics argued that the conventions were dominated increasingly by party bosses and special interests who cut deals out of the eyes of the general public, or the convention as a whole for that matter.

Not surprisingly, around the turn of the twentieth century the progressives started calling for a more open, democratic nomination process. The proposal advocated by the progressives was the direct primary. In primaries, rank-and-file members of the party, not party elites, chose delegates to go to the national convention. By 1916, 20 states, many of them heavily populated, had instituted a primary, but the decline of the progressive movement and the concern by party officials that the nomination process was being taken out of their hands quickly brought to an end this brief period of democratization in the nomination process. Although many states continued to hold primaries, they became a sideshow as the real nomination decisions were once again made by the party elites. Estes Kefauver won virtually every Democratic primary in 1952, only to lose the party's nomination to Adlai Stevenson. In fact, running in primaries was considered a sign of weakness for presidential aspirants.

As the 1960s began, hope for meaningful primaries was on the horizon. John F. Kennedy took his case directly to the people in states such as Wisconsin and West Virginia and persuaded many voters that he would not be beholden to the views of the Pope and party leaders that he was electable. Without convincing performances in these states, Kennedy might not have won the Democratic nomination in 1960. The rise of television also added intrigue to the primaries as the major networks started covering election night results. It appeared that primaries would play a significant role in the 1968 Democratic nomination as well. Senators Eugene McCarthy and Robert Kennedy actively campaigned against the Vietnam War in the primaries, and President Lyndon Johnson's poor showing in the New Hampshire primary against McCarthy was one reason Johnson decided not to run for reelection.[6] However, the rising importance of the primaries quickly came crashing down that year at the Democratic National Convention in Chicago. With television coverage of Vietnam protesters being beaten by police outside the convention hall, inside the hall the party nominated Vice-President Hubert Humphrey, a defender of U.S. involvement in Vietnam, over McCarthy. Humphrey had not participated in a single primary.

The controversy over the 1968 Democratic nomination sparked the nomination process we have today. The problems at the 1968 convention led the Democrats to institute the McGovern–Fraser reforms, which, among other things, passed rules giving "teeth" to the primaries in the delegate selection process and pushed for delegates to reflect the demographics of the party's rank-and-file in a state. The McGovern–Fraser Reforms did not simply affect the Democratic Party; the Republican Party followed suit regarding the proliferation of the importance of primaries in the nomination process. Today, it is virtually impossible for a candidate to earn a party's nomination without the support of rank-and-file members.

Reforms to the Presidential Primary Process

The rise in the number of primaries has made the nomination process far more democratic than was the case under the old systems. However, the increased significance of primaries raises several questions. In the remainder of this chapter I focus on three:

1   Who should be able to participate in a party's primary?
2   How should delegates be allocated?
3   What should the primary schedule look like?

Who Should be Able to Participate in a Party's Primary?

Perhaps the first question that one must address when considering the ideal presidential nomination process is who should be able to participate in that process? Should voting be open only to party members? Should independents be able to vote? What about members of one party voting in the primary of another?

The rules of who can participate in a party primary vary by state. For example, some states hold closed primaries where only registered members of the party are allowed to vote. Others have semiclosed primaries that are open to members of the party and those who are not registered with another party. Finally, some states have open primaries in which any registered voter can participate in a party's primary. One variation of the open primary is the semi-open primary in which voters must declare their partisanship at the time they vote. Not surprisingly, parties prefer closed primaries to keep independents and members of other parties from influencing who their nominee will be. In 2000, for instance, John McCain won the Republican primaries in New Hampshire and Michigan, both of which had open primaries. In each case, the majority of McCain's support came from independents and Democrats; Republicans in both states overwhelmingly supported George W. Bush.

The decision regarding who should be able to participate in a primary is more complex than it may seem. From a democratic standpoint, open primaries are best because people have the greatest opportunity to participate and turnout is higher than in closed primaries.[7] If a person is registered as a Democrat but really likes a Republican, or, conversely, if that person is registered as a Republican and is enamored with a Democrat, should she have the opportunity to help that candidate make it into the general election? Political parties would generally say "no." Open primaries may make it easier to nominate a person who is unacceptable to the rank-and-file party members, even though this candidate may be more electable in a general election. Moreover, the possibility of one party's members sabotaging another's primary is a concern for some. In the 2008 Texas, Ohio, and Indiana Democratic primaries, for example, Rush Limbaugh encouraged Republicans to forego the Republican primary and vote for Hillary Clinton in the Democratic primary instead in order to prolong the Democratic contest.[8]

As with the other issues I discuss in this chapter, there is a definite conflict between the states, which generally want open primaries because they are perceived as more democratic, and the parties, who generally want closed primaries for the reasons listed above. The courts have usually ruled on the side of the parties. Most notably, in *Nader v. Shaffer* (1976), the Supreme Court upheld the constitutionality of closed primaries.[9] Two residents of Connecticut challenged the state's closed primary law as a denial of equal protection, freedom of association, and the right to vote.[10] The Court ruled that "the requirements were not sufficiently onerous to preclude [the plaintiffs] from registering as members of a major party and thereby being allowed to participate in the party's primary. The plaintiffs could, the Court said, register with a party but still make campaign donations or sign petitions for candidates outside the party for which they were registered."[11] What is most important here is that the Court rejected the plaintiffs' claims that their freedom of association was violated, instead ruling that it was the political party's freedom of association that mattered. The ruling was in the best interest of the party, not the citizen.

The Supreme Court also sided with political parties regarding the constitutionality of a different type of open primary, called the blanket primary, in which all candidates' names for an office are listed on one ballot. In 1996, voters in California passed Proposition 198, which instituted the blanket primary in the state. Alaska and Washington were already using similar versions of the blanket primary. Several Californian political parties, including both the state Democratic and Republican parties, challenged Proposition 198 on the grounds that it violated a party's right to freedom of association, or, actually in this case, the freedom *not* to associate. The state contended that, among other things, a blanket primary would elect officials who are more representative of the general public and increase voter turnout. In *California Democratic Party v. Jones* (2000), the Court ruled on the side of the political parties arguing that the parties' freedom of association trumped the benefits of the blanket primary argued by the state.[12] As a result of the ruling, California went back to a closed primary. In Alaska, the state legislature voted in 2001 to abandon the blanket primary, while in Washington the Ninth Circuit Court of Appeals used the precedent set in the *Jones* case to declare the state's blanket primary to be unconstitutional.[13]

In 2004 Washington voters handily adopted a system similar to the blanket primary, with one notable exception. Under the so-called "top-two system" all candidates' names for an office are listed on the ballot, just as with the blanket primary. However, the key difference is that the top-two voter winners face off in the general election, not the top vote winner from each party. Therefore, there is a possibility that two Democrats or two Republicans could face each other in the general election. Although legal challenges remain, to this point the Supreme Court has upheld the top-two system as not violating a party's freedom of association on its face.[14] In 2010, California voters adopted a system similar to Washington's "top-two" election system.

It is understandable why parties believe so strongly in freedom of association, but their concerns about the open primary are misguided. Although there is evidence that crossover primary voting does occur, the voting appears to be more sincere than malicious.[15] If anything, a party benefits from open primaries because they may nominate a candidate that is more electable in the general election. In fact, the electability of Dwight Eisenhower was one reason why Republicans nominated him in 1952 over Robert Taft, even though Taft may have been the "truer" Republican. The goal of political parties is to win elections. They cannot do this with ideological candidates who appeal only to partisans.

How Should the Delegates be Allocated?

Who gets to participate in the nomination process is one debate; how the delegates should be allocated is another. Whether delegates should determine the nominee in the first place is questionable, as I will discuss shortly, but if delegates are going to do so, and there is no evidence that this will change anytime soon, then delegates must be allocated fairly.

The Democratic Party mandates that a state's delegates be allocated proportionally, either by the state as a whole or by congressional district. Under a statewide proportional plan, if Candidate A receives 50 percent of the vote, Candidate B 30 percent of the vote, and Candidate C 20 percent of the vote, and there are 10 delegates at stake, then Candidate A would win five delegates while Candidates B and C would win three and two delegates, respectively. The same rationale applies under a district proportional system, sometimes called a "winner-takes-more" system, except that the winner of the congressional district also receives a bonus delegate. However, a candidate must receive at least 15 percent of the vote, either in the state or the district, depending on the rules, to win delegates.[16] If a candidate earned only 10 percent of the votes, her votes would be discarded and the delegates would be allocated based on the remaining votes. To use another hypothetical example, pretend that of 100 people voting in a primary, 60 voted for Candidate A, 30 for Candidate B, and 10 for Candidate C, and there were nine delegates at stake. Candidate C's votes would not be counted because she did not reach the 15 percent threshold. This leaves 90 votes, of which Candidate A received two-thirds and Candidate B received one-third. Candidate A would then win six delegates and Candidate B three.

The Republican Party does not mandate national guidelines for their state parties, which leads to many different primary and caucus rules. Most notably, some Republican primaries and caucuses are winner-takes-all by state; in other words, if a candidate wins by just one vote, she wins all of the state's delegates. Other state Republican primaries and caucuses use a winner-takes-all by congressional district format, called a "loophole" primary, with bonus delegates going to the statewide winner. And, like the Democrats, some allocate their delegates proportionally, either by state or district.

The argument in favor of a winner-takes-all system is that, theoretically, a nominee should emerge earlier in the primary process, something that parties prefer because they can begin the healing process of a potentially divisive primary season and focus on the general election. Under proportional allocation, a candidate that wins 30 percent of the vote consistently could remain in the race longer because an upset win could put her within "striking distance" of the frontrunner. Under the winner-takes-all scenario, this candidate would likely have received no delegates, making it likely that she would drop out of the race. Writing before the election of Bill Clinton, Emmett H. Buell, Jr. and Lee Sigelman argued that proportional representation prolongs divisive races "well beyond the point of achieving meaningful unity at the nominating convention and may have contributed to Democratic losses in every election except two since 1968."[17]

However, there is minimal evidence at best that nominees emerge earlier in winner-takes-all systems. For example, the 2000 Democratic and Republican nominations were determined on the same day (March 9th) even though the parties operated under different rules. Moreover, the winner-takes-all format could breathe life into a campaign if the candidate is able to pull an upset, as happened in the 1976 Republican nomination race between Gerald Ford and Ronald Reagan. Reagan was able to obtain victories in California, Georgia, Montana, and Texas, several of which had a large number of delegates. His victories in these states prolonged the nomination season. Meanwhile, on the Democratic side, Jimmy Carter's status as the frontrunner was not threatened after losing primaries in Massachusetts and New York to Henry "Scoop" Jackson. Because of proportional allocation, Carter still won a substantial number of delegates, which kept him as the Democratic candidate to beat. Overall, according to political scientist Larry Bartels, Carter was essentially guaranteed the nomination after the California primary 20 weeks into the nomination season. Ford, on the other hand, still had not obtained the nomination at the same point. In other words, under a proportional system Carter secured the nomination more quickly than Ford did under mostly winner-takes-all rules.[18] Furthermore, in the past when Democratic candidates have remained in the race well into June (for example, Jesse Jackson in 1988 or Jerry Brown in 1992), it was not the proportional allocation of delegates that kept them in the race, but a belief that they had a message that needed to be heard. Whether delegates were allocated proportionally or by winner-takes-all, these candidates would have continued their campaigns.

The battle between Barack Obama and Hillary Clinton in 2008 once again raised the issue of whether proportional allocation of delegates prolongs the nomination season. However, it was not the proportional allocation of delegates that extended the nomination, but the fact that two popular candidates were running against each other, neither of whom was able to deliver a knockout blow. This inability to do so was because Obama would win a state, then Clinton would win a state. This process seemed to continue over and over. In fact, political scientist Brian Arbour "re-ran" the 2008 Democratic nomination contest using Republican rules for delegate allocation in each state. Had the Democrats actually used Republican rules, Arbour finds that the nomination battle would have been even more prolonged. As Arbour writes, "[I]n a close contest fought over every state and territory, where the winner of the popular vote remains very close, it is the closeness of the results that determines these outcomes, not the rules."[19]

Allocating delegates proportionally—either by district or by state—more accurately reflects the wishes of voters and, as a result, should be adopted by the parties in all primaries and caucuses.[20] As I discuss in the chapter on the Electoral College, winner-takes-all systems exaggerate the mandate of the winner. For example, "in 1998, George H.W. Bush won 59 percent of the popular vote in states holding some type of winner-takes-all voting on Super Tuesday but won 97 percent of the delegates."[21] As long as a threshold exists, the delegate allocation will never be perfectly proportional to the vote total because votes for the candidates who fail to meet the threshold will not be counted; but it is far more so than under a winner-takes-all system. Furthermore, parties actually benefit from allocating delegates proportionally because they nominate candidates who will likely have broader support in the general election under these rules.[22]

The discussion to this point has focused on the allocation of so-called "pledged delegates." However, during the 1980s the Democrats added what came to be known as "superdelegates." Superdelegates are elected officials, party leaders, and the like who receive a vote for the nomination. They have tended to comprise between 15 and 20 percent of the delegates at the Democratic convention. Until 2008, they had never played a significant role in determining the nomination. Most people paid little attention to superdelegates—indeed, most people probably were not even aware of their existence. Yet, when neither Barack Obama nor Hillary Clinton was able to win a majority of the total delegates based on the pledged delegates (those elected in primaries and caucuses) alone, it was the superdelegates that ultimately determined the nomination.

Superdelegates can vote for whoever they want and can change their minds as often as they want until the actual vote takes place. Initially, it appeared that Clinton would receive the majority of the superdelegates because of the number of IOUs she had obtained over time, initially as First Lady and then as a senator from New York. However, with Obama's surprise showing, many superdelegates who initially withheld support from either candidate broke to Obama. Additionally, some early Clinton superdelegates decided to vote for Obama because he had won more of the overall popular vote.

Even though it was the superdelegates who ultimately gave Obama the delegates needed to win the nomination, the 2008 Democratic nomination illustrated the uselessness of superdelegates. Had superdelegates supported Clinton in numbers large enough to give her the nomination, the party may have been fractured beyond repair for the general election since Obama won more pledge delegates and the popular vote. Rank-and-file Democrats may have felt that, similar to 1968, the party elite "stole" the nomination from them and may have been less likely to go to the polls in the general election. Because of the controversy that would surround such a decision, most superdelegates simply vote the way their state or district voted. This makes superdelegates essentially irrelevant because they are simply confirming the vote that already took place. Democrats are in the process of rethinking the concept of the superdelegate. It is unlikely that they will be eliminated entirely, but instead be lessened in numbers. However, I do not see a compelling reason for them to remain.[23]

What Should the Primary Schedule Look Like?

Even if proportional allocation of delegates keeps a frontrunner from emerging or superdelegates overturn the will of rank-and-file members, a simple, smart reform would alleviate these problems. The current schedule of presidential primaries and caucuses needs to be scrapped; instead, we should nominate a party's presidential candidate as we do for almost all other offices in almost all other elections, on a single day.[24] In other words, we should move to a national primary.

Perhaps the strangest aspect of the presidential nomination process is the schedule in which the primaries and caucuses take place. Instead of deciding the nomination in one day, the current system spreads the nomination process over several months. Each state determines when their presidential primary or caucus will be. Some states combine the presidential primary with primaries for other offices; other states do not. As I discuss in greater detail momentarily, there is a mad rush for states to move their primaries or caucuses earlier in the election season to keep from being shut out of the nomination process. However, one tradition remains: Iowa and New Hampshire always come first.

Since 1952, New Hampshire has held the first primary; in fact, the state constitution mandates that this be the case. Iowa conducts its caucus even before the New Hampshire primary. Initially, going first was not a big deal. As noted, primaries were essentially irrelevant. That changed after the McGovern–Fraser Reforms gave the primaries and caucuses more control over the nomination process. Now, going first mattered, and it mattered a lot. Nowhere is this better illustrated than with the Democratic nomination of Georgia governor Jimmy Carter in 1976. Carter was perceived as an outsider from the beginning. He was running in a saturated field of much better known candidates, including governor George Wallace, senators Henry Jackson, Fred Harris, and Birch Bayh, and representative Mo Udall. Hubert Humphrey, perhaps the best known of the lot, was not officially running, but indicated that he would accept the nomination. In a poll conducted in December of 1975, Carter was carrying less than 5 percent of the vote nationwide.[25]

Carter's campaign understood the importance of the Iowa caucuses. He spent a considerable amount of time in the state, building a well-organized campaign. His rural background appealed to many Iowans. As a result, he pulled a surprise victory on the night of the caucus, easily defeating his main competition, Bayh, by two to one. Immediately thereafter, Carter was labeled as a frontrunner by the press.[26] Although Carter held his own or won caucuses in Mississippi, Maine, and Oklahoma, the next major test for his candidacy was the New Hampshire primary, where he pulled an upset victory. With impressive victories in Florida, Illinois, and North Carolina, the rest of the field dwindled, eventually giving Carter the nomination.

The 1976 Carter case is the main reason why some people believe that the presidential primary process should be spread over the course of several months. The Iowa caucus took place on January 21st; Carter did not receive the delegates needed to win the nomination until the Ohio primary on June 8th. The length of the primary season allowed Carter to spend much of his early efforts in Iowa and New Hampshire. By doing well there, he emerged as a serious candidate. Because the primaries and caucuses occurred over several months, voters had the opportunity to really "vet" Carter, to learn more about a candidate who was previously virtually unknown nationwide.

Under a nomination system that takes place over several months, outsider candidates have time to build a fundraising base. People give money to candidates who have a legitimate shot at winning. Few people saw Carter as a serious candidate before Iowa. His success is Iowa made him viable, and with viability came money. Had Carter run in a national primary, he would have likely never emerged as a serious candidate; therefore, he would have had great difficulty raising money. "[The Carter campaign] *did* have enough money to wage a vigorous campaign in Iowa and New Hampshire," write Andrew Busch and William Mayer, "and if successful there, they believed, they could then raise the money necessary to contest the next round of primaries, which, if they kept winning, would allow them to raise more money for still later primaries, and so on through the final primaries and on into the convention."[27]

Another advantage of an expansive primary season is that it encourages "retail politics." If you live in Iowa or New Hampshire, there is a good chance that you have met several of the candidates personally. Candidates do not win in Iowa or New Hampshire by advertising on television; they win by talking with people in local diners, fire halls, and living rooms.[28] This gives voters in Iowa and New Hampshire the opportunity to get to know the candidates better than one can in a 30-second spot on television. Moreover, Iowans and New Hampshirites take their job evaluating the candidates seriously. There is great state pride in being the first primary or caucus. These states certainly benefit from going first as well. As Busch and Mayer note, in addition to the obvious perks of having influence over the nomination and getting attention from candidates, the states reap economic benefits from going first and may receive special policy concessions (for example, generous federal ethanol subsidies).[29]

Other states have not sat by idly and allowed Iowa and New Hampshire— two states that do not represent the rest of the country demographically—to have the nomination spotlight all to themselves. Perhaps the greatest consequence of the McGovern–Fraser Reforms has been the frontloading of primaries. There has been a mad rush by many states to move their primaries or caucuses earlier in the season, especially in recent elections. Heavily populated states, such as California, New York, Florida, Illinois, Michigan, and New Jersey, tired of having little influence over the party's nomination. Many of these states initially held their primaries in June when the nomination was essentially already determined or at least the field had been significantly winnowed. The only way to fix this problem is to schedule the primary earlier. For example, in 1996, California moved its primary to March 26th, but was still kept from having an influence over who the Republican Party's nominee would be.[30] By the time of the primary, already 65 percent of the delegates had been allocated.[31] So, four years later the state moved its primary to the first

Tuesday in March (the 7th). In 2004, the primary took place on March 2nd. Even with the earlier primary dates, California's primaries had no impact on the nomination process. In 2004, for instance, my wife told me, I am sure much to her chagrin today, that she was planning to vote after work for John Edwards (we lived in California at the time). By the time she got off work that day, Edwards had already dropped out of the race based on his performances in primaries held earlier in the day. In other words, California had not finished voting, but John Kerry had already secured the nomination. Because of concerns over increased frontloading, the parties attempted to stem the tide by offering bonus delegates to states that held their primaries or caucuses after a certain date; there were few takers because the bonus delegates were not enough to overcome the advantages of holding a primary or caucus earlier in the nomination season.

In 2008, frontloading was out of control more than ever. In an attempt to stem the tide of frontloading, the Democratic and Republican parties passed a rule mandating that no state caucus or primary could be held before February 5th. The Democrats made exceptions for Iowa and New Hampshire, and also for Nevada and South Carolina. According to the Democratic rules, any non-exempt state that held its primary or caucus before February 5th would be stripped of its delegates. The Republican Party made no exceptions to the February 5th rule, but would only eliminate half of the delegates from states that violated the provision.

The February 5th rule did not have the intended effect. On the Republican side, Iowa, Wyoming, New Hampshire, Michigan, Nevada, South Carolina, Florida, and Maine all scheduled their primaries or caucuses before February 5th (remember, it is the state, not the party that sets the dates of elections).[32] On the Democratic side, most notably Michigan and Florida scheduled their primaries in violation of party rules. A number of other states abided by the parties' rules, but moved their primaries or caucuses to February 5th. States including California, Illinois, New Jersey, and New York passed laws moving their primaries to the 5th, which sparked another wave of states to push up the date of their primaries or caucuses. In fact, New Jersey, which had previously held its primary in June, initially moved its primary for 2008 to February 26th only to vote again to schedule the primary on the 5th after California and New York scheduled their primaries on that day. Altogether, voters in 24 states went to the polls on February 5, 2008.

The two parties are working to stem the tide of frontloading in 2012. The parties have adopted a so-called "pre-primary window" where Iowa, New Hampshire, South Carolina, and Nevada can hold their nomination contents at the beginning of February instead of January, as was the case in 2008. The remaining states would then not be able to hold their nomination contests before the first Tuesday in March. The Republican party also adopted a rule that any state whose nomination contest is held in March must allocate its delegates proportionally. States whose nomination contest takes place in April can allocate on a winner-takes-all basis. This rule is designed to encourage states to hold nomination contest later in the year. Still, it is important to remember that it is the states, not the parties, that schedule dates for the primaries and caucuses and, as 2008 illustrated, the wishes of the parties are not always granted.

Because of the concern over frontloading, scholars and practitioners have proposed numerous reforms to the current system. They range from holding a national primary to drawing states out of a hat to determine the order in which they would vote. Since there are so many possibilities, I will focus on the four most prominent reforms offered: regional primaries, the Delaware and Ohio Plans, and a national primary.

Regional Primaries

One possible solution to the problem of frontloading would be to enact a series of regional primaries, a plan that has been endorsed by the National Association of Secretaries of State. This idea was first tested in 1988 when 20 states, most of which were located in the South, held their primaries and caucuses on the same day in early March. While there are slight variations of this proposal, the country would be split into four regions (or six under some proposals). All states in that region would hold their primaries and caucuses on the same day. The four election dates would be scheduled about a month apart giving candidates enough time to campaign in all regions. The regions would be rotated so that if, say, the South went first in 2012, it would go last in 2016, third in 2020, and so on. The advantage of the regional primary would be that it would keep the same states from having the most influence year after year, although many regional primary proposals still exclude Iowa and New Hampshire allowing them to continue their first-in-the-nation status. Costs of campaigning might decrease as well, since candidates will be in the same region for a month. They will not, for example, have to jet off from California, to New York, and then to Florida.

The idea for regional primaries has come close to being enacted informally but it has never received much support from party leaders, although, as I note momentarily, this may be starting to change. I have already mentioned the Super Tuesday primaries in 1988, which were composed primarily of southern states. New England states, with the exception of New Hampshire, have generally held their primaries on the same date, as have several of the Industrial Midwest states. However, increased frontloading may make these "informal" regional primaries obsolete. The Democratic party is considering adopting a rule that would give additional delegates to states that join a regional or sub-regional primary. Whether such a rule will be adopted and, if so, whether it will be successful remains to be seen.

Although the regional primary eliminates the problem of frontloading, it does raise the problem that a candidate from the region whose primaries go first could be unfairly advantaged. A regional plan would allocate roughly 25 percent of the delegates each election day, assuming there are four regions, so a candidate from, for example, the South, might already have a firm grasp on the nomination if southern states held their primaries and caucuses first. Conversely, a candidate whose home residence is from outside of the first region could be doomed. Additionally, because both parties usually only have primaries when there is no incumbent, there is no guarantee that when a region goes first, that partisans in a region will get to vote first. For example, if President Obama is not challenged in 2012 and the South goes first, it will be four cycles again before Democrats in that region get to influence the process. A further problem with the regional primaries plan is that it would not shorten the nomination season. The process would take place over several months.

The Delaware and Ohio Plans

Another idea that once gained some traction among Republicans is the "Delaware Plan." Under this proposal, state primaries and caucuses would be held in ascending order, based on the state's population. Again, there would likely be four primary dates with the least populated states going first and the most populated states last. This would essentially "backload" the delegate selection process. Because the largest states come last, no candidate could secure the nomination until all four groups of states had voted. In other words, a greater number of people would have a voice under the Delaware Plan than is the case under the current system or even under a series of regional primaries.

At the 2000 Republican National Convention, it looked as though the Delaware Plan might pass and be implemented in 2004. The plan, called the Delaware Plan because the Delaware Republican Party created it, was supported by a GOP commission studying reform of the nomination process. It later received the backing of the Republican National Committee. Yet, the Delaware Plan did not have universal support. Not surprisingly, heavily populated states balked at the idea, claiming that their ability to influence the party's nomination was hindered. Even though the nomination may not have been secured under the Delaware Plan by the time the most heavily populated states voted, the field could be significantly winnowed. Fearing an intense fight at the Republican National Convention in 2000 over the plan, George W. Bush came out against the plan, which effectively brought to an end any hope of its passage. Democrats have long been skeptical of a proposal like the Delaware Plan because many of the least populated states are racially and ethnically homogenous. In other words, the states with initial input would not look demographically like the party as a whole.

In 2008, Republicans again came close to adopting a nomination scheduling reform, this time called the Ohio Plan. Under the Ohio plan, the least populated states and territories would always hold their nomination contests on the same day and at the beginning of the nomination season. These contests would be followed by three pods comprising the remaining states that would rotate each election cycle. So, Pod Z, which included Florida, Georgia, Illinois, Michigan, New York, Ohio, and Pennsylvania, might go last in 2012, but second in 2016. Like the Delaware Plan, the Ohio Plan was also controversial and John McCain took it off the table at the party's national convention.

A National Primary

Perhaps the most common proposal put forth—and the most popular in the eyes of the public—is to hold a national primary. As with the general election, everyone would vote on the same date. There could be two possible national primary plans. One would be to eliminate delegates altogether and simply have the candidate who received the most votes obtain the nomination. The second plan, which would technically be a national primary and caucus, keeps the delegate selection process as it is now, but would have all states hold their primaries and caucuses on the same day. With this plan, states like Iowa and Nevada could retain the caucuses in which they believe so strongly. To me, either of these plans makes more sense than the current system.

An important benefit of a national primary is that turnout would likely increase because everyone would have a voice in who the nominee would be. The current nomination system encourages voter disengagement and disenfranchisement. In 2000, turnout in the Republican and Democratic New Hampshire primaries was 52 percent and 40 percent, respectively. In those 23 Republican primaries and 22 Democratic primaries held after March 9th, when the two parties' nominees were already known, turnout was only 16 percent.[33] In the 2004 Idaho Democratic primary, only 379 people turned out to vote![34] The 2008 primary season saw a record-shattering 58.7 million people vote in a primary or caucus.[35] This can be attributed primarily to the intense battle on the Democratic side where voters in virtually all states had a say in who the nominee would be. However, because the Republican nomination was decided much earlier, turnout was not nearly as high in those contests after February 5. For example, while more than 2.3 million people voted in Pennsylvania's Democratic primary on April 22, only about 800,000 voted on the Republican side. In Indiana, a traditionally strong Republican state, more than 1.2 million people voted in the Democratic primary on May 6 compared to roughly 400,000 in the Republican contest.[36] These disparities would likely not exist in a national primary.

Another advantage of a national primary is that it would significantly shorten the campaign season. Campaigns in the United States, especially for president, are far longer than in other countries. Presidential hopefuls must begin contemplating a campaign almost immediately after the last presidential election. The length of the campaign season has the potential to make voters fatigued and discourage the candidacies of attractive aspirants who do not want to go through the grueling process. Indeed, as I write, more than a year and a half before the 2012 Iowa caucus, we have already seen a great deal of speculation about who will run for the Republican nomination.

With a national primary, the election could be held some time in, say, June, preferably in conjunction with primaries for other offices to reduce the number of times people are asked to vote. This would shorten the campaign season by several months, but still give the parties a chance to hold their national conventions and allow people enough time to assess the candidates in the general election. A further strength of the national primary is that it would bring national issues to the forefront, instead of issues that are popular in Iowa and New Hampshire. As Stephen Wayne writes, "Candidates for the nation's highest office would be forced to discuss the problems they would most likely address during the general election campaign and would most likely confront as president."[37] Additionally, a national primary proposal that removes delegates from the process is the reform that is most consistent with the principle of "one person, one vote."[38]

There are several arguments against a national primary, most of which are flawed and many of which are becoming irrelevant given the current front-loaded calendar. One claim against a national primary is that it will unfairly benefit establishment candidates; the Jimmy Carters of the world will not have a chance to build momentum with an early-upset victory. Thomas Patterson goes so far as to write, "The election would be a cakewalk for a well-known, well-funded candidate backed by party leaders."[39] After the Democratic party's nomination of Barack Obama in 2008, I lost count of the number of people who told me that he could not have beaten Hillary Clinton, the establishment candidate, in a national primary.

There are two flaws with the argument that establishment candidates would have an unfair advantage in a national primary. First, well-known, well-funded candidates backed by party leaders have already done quite well under the current system; Jimmy Carter and Barack Obama are the exceptions, not the rule. Between 1976 and 2000, some years in which frontloading was prominent and some in which it was less so, no candidate who has neither led in the last national poll prior to the Iowa caucus nor raised the most money prior to the election year has won his party's nomination.[40] In 2004, Howard Dean out-raised his opponents during the previous year and looked poised to win in Iowa. Instead, he lost the nomination to Senator John Kerry. However, it is hard to argue that Kerry was the anti-establishment candidate; he had been a senator for 20 years. So, anti-establishment candidates are not having much success to begin with.

Second, it is not entirely clear to me that establishment candidates automatically win under a national primary. As I said, a number of people have pointed to the Democratic nomination in 2008 as an argument against a national primary because of the feeling that Obama could not have won under such a system. I do not view this argument as being particularly persuasive. Simply because Clinton, not Obama, may have won in a national primary is a weak rationale against such a reform. No nomination system will benefit all candidates equally and I am skeptical of those who make an argument solely because their favored candidate would not win. Additionally, there is certainly no evidence that Obama would have definitely lost under a national primary (just as there is no evidence that he would have won). We simply cannot know. However, he had raised a significant amount of money and had strong organizations in numerous states. Clearly, he would have been competitive. Finally, and perhaps more importantly, Obama won the nomination under the calendar that approximated a national primary more closely than any other nomination season.

Opponents of a national primary are also concerned that voters will not have enough time to learn about the candidates; the nomination process will be over just as soon as it starts. Because of the large number of presidential aspirants in the two major parties, the argument goes, an extended primary season allows the voters to vet the candidates. I have never understood this argument. While it is true that more candidates enter presidential primaries than primaries for other offices, the field is almost always quickly narrowed to three or four legitimate candidates. Even with a national primary, campaigning would still begin several months beforehand, giving voters plenty of time to assess the candidates' strengths and weaknesses. There is no reason why a few states' residents who hold their primaries and caucuses early, and do not reflect the rest of the country demographically, should determine the choices for residents of states who hold their primaries or caucuses later in the year.

In addition to keeping anti-establishment candidates from emerging and giving voters enough time to vet the candidates, critics argue that a national primary will increase the cost of campaigns that are already spiraling out of control. Under a regional primary system, for example, travel costs would be cut because candidates could remain in one geographic area. However, it is hard to believe that any plan will stem the wave of candidate spending. In the arms race for campaign money, no candidate can have enough. A different primary schedule is not going to lessen the need to fundraise constantly.

Another issue that could arise under a national primary is that ideological candidates who are unelectable in the general election would be more likely to win the nomination. If there are six or seven legitimate candidates, the theory goes, then a candidate who is strongly supported by a small faction in the party could win. However, this becomes less of a concern if open primaries are used. Also, empirical research indicates that parties have learned not to repeat the Goldwater or McGovern mistakes from previous nominations. Indeed, voters in primaries often act as "sophisticated voters," choosing the candidate with the best chance to win in the general election; not the candidate that most closely reflects their interests.[41] This may have been one reason why the Democrats chose to nominate John Kerry instead of Howard Dean in 2004.

Additionally, the worry about an extreme ideological candidate emerging from the primaries can easily be addressed by the rules of the primaries. If the national primary plan eliminates delegates—and most proposals do—then a rule can be instituted to require that a candidate receive a majority of the vote to be nominated. If no candidate receives a majority of the vote—certainly a possibility given the fact that there are likely to be three or four viable candidates—then there are two options. First, parties could hold a runoff primary between the candidates receiving the two highest vote totals. This concept is regularly used in several states' primaries, including Louisiana and Georgia, as well as in many local elections. There are three problems with holding a runoff. First, it will make voters have to go to the polls once more, and, as I argued in Chapter 2, Americans are already asked to vote too often. Second, the costs of elections increase, both in terms of campaigning and election administration. Third, by holding another election, the campaign season must be extended.

However, there is a second runoff option that gets around these problems; that is, an instant runoff can be held. Instant runoff voting (IRV) is used in some local elections, including those in San Francisco and Minneapolis. Some states, such as Louisiana and South Carolina, use IRV for overseas voters in federal or state runoff elections. Admittedly, IRV has not been tried on as grand a scale as a presidential election, but it is becoming a more common voting system at the state and, especially, local level.

Here is a hypothetical example of how IRV works. Instead of voting for only one candidate, voters can rank order their candidates. Pretend that after tallying everyone's first vote choice, the results are as follows:

Candidate A	100 votes (40%)
Candidate B	75 votes (30%)
Candidate C	40 votes (16%)
Candidate D	35 votes (14%)

Since no candidate receives a majority of the vote, Candidate D is removed from the race because of her last place finish. We then look at the second choice of the 35 people who voted for Candidate D. Say 30 of them supported Candidate A as their second choice and the remaining 5 votes supported Candidate B. The updated tally is:

Candidate A	130 votes (52%)
Candidate B	80 votes (32%)
Candidate C	40 votes (16%)

Candidate A now has a majority of the votes, so she would win the nomination. If after the second round, Candidate A still did not have a majority, Candidate C would be dropped and the process would continue until someone held a majority of the vote.

In addition to lessening the possibility of voter fatigue and lowering the costs of elections, IRV is positive because it allows voters to express their true preferences. No longer is a vote wasted. There is a belief that IRV will discourage negative campaigning because coalition building becomes more important. In our hypothetical example, Candidate A is not going to want to upset Candidate D's voters because she may need them to win a majority. However, I have seen no empirical studies to indicate whether IRV does promote more positive campaigns, and it is not clear to me that the elimination of negative advertising is positive.[42] Because IRV is a possible reform to the Electoral College as well, I turn more to the strengths and weaknesses of it in the next chapter. For now, I want to make the point that an unacceptable candidate is not likely to emerge from a national primary.

Finally, opponents of a national primary argue that it will make the parties' national conventions irrelevant.[43] This argument makes no sense. If the point of a national convention is to choose the party's nominee, then no convention in the last several presidential election cycles has been relevant. Because of the importance of the primaries and caucuses in choosing delegates, we know well in advance of the convention who the parties' nominees will be. The delegate roll call is nothing more than a symbolic event.

If delegates were eliminated from the presidential selection process, the conventions could still serve as an important launching point of a presidential campaign. States could continue to send delegates to vote on the party platform as well. One possibility, however, that I mentioned previously is that delegates could still be elected the same way they are currently, even under a national primary. If this was the case, then it is likely that the convention would be more important than at any time in the last 40 years because the nomination may no longer be a foregone conclusion. Each party requires that their nominee receive a majority of delegates. Under a national primary, it would be harder for one candidate to do so because she would not be able to obtain momentum the same way that she currently can. For example, a win in Iowa could not provide a boost in Nevada. Instead, we would be more likely to see the old brokered conventions of the past where negotiations occur and the party's candidate is actually nominated at the convention. Parties would not want such a plan, however, because it would undermine their ability to appear united.

I have never much cared that conventions are not responsible for the nomination of presidential candidates in anymore than a symbolic way. Even though the nominations are foregone conclusions at today's conventions, they are not meaningless. Conventions allow parties to debate and pass their party's platform. More importantly, they present the greatest opportunity in the campaign season for the party's nominee to present him/herself to the voters. The importance of these factors would not change under a national primary.

I should briefly mention one other option to reforming presidential primaries, which is eliminating the process altogether. There are some benefits to having party leaders choose the party's nominees instead of rank-and-file members. First, it would reduce the number of times in which people are asked to vote, which is consistent with my argument about making democracy less burdensome. Second, enormous amounts of money would be saved because candidates would no longer have to raise money the same way they do now. In some cases, such as in Georgia, election administration costs would be saved as well because the state holds its presidential primary on a different date than its primaries for other offices. Third, from a party's point of view, eliminating primaries would solve the problems of nonparty members potentially influencing who the party's nominee will be. Fourth, allowing party leaders to choose their nominee would appease those who believe that conventions are no longer relevant. Finally, some argue that party leaders will actually select less ideological candidates who have a better chance to win in a general election.

The problem with such a move, however, is that the process no longer is transparent—another criterion that is important in a model electoral democracy. Deals are more likely to be made outside of the public's eye. Moreover, allowing the party leaders to determine the party's nominee is not democratic; rank-and-file members should have a voice in who will represent the party in the general election. There are often significant differences regarding the positions on issues candidates of the same party take as well as personal characteristics, such as leadership abilities and experience. Sarah Palin is not Mitt Romney; Hillary Clinton is not Barack Obama. The party-in-the-electorate, the people who identify with a political party, is an integral part of a political party. Without them, there would be no party; therefore, they should have a voice in who represents the party.[44]

Because of the enormous coordination obstacles between parties at all levels of government and the states, radically reformulating the presidential nominating process is a challenge. Discussing the prospects for major change, Rhodes Cook writes, "[D]on't bet on it. The smart money is not on any radical change, but a continuation of the gradually evolving system that is already in place—where the parties set the basic ground rules, the states have plenty of flexibility, and most of the voters have a role that is marginal at best."[45] Cook is probably correct that radical change may not be on the horizon. Coordination between the parties and states over the scheduling of primaries is quite difficult. States want to protect their voters' interests. Less populated states would not likely sign on to a national primary for fear that they would be ignored. More populated states might resist a regional primary because of the fact that at some point they will have to come last. The only way to coordinate reform would be by the national government stepping in and passing a law. This is unlikely to happen, however. Over the years several bills have been introduced in Congress to reform the primary system, but none have gained much traction primarily because the law would have to be passed by legislators who might be working against the best interests of their states. Even if Congress passed and the president signed a bill that enacted primary reform, there are constitutional questions regarding whether Congress has this power.[46]

In this chapter I have argued that the presidential nomination process needs to be significantly overhauled. Primaries should be open and held on the same day. If delegates are going to continue to be selected, then they should be allocated on a proportional basis and superdelegates should be eliminated. While the presidential nomination process is far from perfect, neither is the institution in which we elect our presidents. I now turn to the question of the Electoral College.

Chapter 9

The Electoral College

Any book assessing the state of American electoral democracy would be incomplete without a discussion of one of the most controversial and unique aspects of American democracy: the Electoral College. Supporters of many of the other subjects covered in this book, including the frequency of elections, voting for numerous offices, and direct democracy, do so because they believe those aspects of the American electoral system promote more democracy. To its critics, however, the Electoral College is inherently undemocratic. First, there is no guarantee that the majority, or even the plurality, winner of the popular vote will become president. Second, according to the Constitution, there is not even a guarantee that the people will get to vote for president! Each state determines how it will choose its electors. They can do so through a popular vote, as all states currently do, but there is nothing that requires direct citizen input. If a state legislature decides it wants to appoint electors, as many state legislatures did immediately after the ratification of the Constitution, it is free to do so (although it would certainly face massive opposition from the public). As a result, perhaps no aspect of the Constitution receives more criticism than the Electoral College.

And, it should. In this chapter, I examine the arguments made in favor of the Electoral College and point out the flaws with those claims. I then outline the various reforms to the Electoral College that scholars and practitioners have suggested and look at their strengths and weaknesses. In particular, I argue in favor of a plurality election with an instant runoff. However, since the Electoral College seems to be here for the foreseeable future, two reforms are needed to improve the current system: the elimination of both "faithless electors" and the House contingency plan to select a president if no candidate receives a majority of the electoral vote. Before laying out my argument, a brief history of how we ended up with such a unique system is in order.

What is the Electoral College? Why Do We Have It?

When you vote in a presidential election you are casting your vote not for a presidential candidate, but for an elector(s) pledged to support that candidate;

this is similar to the delegate selection process discussed in the previous chapter. Each state gets a number of electoral votes, equal to their representation in the House of Representatives, plus two bonus electoral votes for Senate representation. So, for instance, California has 55 electoral votes today, while Wyoming has three. The ratification of the Twenty-third Amendment in 1961 gave the District of Columbia three electoral votes as well. With the exception of Maine and Nebraska, each state then normally pledges all of its electoral votes to the person who wins the most votes in the state (as I discuss shortly, Maine and Nebraska divide their electoral votes by congressional district, and the winner of the state gets the two remaining electoral votes). The first person to get 270 electoral votes (a bare majority) wins.

If no candidate reaches 270 votes, then the election is sent to the House of Representatives. Once in the House, each state gets to vote for one of the three candidates who won the most electoral votes.[1] A candidate must receive votes from a majority of states to be elected. This contingency plan gives the less populated states enormous power because Wyoming has the same influence as California. The Wyoming representative has massive sway because, since Wyoming only has one representative, her vote decides how the state votes; in California, a representative would be only one of 53 votes. The last time an election was decided by the House was in the controversial election of 1824 when Andrew Jackson won both the popular and electoral vote, but failed to win a majority of the electoral vote. Instead, the House elected John Quincy Adams. Given the closeness of the 2000 presidential election, some people worried that the House would decide the outcome of that election.

No other country in the world elects its executive in this manner. Once I had the opportunity to give a talk on the Electoral College to a group of Mexican politicians who were visiting the United States to study its democracy. As I was explaining how the Electoral College worked, I noticed that several of the politicians had quizzical expressions on their faces. I thought that perhaps the translator was not translating what I was saying correctly. After I finished the talk, one of the participants immediately raised his hand to ask a question—or perhaps, more accurately, make a statement. "I don't understand how Americans can argue that their democracy is a model for others to follow," the politician said, "when they have a process such as this to elect their president." I quickly realized that there was not a problem with the translation after all.

The question is how did the United States end up with a system as distinct as the Electoral College? One might expect that the Electoral College was one of the great debates among the founders at the constitutional convention. In reality, the Electoral College was almost an afterthought. The founders were much more concerned with questions related to states' rights and representation in the legislative branch than they were with the selection of the president.

This is not to imply that the Electoral College was the only proposal put forth regarding the presidential selection process. In fact, other ideas were vigorously debated well before the idea of the Electoral College even emerged.[2] Some of the participants at the convention believed that the Congress should choose the executive, a proposal that convention participants initially passed.[3] After more thought, James Madison, Gouverneur Morris, and James Wilson, in particular, were concerned that Congress selecting the executive would violate the systems of checks and balances and separation of powers that they so strongly supported. "He [the executive] will be the mere creature of the legislature if appointed and impeachable by that body," argued Morris.[4] Eventually, the rest of the convention agreed and the Congress selection plan was overturned.[5]

Wilson believed that the people should vote directly for the executive. This idea was met with skepticism because there was concern that the average American was not capable of making such an important decision. "The people 'will never be sufficiently informed of characters' to make a good choice," claimed Roger Sherman.[6] Moreover, a direct election did not appeal to less populated states that were concerned that they would be irrelevant in electing the president. Only Pennsylvania (Wilson's home state) ultimately voted for the direct election of the president.[7]

After much frustration and many proposals, the convention finally settled on the Electoral College, initially proposed by Wilson, just two weeks before adjourning. While ultimately adopted, the Electoral College was controversial from the start. Thomas Jefferson called it "the most dangerous blot in our Constitution."[8] Historians Christopher Collier and James Lincoln Collier refer to it as "a Rube Goldberg machine." They write that the Electoral College was "jerry-rigged out of odds and ends of parliamentary junk pressed together by contending interests."[9] Donald Lutz and his colleagues state that "the Convention delegates 'backed into' the final solution," and that "no coherent theory supported this solution."[10] Although not a flawless system, the convention delegates assumed that George Washington would be elected to as many terms as he wanted. Again, they were more concerned with the long-term effects of other issues.[11] And, the Electoral College was an acceptable compromise for both more populated and less populated states. The most populated states benefited from the proposal because they would have the greatest number of electoral votes, but the least populated states received more influence than they otherwise would have under other proposals because of the two "bonus" electors that each state received. Perhaps the even bigger advantage of the Electoral College from the point of view of the less populated states was that the House, again with each state getting one vote, would ultimately decide the election if no candidate received a majority of the electoral vote. Because parties did not exist at the time of the creation of the Electoral College, many delegates believed that the House would regularly decide presidential elections, whenever, of course, Washington decided not to run, because several candidates would likely throw their hats into the ring, making it difficult for any one candidate to receive a majority of the electoral vote.

Arguments in Favor of the Electoral College and Why They are Flawed

Supporters of the Electoral College generally put forth four main arguments in favor of the institution:

1   It is consistent with the federal nature of the Constitution.
2   It forces candidates to receive broad support, hence protecting less popu-lated states.
3   It reduces fraud and produces a clear winner in a short period of time.
4   It protects the American two-party system.

I now address each of these claims:

The Electoral College is Consistent with and Preserves Federalism

Though the Electoral College may have found its way into the Constitution through the back door, proponents of the system argue that it is grounded in principles advocated at the convention: mainly federalism and separation of powers. I have already noted the founders' concerns about giving Congress the power to choose the executive, but supporters believe that the Electoral College fits nicely with the founders' emphasis on creating a federal, rather than national, system of government as well. It allows states to determine their own rules regarding the selection of electors. Paul Schumaker and Burdett Loomis write:

> By distributing 436 electors to the states (and the District) on the basis of their populations, it gives great weight to the idea that we are a nation of individual citizens, who should all count equally in holding our presidents accountable through votes. By allocating 102 electors to the states (and the District) simply because they are states, it also recognizes that we are a nation of states, each of which should also count equally in the presiden-tial election process. Arguments that the Electoral College is unfair in giving more value to the votes of citizens of small states are therefore problematic because they assume that we are simply a nation of individual citizens. As a nation of states, each state has a role to play in the process of electing the most powerful national authority.[12]

The problem with this argument is that the founders did not adopt the Electoral College because they believed it had a federal nature; they adopted it as a compromise between large and small states, slave and free states, and because neither the option of the people nor the Congress deciding the presi-dent was appealing to the majority of delegates.[13] "The chief virtue of the

Electoral College," writes historian Jack Rakove, "was that it replicated other political compromises that the Constitutional Convention had already made," not that it promoted federalism.[14]

Furthermore, it is unclear exactly what the presidency has to do with federalism since it is the only truly national office that is elected; it is congressional representation that is more in line with the notion of federalism. Finally, were the Electoral College abolished, it is tough to see how federalism would be threatened. Electoral College scholar Neil Peirce sums up this view: "The vitality of federalism rests chiefly on the constitutionally mandated system of congressional representation and the will and capacity of state and local governments to address compelling problems," writes Peirce, "not on the hocuspocus of an eighteenth-century vote count system."[15]

The Electoral College Forces Candidates to Earn Broad Support

Another argument in favor of the institution is that the Electoral College forces candidates to have broad support from a variety of states, not just the backing of people in the country's urban centers. "The Electoral College is an 'alloy' of popular will," writes political theorist Gary Glenn. "That means popular election of the president through the Electoral College makes popular election fairer to the interests of geographical minorities (small states), and hence elects presidents by broader and more diverse interests than would direct national election. It produces presidents more likely to govern for 'the general good' instead of the will of 'more' of the national popular vote."[16]

Yet, there is scant empirical evidence that the Electoral College does what Glenn says it does. Candidates do not win presidential elections by racking up wins in a number of scarcely-populated states; they win by carrying a number of battleground states. A quick look at where a presidential candidate's campaign undermines the "broad support" argument. In 2008, presidential and vice-presidential candidates skipped ten states entirely (presidential candidates McCain and Obama did not make a single visit to 14 states and several others were only visited once).[17] Even with the Democratic Party's fifty-state strategy, candidates Obama and Biden failed to make appearances in 17 states.

The number of states ignored by the presidential and vice-presidential candidates in 2008 was actually less than in previous contests. In 2004, presidential and vice-presidential candidates did not appear in 20 states, and eight others received three visits or fewer (mostly by the vice-presidential candidates).[18] On the other hand, candidates made 84 trips to Florida, 63 to Ohio, 40 to Wisconsin, and 36 to Pennsylvania.[19] In 2000, presidential and vice-presidential candidates visited Florida 61 times, Michigan 43 times, and Pennsylvania 42 times; they never visited Alaska, North Dakota, South Dakota, Montana, Rhode Island, Hawaii, Nebraska, Utah, Kansas, Oklahoma, South Carolina and Virginia. Three other states received only one visit and the candidates visited five other states three times or fewer.[20] In 1996, Bill Clinton did not visit 19 of the 50 states, while Bob Dole skipped 29 states.[21] It is hard to argue that this is evidence of broad support.

In fact, abolishing the Electoral College in favor of a popular vote election might actually make candidates visit states that they otherwise ignore. Take Alabama, for instance, a medium-populated state that rarely receives visits from presidential contenders.[22] The reason Alabama is not a frequent stop during a presidential campaign is clear; the state is not in play. The Republican candidate will win the state, so there is no reason for either party's candidate to visit. It does not matter if the Republican candidate wins the state with 55 percent of the vote or 75 percent of the vote; he is going to win all 9 of the state's electoral votes. In a popular vote election, it does matter if the Republican candidate wins 55 percent or 75 percent of the vote because all votes are counted in the same pool; every vote matters, so there is incentive to campaign for every vote. Even the Democratic candidate might visit Alabama in hopes of picking up extra votes.

Along with making candidates win broad support, proponents of the Electoral College argue that it protects the interest of less populated states. The argument goes that because each state gets two bonus electors, the less populated states have more influence than they would have under a popular vote election; therefore, less populated states cannot be ignored and their interests can be protected. I just showed that less populated states *can* be ignored under the Electoral College, but let's assume for a minute that they are not. It is unclear to me exactly what a "small" state interest is. As presidential scholar George Edwards notes, even the least populated states have significant diversity.[23]

Furthermore, it is difficult to think of a common interest between less populated states. It is not clear what a state like Wyoming or Rhode Island have in common besides their small populations. Indeed, these states regularly support opposing presidential candidates, indicating that they are more different than alike. If we were going to try to find a common interest between less populated states, I guess one might say that it is agriculture, because most of these states are predominantly rural. It is hard to argue that agriculture interests would suffer, though, if the Electoral College were abandoned. "The market value of the agricultural production of California, Texas, Florida, and Illinois exceeds that of all seventeen of the smallest states combined."[24]

Even if there is such a thing as a small state interest, it is not taking a part in presidential elections under the Electoral College. "[N]owhere in the vast literature on voting in presidential elections has anyone found that voters choose candidates on the basis of their stands on state and local issues," writes Edwards. "Indeed, candidates avoid such issues, because they do not want to be seen in the rest of the country as pandering to special interests."[25]

And, why is it that we are only concerned about protecting local interests in presidential elections? If local interests need protection anywhere, it would be in gubernatorial elections. Do you think people in Centralia, IL have the same concerns as the people in Chicago? Yet, residents of Centralia are forced to accept the outcome of gubernatorial elections that are basically decided by a bloc of voters in Chicago. No doubt, just about every state in the Union has a similar example.

Finally, I am not sure why we are so concerned about protecting less populated states in the presidential selection process; they are more than represented in the U.S. Senate. Because of the filibuster and the fact that any bill that is signed into law has to be approved by the Senate, less populated states can hold legislation hostage. There is a reason why Delaware is "the first state;" Delaware's legislature knew that they were getting a good deal under the Constitution. Interestingly, senators from less populated states rarely vote as a bloc, indicating that there probably are no issues that unite them.

Founding Father James Wilson, one of the strongest advocates at the time of a direct vote, said it best: "Can we forget for whom we are forming a government? Is it for *men*, or for the imaginary beings called *States?*"[26] Indeed, the founders chose to begin the Preamble to the Constitution with "We the People," not "We the 13 states."

The Electoral College Reduces Fraud

Another advantage of the Electoral College, according to advocates, is that it reduces fraud and ensures that a national recount crisis will not occur. Imagine if what happened in Florida in 2000 happened on a national stage. The Electoral College makes a national recount moot because it is not the popular vote that matters but the electoral vote. In addition, because so few states influence the outcome of the election, candidates do not ask for recounts, meaning that fraud is contained at the local level. Writing about the possibility of a national recount, Norman Ornstein states "[T]hree (or four) crises out of more than 50 presidential elections is remarkably small. And the drive for reform, based on the actual crises or the threat of another precipitated by the Electoral College, tends to ignore the crises that could be generated by direct national popular vote for the president."[27]

If anything, fraud and concerns over recounts are heightened *because* of the Electoral College. "Direct election would create a *disincentive* for fraud," claims Edwards, "because altering an election outcome through fraud would require an organized effort of proportions never witnessed in the United States. And because no one in any state could know that his or her efforts at fraud would make a difference in the election, there would be little reason to risk trying."[28] Law professor Jamin Raskin concurs. "The fact that we conduct not one national election for president but 51 different contests for presidential electors creates a recurring incentive for strategic mischief by partisan actors in the states, who need only suppress a relatively small number of votes to swing all of a state's electors—and thereby potentially the entire election—into the desired column," writes Raskin.[29] Furthermore, it is more likely that a state will require a recount than the nation as a whole. A recount was needed in Florida because 537 votes separated Bush and Gore. Recounts could have occurred in Iowa, New Mexico, and Wisconsin as well, because only a few hundred votes separated the candidates. Yet, there was no need for a recount nationwide since Gore had more than a 537,000-vote lead over Bush.[30]

The Electoral College Protects the Two-Party System

If you are a supporter of a two-party system, proponents of the Electoral College assert, then you must back the Electoral College because its abolishment would lead to the rise of competitive third parties. There is no doubt that, because of the winner-takes-all allocation of electors, the Electoral College benefits the two major parties. Eliminating it, however, is not going to lead to the demise of the two-party system in the United States. In elections for other federal, state, and local offices the two-party system remains entrenched; an Electoral College elects none of those offices. There are too many institutional and cultural barriers to a third-party system in the United States (see Chapter 11), the Electoral College is but one. There is "no reliable, convincing evidence to suggest that changing the presidential election system, in and of itself, would alter significantly the party system in a predictable manner," writes Allan Cigler and his colleagues. "There are simply too many other factors that reinforce our system of two-party dominance beside Electoral College rules."[31]

If anything, third parties may wreak more havoc under the Electoral College. If a strong regional candidate, such as George Wallace, can win enough electoral votes to throw the election into the House, then that candidate will have enormous negotiating power. Wallace won 46 electoral votes in 1968. Had he won a few other southern states and/or Hubert Humphrey defeated Nixon in one or two others, the House would have decided the election.

A Dated Argument

There is one argument in favor of the Electoral College that my students regularly make that definitely no longer holds water. They often reference the founders' concerns that the people would be incapable of making such an important decision as choosing the president. It is problematic to compare the capabilities of today's voters with those at the time of the founding. Information is far more readily available now than it was back then and empirical evidence indicates that people are capable of casting informed votes in presidential elections.[32] But, let us assume that people are not casting informed votes. The Electoral College no longer provides a buffer because all states today choose their electors via popular vote; informed, engaged elites are not responsible for selecting electors as some founders had initially envisioned.[33]

The Reasons for Change

The most obvious defect of the Electoral College is the fact that, as we saw in 2000, a national popular vote winner may not win a majority of the electoral vote. Al Gore defeated George W. Bush by more than 537,000 popular votes, but lost the electoral vote 271–266. Before 2000, the popular vote winner failed to win the electoral vote three other times (1824, 1876, and 1888), but it has almost happened several other times including 1960 and 1976.[34] If a democracy is supposed to be "government by the people," then it is problematic when the choice of the plurality of voters is not elected as is the case in every other election—federal, state, or local.

Critics of this argument, most notably public choice theorists, claim that it is impossible to measure the national popular will. As I noted in Chapter 5, ballot access requirements may screen out attractive candidates or the rigors of running for the presidency may do so. In other words, the choices the voters have may not represent who they really want. Furthermore, not everyone votes in an election, meaning that the wishes of nonvoters are not represented in the "popular will." Both of these claims are true, but they are also true for every other office for which Americans are asked to vote. No one seems to question whether senators, governors, or representatives reflect the popular will of the people; therefore, I am not sure the argument should apply to the president. The popular vote in presidential elections reflects the public will of voters based on the choices with which they were presented, no different than any other elected office in the country.

Moreover, the Electoral College is inconsistent with the cherished principle of "one person, one vote." Under the Electoral College, not everyone's vote counts equally on a national level. Because of the two bonus electors, electors in Rhode Island represent fewer people than electors in New York. Politically engaged citizens in heavily populated states, then, are disadvantaged simply on the basis of where they live. Furthermore, some people's votes count more than others because turnout is not constant in the states. A vote will count less in a state like Wisconsin or Minnesota where turnout is traditionally high than a vote in a similarly populated state like Georgia where turnout is generally low. "States have no interest, as states, in the election of a president," writes Rakove, "only citizens do, and the vote of a citizen in Coeur d'Alene should count equally with one in Detroit."[35]

The idea of "one person, one vote" has appeared several times in this book. Interestingly, the U.S. Senate violates this notion inherently since representation is equal. Why not argue then that the Senate is undemocratic? Some people do,[36] but one does not have to abolish the Senate to defend the principle of "one person, one vote" for president. Again, George Edwards best sums up the response to the argument comparing "one person, one vote" in Senate and presidential elections. "The Senate is explicitly designed to represent states and the interests within them," writes Edwards. "The presidency is designed to do something quite different. The president is to rise above parochial interests and represent the nation as a whole, not one part of it."[37]

Another problem with the Electoral College is that with the current winner-takes-all rules used in 48 states and the District of Columbia, the Electoral College discourages participation. The state of Kansas, for example, has voted for the Republican candidate in every election since 1964, when all but the Deep South and Arizona voted for Democrat Lyndon Johnson. As a result, Kansas is ignored in presidential elections. Voters are not encouraged to go to the polls there the same way that they would be in the neighboring state of Missouri, whose electoral votes are usually up for grabs. Recall that in the Calculus of Voting equation, discussed in Chapter 1, potential voters consider the probability that their votes will matter when deciding whether to participate. In Kansas and many other states in the Union, the presidential election is not in play, so the incentive to vote is minimal. In a competitive popular vote election, the votes of people in uncompetitive presidential election states will matter, giving people a reason to participate. Indeed, research finds that voter turnout is greater in battleground states than in non-battleground states, either because of the perception that a vote matters more in a battleground state or because voters are exposed to more information about the candidates.[38]

Finally, again because of the winner-takes-all rules, the Electoral College exaggerates the winning candidate's victory. In 1980, Ronald Reagan barely won 50 percent of the vote, but carried more than 90 percent of the electoral votes. Clearly the electoral count is not a true reflection of public support. Advocates of the Electoral College argue that an exaggerated electoral vote victory is positive, because it gives the president a better opportunity to claim a mandate. The problem is that there is little evidence that presidents who win the electoral vote count in a landslide are any more successful than presidents who win by a closer margin; or, conversely, that presidents who win the electoral vote count by a slim margin are less successful than those with a significant electoral vote victory.[39]

A brief word must be said about one argument made by people, mostly Democrats, who support abolishing the Electoral College, which does not pass muster. Many Democrats have long believed that the Electoral College was biased in favor of Republicans; the fact that Al Gore won the popular vote but lost the electoral vote further solidified this feeling. It is true that Republican candidates generally win more states than Democratic candidates, but Bill Clinton and Barack Obama did quite well under the Electoral College. Moreover, had George W. Bush lost Ohio in 2004, we would have seen 2000 all over again, only with the results reversed. Bush would have won the popular vote, but lost the electoral vote. In fact, Kerry consultant Mark Mellman's research indicated that the Electoral College favored Kerry over Bush.[40] Even in the 2000 presidential election that renewed the controversy over the Electoral College, preelection polls made it appear that George Bush would win the popular vote, but lose the election (the opposite of what actually happened). In sum, there is no compelling evidence that the Electoral College favors one of the major parties over the other.

Attempts to Reform the Electoral College

Because of the issues just raised, no aspect of the Constitution has received more calls for amendment than the Electoral College. The controversy surrounding the Electoral College has led to more than 700 separate proposals for either amending or entirely abolishing the institution.[41] It would obviously be impossible to discuss every plan, and many of them are redundant, but I will examine the strengths and weaknesses of some of the most prominent ideas.[42]

Amending the Electoral College

There are many scholars and practitioners who believe that the basic framework of the Electoral College is sound, but that the institution needs some tweaking. Perhaps the most common reform for amending the Electoral College is the district plan. Indeed, two states—Maine and Nebraska—already use this system for allocating their electors.[43] Under the district plan, supported by James Madison at the Constitutional Convention, the candidate who wins the plurality vote in each congressional district obtains that district's electoral vote and the candidate who wins the statewide vote receives the two bonus electoral votes given to each state because of senatorial representation. The rest of the Electoral College remains intact. The argument in favor of the district plan is that it makes the Electoral College more reflective of the nationwide vote.[44] There are heavily Republican areas in California, for instance, as are there strongly Democratic districts in Texas. Under the current winner-takes-all system, these areas do not matter. It makes little sense for a presidential candidate to campaign in a state that he knows he is going to lose. Under the district plan, a candidate might actually visit states that he otherwise would ignore because certain congressional districts are competitive or benefit the candidate's party.

One problem with the district plan, however, is that it does not eliminate the possibility that the plurality vote winner could lose the election. Indeed, if the district system had been in place nationwide in 1960, Richard Nixon would have defeated John Kennedy, the popular vote winner, by 33 electoral votes instead of losing to him by 84 electoral votes.[45] Al Gore would have lost the electoral vote by an even larger margin in 2000 under a district system, while still winning the popular vote.[46] Moreover, allocating electors by congressional district would make the redistricting process discussed in Chapter 7 even more political as parties would push for drawing districts that would benefit their presidential candidates. Finally, it is likely that such a plan would simply create battleground districts instead of battleground states. California may have Republican districts and Texas Democratic districts, but there would still be little incentive to visit those districts because most are strongly in favor of one party or the other.

A similar reform to the district plan is the proportional plan, which was rejected by voters in Colorado in 2004. Under this proposal, again, the crux of the Electoral College remains in place, but electoral votes would be allocated proportionally, based on the popular vote in a state.[47] In other words, if a state has 10 electoral votes and Candidate A receives 60 percent of the vote and Candidate B the remaining 40 percent, then Candidate A wins 6 electoral votes while candidate B wins 4; under the current system Candidate A wins all 10 votes. This is a clear example, but not all election results would be as clean. Pretend Candidate A won 65 percent of the vote and Candidate B won 35 percent. Would Candidate A then win 6.5 electoral votes? Would you round up or down? If so, then Candidate A would receive 7 electoral votes and Candidate B 4, but there are only 10 electoral votes. You can see how complex such a system could be. While it would be complicated to allocate the electors in a proportional system, certainly it can be done. As I stated in the previous chapter, delegates during presidential primaries are often allocated proportionally.

The most obvious advantage of the proportional plan is that the electoral vote would be more reflective of the popular vote, even more so than under a district plan. As under the district plan, a proportional plan might encourage candidates to visit states they otherwise would not. For example, now it would matter if a candidate won 40 percent of the vote in a state instead of 30 percent. And, candidates would no longer just visit competitive congressional districts as they would under the district plan.

Although these are positive aspects of the proportional plan, there is one major problem. Allocating electoral votes proportionally would make it extremely difficult for a candidate to receive a majority of the electoral votes because minor party candidates would no longer be shut out. A third-party candidate who receives 10 percent of the vote in a state would receive 10 percent of the state's electoral votes, which in a close race could be enough to throw the election into the House of Representatives. If electors were allocated proportionally, then half of the presidential elections between 1956 and 2000 would have ended up in the House.[48] This percentage likely would have been even greater because, in reality, third-party candidates were hurt by the winner-takes-all rules. If a proportional system had been in place, then minor party candidates would have done better because people would be less likely to feel that they were wasting their votes. This would make it even more difficult for one candidate to receive a majority of the electoral vote.

Having a candidate fail to win a majority of the electoral vote leads to one of two undesirable results. First, a third party can essentially hijack an election unless one of the two major party candidates meets its needs. For example, in 1968, George Wallace could have received significant concessions from either Hubert Humphrey or Richard Nixon in return for support from Wallace's electors. A fringe candidate then would have determined the outcome of an election and received who knows what kinds of promises from the incoming administration. If a third-party candidate did not instruct his electors to support one of the two major party candidates, then, as I noted earlier, the election would be decided in the House of Representatives where each state receives one vote, regardless of its population. It is hard to think of a less democratic solution than Wyoming and Delaware having as much influence as California and Texas in determining who the president will be. If a proportional plan were to be enacted, then states should require a threshold that candidates must pass to win electoral votes, as the Democrats do in their presidential primaries and caucuses. The problem is that once a threshold is implemented, then the vote is not a true reflection of the people thereby eliminating the main advantage of the proportional plan.

Abolishing the Electoral College

While the district and proportional plans each have some positives, ultimately they still keep the thrust of the Electoral College intact. Under each plan, the notion of "one person, one vote" would still be violated. Therefore, the only acceptable solution is to abolish the Electoral College. The question is: if the Electoral College is abolished, then what would replace it? The obvious answer is a popular vote election that is used in all other federal elections, but there is considerable debate among advocates of eliminating the Electoral College regarding the rules of a popular vote election.

One possibility would be for the candidate with the most votes to win the election. This election would look no different than most of the elections in the United States. An advantage of a plurality vote winner election is that it is most consistent with the principle of "one person, one vote;" every person's vote counts equally. From a democratic standpoint then, this suggestion might be fairest. The problem with the plurality vote winner proposal, however, is that a candidate could win the election with the support of a small fraction of the public. If several viable candidates decided to run, then a candidate who receives one-third or even one-quarter of the vote could win. This could result in the election of an extremely polarizing figure who has strong support among a minority of voters. The chance of a fringe candidate being elected is a concern, but I am not convinced that the possibilities of such a candidate being elected are as great as some have argued. With the exception of Louisiana, every gubernatorial election in the country uses this system and it works well. Parties keep the number of viable candidates to a minimum, and rarely do you see a gubernatorial candidate elected without significant support. Moreover, the Electoral College does not ensure a majority vote winner. Not only can a candidate win the electoral vote but lose the popular vote, candidates who win the electoral vote can be elected with far less than a majority of the popular vote. Bill Clinton carried only 43 percent of the popular vote when elected in 1992; Abraham Lincoln won less than 40 percent of the vote on his way to victory in 1860. In fact, in roughly 40 percent of the presidential elections since 1824 the winning candidate did not receive a majority of the vote.

One way to get around the problem of popular vote winners not receiving a majority is to hold a runoff election. I discussed this possibility as it relates to the reform of the presidential nomination process in the previous chapter. Under such a system—used in the state of Louisiana for example—the top two vote winners would face each other in another election several weeks later. The advantage of a runoff would be that, like under the plurality vote system, all votes would be counted equally, but the winner could also claim support from the majority of voters. However, the downside of this reform is that it would extend an already too long election season and infuse even more money into presidential elections. Two candidates would likely have to spend obscene amounts of money three times during the year (to win the primary, to get into a runoff, and to win the runoff). Often, the runoff would simply be a repeat election of the previous election held, because there are almost always only two candidates who have a legitimate chance of winning, although it is possible that more legitimate candidates would emerge since the Electoral College would be abolished. For example, in 2000 the runoff would have been a repeat of the race between Al Gore and George W. Bush. In other words, voters would have been exposed to another month of campaign commercials and stump speeches from the same candidates who they had probably already heard too much from.[49] As noted in the preceding paragraph, winning presidential candidates often do not receive a majority of the vote, making the possibility of a runoff likely.

One solution to this problem is to hold an instant runoff vote (IRV) as I discussed in the last chapter. Again, under this system a candidate would have to win a majority of the vote to be elected, just as she would under the previous proposal mentioned, but a separate runoff election would not take place. Instead, voters would have the opportunity to rank-order their preferences and vote totals would be recalculated until one candidate emerged with a majority of the vote.[50] There are potential problems with an IRV as well. First, IRV might be more confusing to voters who are not used to casting a ballot for more than one candidate for an office. The information costs of voting might increase as well because an IRV would likely encourage more candidates to run for office, as would the two previous reforms, meaning that instead of studying the positions of two candidates, voters might have to consider the positions of three, four, five, or more candidates. Another concern with IRV is that some of the voting systems discussed in Chapter 6 might not be compatible with allowing people to rank-order their candidate preferences; and even if they are compatible, they still would be more likely to confuse voters. One final concern among some people with IRV, as opposed to a plurality election or a regular runoff, is that it would undermine the two-party system. The winner-takes-all rules of the Electoral College virtually guarantee that only a Democrat or Republican can win. IRV would encourage more third-party candidates or candidates of the two major parties who did not win the nomination, but choose to run as independents, because no longer would a person's vote be wasted. For example, people could comfortably vote for Ralph Nader because Al Gore would not be hurt by their vote (assuming they voted Gore as their second choice).

Of these potential problems, the only one that concerns me is the compatibility of voting systems. IRV may initially confuse some voters, but it is not an overly difficult concept to understand. The number of candidates may increase, but I am not sure to an unmanageable amount. Again, party loyalty would keep some candidates from running and most elections, even ones such as the 2003 California gubernatorial recall that had 134 candidates listed on the ballot, would be quickly parsed down to only a few legitimate contenders. As I noted earlier, the two-party system would not be affected because of the other institutional and cultural barriers to competitive third parties. Ralph Nader might have won more votes in 2000 had IRV been in place, but not enough to undermine the two-party system. The compatibility of some voting machines is a concern, but it is not an obstacle that cannot be overcome. For example, Arkansas, Louisiana, and South Carolina currently use IRV for overseas voting. San Francisco, CA and Minneapolis, MN have also adopted IRV for most city elections.

IRV is advantageous because it will eliminate wasted votes, may bring more people to the polls, and, because a majority winner will occur, is a better reflection of the popular will. Furthermore, because a majority is needed to win, IRV will keep extremist candidates from ascending to the presidency. Some scholars even argue that the system will make fraud much more complicated to carry out.[51]

The Future of the Electoral College

Although IRV has some definite benefits and is gaining traction in states and localities around the country, the chances of it being enacted to select the president are remote. In fact, the abolishment of the Electoral College at all seems highly unlikely. As controversial as the Electoral College is, one must go all the way back to 1803 to find an amendment simply modifying the Electoral College.[52] To enact any one of the abolishment reforms would require a constitutional amendment. In other words, two-thirds of both the House and the Senate would have to support such a proposal and then three-fourths of the state legislatures must do so. This is simply not going to happen; too many states benefit from the current system and opposition in only 13 of the 99 state legislatures would be enough to block an amendment.[53] Because of the two bonus electors, less populated states believe—even if it is not true—that they are represented more than they otherwise would be under a popular vote or runoff. Furthermore, more heavily populated, politically competitive states—battleground states—would resist abolishing the Electoral College because they are so important under the current system. Look at the attention that states like Florida, Ohio, and Pennsylvania have received in previous presidential elections.

Certainly these states would not be ignored in a popular vote election, but they would not garner as much attention as they currently do. Heavily populated, politically uncompetitive states, such as California, Texas, New York, and Illinois, which are ignored under the Electoral College would become just as important, if not more so, in a popular vote election than the current battleground states. Quickly doing the math makes it clear that three-fourths of the states would not be on board with abolishing the Electoral College because they benefit too much from it. After 2000, many people thought that it spelled the end for the Electoral College. Even with a popular vote winner losing the election, it was never close to being eliminated. If the Electoral College was not abolished after the issues surrounding the 2000 election, then it is difficult to see a scenario that would lead to its demise.

Recently, a new proposal to "amend" the Electoral College has received some support. I put the word "amend" in quotations because the proposal is essentially a backdoor way to abolish the Electoral College without having to change the Constitution. An organization named FairVote, which has former presidential candidates John Anderson and Birch Bayh among other known politicians on their advisory board, has pushed an interesting plan—if you are opposed to the Electoral College—to enact a national popular vote. Briefly, this is how the plan works. Remember that the Constitution mandates that state legislatures determine how electors will be selected. Every state but Maine and Nebraska relies on the popular vote within the state to determine which candidate's electors are seated. Under FairVote's plan, the state legislature would ignore the state popular vote and choose electors based on the national popular vote. Let's use the 2000 presidential election as an example. Pretend that the state of Florida adopted FairVote's plans. The controversy surrounding the Florida election would be moot since Al Gore won the national popular vote. Instead of choosing Bush electors, because he won the popular vote in the state, Florida would have chosen Gore electors, because he won the popular vote nationally. This would have allowed Gore to win the electoral vote and, hence, the election.

The aspect of FairVote's plan that is so unique is that, as I said earlier, the Electoral College will not be abolished; therefore the proposal does not require a constitutional amendment. If FairVote can get enough states to pass the policy, then it will guarantee that a popular vote winner will not lose the electoral vote. In a sense, the Electoral College is abolished while still remaining on the books.

Not surprisingly, supporters of the Electoral College have criticized FairVote's proposal, but the organization has had some success pushing their plan. At the time of this writing, six states (Hawaii, Illinois, Maryland, Massachusetts, New Jersey, and Washington) and the District of Columbia have already signed the proposal into law. In four other states (California, Colorado, Rhode Island, and Vermont), the proposal has passed both bodies in the state legislature; in nine others the bill has passed one legislative body. The chances of

FairVote's plan passing, however, are remote. As I noted, there are several states that benefit too much under the Electoral College to enact this plan; legislators will likely see it as what it is—a backdoor way to abolish the Electoral College. Also, even in the states where the plan has passed, it will only go into effect if enough other states comprising 270 electoral votes approve the legislation; again, this is unlikely to happen. Moreover, the constitutionality of the plan is debated.[54] Finally, it is not clear that just because a state has adopted the legislation, it could be forced to follow through on its commitment. I have a hard time believing that had FairVote's plan been in place during the 2008 presidential election and had Barack Obama lost the popular vote, Illinois would have stood by its commitment and seated electors for John McCain. Moreover, it is not clear to me, even as an opponent of the Electoral College, why a state would want to go against the wishes of a plurality of its voters.

Since the Electoral College will not be abolished, there are two amendments that must be made to it. First, the Constitution gives electors the freedom to vote as they see fit; they do not have to pledge to vote for the popular vote winner in a state. These so-called "faithless electors" have voted against the wishes of a state (or the District of Columbia) only a handful of times in the course of the country's history and have never influenced the outcome of an election. The last time an elector did not follow the wishes of the popular vote was in 2004 when an elector from Minnesota voted for John Edwards for both president and vice-president.[55] In 2000, an elector from the District of Columbia submitted a blank ballot instead of voting for Al Gore to protest the area's lack of representation in Congress. Even though faithless electors have never turned an election, there is no reason to give one person such power. Moreover, if an election ever was decided by a faithless elector's vote, the legitimacy of the election would be completely undermined.

Not everyone is convinced that faithless electors are problematic. "[O]ur political system has always had a place of honor for the maverick—the freethinking human who refuses to succumb to the party line or popular pressure," write Paul Schumaker and Burdett Loomis. "For example, the decision of Vermont Senator James Jeffords to change his party affiliation from Republican to Independent in May 2001, and thus change control of the Senate from Republican to Democratic, resembles the action of a rogue elector. For many of us, politics is a human endeavor and humans should exercise individual judgment."[56] However, the Jeffords example is a weak analogy. Residents of Vermont could vote Jeffords out of office when he came up for reelection if they were upset with his decision (Jeffords retired before voters had the chance), but there is no opportunity for voters to punish a faithless elector. Furthermore, the voters of Vermont likely recognized Jeffords' maverick tendencies when they elected (and reelected) him; no one knows enough about the electors—indeed the overwhelming majority of people have no idea who they even are—to know if the elector might exercise her own judgment. Lastly, one person should not have the ability to determine the outcome of an election for an entire country, especially considering that electors are not necessarily the "cream of the crop" as the founders had envisioned, but the most loyally partisan and biggest donors instead. Simply because a person gives a substantial amount of money to a political party should not give him the right to vote however he wants as an elector. Because of concern over faithless electors, 29 states plus the District of Columbia "force" an elector to vote for the state's popular vote winner.[57] However, these faithless elector laws are not likely to hold up in court if challenged and, indeed, seem difficult to enforce given the faithless elector in the District of Columbia in 2000. Admittedly, the chances of a faithless elector determining the outcome of an election are extremely miniscule, but there is no reason to allow the possibility, however remote it may be.

The second reform that is needed if the Electoral College is to remain in place is that each state in the House of Representatives should not be given one vote to determine the winner of a presidential election if no candidate receives a majority of the electoral vote. Prominent constitutional scholar Sanford Levinson refers to this provision as "the most dubious feature of the Constitution."[58] Again, it is rare that no candidate receives a majority of the electoral vote; in fact, it has only occurred twice and not since 1824. Still, it has come close in some recent elections (1948, 1960, 2000)[59] and if the proportional allocation of delegates mentioned previously is enacted in some states, it would be more commonplace. It simply makes no sense to give Wyoming as much of a say as California, or Rhode Island as much of a voice as Texas. The seven states that have one representative can provide 27 percent of the votes needed to be president. Moreover, this contingency violates the principle of separation of powers by giving the House the power to determine the president. And, since the Senate gets to choose the vice-president if no candidate receives a majority of the electoral vote, there is a possibility that the president could be a member of one party and the vice-president a member of the other; certainly not the best condition for governing.[60]

The easiest way to get around this problem would simply be to eliminate the requirement that a candidate receive a majority of the electoral vote. This might undermine a president elect's mandate, but no more so than if the candidate did not win the popular vote, but is elected president. If one insists on giving the House the final say, then each member should receive a vote instead of each delegation. However, the chances of eliminating the House contingency provision are admittedly small. A small number of states can thwart a constitutional amendment, and I cannot see a reason why Wyoming, the Dakotas, Delaware, Rhode Island, and other less populated states would want to give up the power they would have should an election be decided in the House.

In sum, however frustrating the Electoral College may be to it detractors, it seems extremely unlikely that substantial reform will be made to it anytime soon.

Chapter 10

Campaign Finance

Have you ever thought about running for office? If so, you either better be independently wealthy or able to raise a heck of a lot of money. It does not matter how much leadership ability or integrity you have or how intelligent, qualified, experienced, charismatic, or good-looking you are, if your campaign does not have money then you simply cannot win. Mark Hanna, the famous political consultant, once quipped, "There are two things that are important in politics. The first is money and I can't remember what the second one is."[1] While Hanna was speaking about politics during the early twentieth century, his words ring true even more so today. Without money, campaigns cannot buy airtime (either radio or television), send direct mail, hire consultants, or conduct polls. Voter mobilization efforts become more difficult. Without money, it even becomes hard to raise money.

Because of the importance of money to campaigns, not surprisingly we see a lot of it spent at all levels of government by candidates, political parties, and other political organizations. The amount of money entering the system has alarmed campaign reformers who feel that money buys elections for candidates and buys influence for organizations such as labor or corporations. As a result, they have pushed to the limit the amount of money that can be spent by campaigns, the amount of money that can be donated to campaigns, and the amount of advertising that is done by political groups. Others claim that these measures are not enough. Instead, they believe that elections should be publicly funded. Without candidates having to raise money, the argument goes, the chance for corruption declines significantly and elections become fairer because the incumbent fundraising advantage is eliminated.

Throughout this book I have often sided with the views of reformers. I supported same-day voter registration, the elimination of judicial elections and the Electoral College, and a nonpartisan redistricting process, to name only a few examples. In this case, however, I do not side with the "traditional reformers." In this chapter I put forth a reform to campaign finance law as well, but not for the reforms that are normally proposed. Instead of adding more restrictions to campaign finance, I think we should consider eliminating all restrictions with the exception of disclosure. Money is needed to win elections, but it does not guarantee victory. Moreover, eliminating campaign finance restrictions might actually *help* challengers by making elections *fairer* and will significantly shorten campaign seasons that are already way too long.

I must admit that of all the arguments in this book, I am least sure that I am correct regarding this one. Campaign finance is a complex, difficult issue. And with any reform, we often cannot be sure exactly what the consequences of the reform will be. Still, the current system of campaign finance does not work and alternatives are needed. I am not convinced that the proposals put forth by the campaign finance reform community are viable or will have the intended effects. Therefore, we need to seriously consider eliminating contributions limits. However, before making my case and discussing the flaws of the traditional campaign finance reforms, a brief history is needed in order to help us understand how we got the system we have in place today.

A Brief History of Campaign Finance Reform

Although campaign finance laws have been on the books for some time, serious attempts to control the role of money in elections are barely 30 years old.[2] Before the 1970s, there was virtually no regulation of money in federal elections.[3] Individuals could donate as much money as they wanted to a candidate's campaign and loopholes allowed candidates to ignore the requirement to disclose from where their campaign contributions came. In 1971, Congress took the first steps to "put teeth" into campaign finance laws and alleviate the role of money in federal elections by passing the Federal Election Campaign Act (FECA) and the Revenue Act. Among other things, the FECA limited candidate spending on media advertisements and permitted the creation of political action committees (PACs), who could solicit individual donations that could then be contributed to federal campaigns. The Revenue Act established the public financing system for presidential elections that will be discussed in greater detail shortly.

After the Watergate scandal, Congress decided that it had to go further to combat the real—or perceived—corruption that was caused by money in federal elections, and, in 1974, amended FECA. The amendments were designed to keep wealthy donors from unduly influencing an election by donating millions of dollars to a candidate. There was widespread concern that presidential and congressional candidates were for sale. The feeling was that a significant individual donation to a candidate might be enough to buy a politician's vote or influence the issue agenda.

As a result, the FECA amendments limited individual contributions to all federal candidates and political parties. Individuals could donate no more than $1,000 to a candidate during each primary and general election, and could contribute no more than $25,000 per calendar year to candidates, political parties, and PACs.[4] However, the FECA amendments did not stop with simply restricting individual donations. They enacted mandatory spending limits for congressional campaigns and restricted the amount of money that candidates for federal office could donate to their own campaigns. In addition, the amendments limited the amount of money that individuals could spend, independently of a candidate or party, to try to influence the outcome of an election. The 1974 amendments also created the Federal Election Commission (FEC) to administer and enforce FECA and its amendments and required the disclosure of campaign donations of more than $250.

Not surprisingly, the amendments were controversial as many citizens viewed them as an assault on free speech. In their eyes, money was a form of speech. Campaign donations were considered an expression of support for a candidate. Moreover, the limits on individual spending were also viewed as restricting a person's freedom. Almost immediately after the amendments were signed into law, they were challenged in court, ironically by one of the most conservative members of Congress—Senator James L. Buckley of New York—and previously one of the most liberal members of Congress—former Minnesota senator Eugene McCarthy. The lawsuit resulted in what remains today as the most influential court decision regarding campaign finance law: *Buckley v. Valeo*.[5] In *Buckley*, the Supreme Court upheld some of the FECA amendments, but declared others to be unconstitutional.

At stake in *Buckley* was a battle between protecting free speech and eliminating corruption, or at least the appearance of it. The ruling frustrated both reformers and those challenging the law. The Court distinguished between limiting direct political contributions to candidates and limiting political expenditures by candidates and individuals. According to the Court, capping individual contributions to a candidate was constitutional because it could stem corruption, or simply the appearance of corruption, in the electoral process.[6] With regard to freedom of expression, the Court argued that it was the act of contributing itself, not the amount that was contributed, which was the important expression of free speech. Therefore, as long as individuals could donate money to candidates, the amount of their contributions could be restricted to a level reasonably calculated to avoid vote buying in Congress. Furthermore, individual contributions could be limited because there were still other outlets for people to express their views, such as independent advocacy on behalf of ideas or candidates.

The Court took the opposite stance regarding the spending limits for congressional campaigns as well as the restrictions placed on independent spending by individuals or associations and a candidate's ability to donate money to her campaign. Here, the Court reasoned that the goal of curtailing corruption did not logically justify limits on expenditures. It ruled that campaign-spending limits were unconstitutional because such restrictions directly limited the ability of a candidate to speak and diminished the marketplace of ideas. For candidates to get their views heard, they need money to promote those views. If a campaign is restricted in terms of how much it can spend, then the voters lose out because their ability to learn about a candidate is hampered. Likewise, individuals who did not coordinate their spending with a candidate—called an "independent expenditure"—were free to spend unlimited personal funds to express their own views on policy and candidates. The absence of coordination removed the opportunity for quid pro quo between the spender and a candidate, the Court held, and the Court struck limits on candidates' use of personal funds because candidates cannot "corrupt" themselves. According to the Court:

> A restriction on the amount of money a person or group can spend on political communication during a campaign necessarily reduces the quantity of expression by restricting the number of issues discussed, the depth of their exploration, and the size of the audience reached. This is because virtually every means of communicating in today's mass society requires the expenditure of money.[7]

Finally, *Buckley* created the controversial distinction between express advocacy and issue advocacy ads that, as we will see, have become an important part of the current debate regarding campaign finance reform. For an ad to be considered "express advocacy," it must contain so-called "magic words," such as "vote for," "elect," "Jones for Congress," "vote against," "defeat," and the like. In other words, the ad must explicitly attempt to persuade a person to vote a certain way. Issue advocacy ads may mention a candidate, but do not contain any specific call for the election or defeat of that person. In theory, they discuss public policy and may mention a public official who is involved in making the policy. Over time, issue advocacy developed into subtle election-related messages, such as an ad about environmental policy that ends with a phrase along the lines of "Call Congressman Jones' office and tell him that you find his environmental record to be deplorable." The intent of the ad is clear, but no magic words are actually used. According to the Court in *Buckley*, only express advocacy ads fell under the jurisdiction of the FEC; therefore, only express advocacy ads could be regulated.

In 1979, Congress once again amended the FECA by including a provision that would eventually lead to significant amounts of unregulated money entering campaigns. As an attempt to strengthen state and local party organizations that were thought to be on the wane, Congress passed a statute allowing parties to accept and spend what came to be known as "soft money." Soft money is individual, corporate, or union gifts that parties could use for grass-roots party building activities such as voter registration or get-out-the-vote drives, but not to support specific candidates or campaigns. Most importantly, soft money was unregulated and unlimited. So, while a person was limited by the amount of hard money—regulated money donated directly to parties or candidates—she could donate, she could now give potentially millions of dollars in soft money to the political parties.

While unintentional, soft money opened a huge loophole in campaign finance rules. Individuals limited to a $1,000 contribution to candidates could now funnel considerably more money through the political parties under the guise of soft money. Parties would then turn around and spend this money on issue advocacy ads and argued that such ads constituted party building activity because they promoted the party. The amount of soft money raised by the parties went through the roof. In the 1991–1992 election cycle, soft money accounted for roughly 16 percent of the funds raised by both parties. By the 2001–2002 cycle, soft money comprised 53 percent and 36 percent of the money raised by the Democratic and Republican parties, respectively; in all, the two major parties raised slightly less than $500 million in soft money donations.[8]

The infusion of soft money into the system along with increased independent spending by interest groups again brought campaign finance reform to the forefront in the late 1990s. In order to close some of the loopholes, senators John McCain (R-AZ) and Russell Feingold (D-WI) introduced a bill that would eliminate soft money from the parties and severely restrict issue ads and electioneering by independent groups. While the bill passed the Senate, a similar version languished in the House. Then, with the scandals surrounding corporations like Enron and Worldcom who donated millions of dollars to candidates from both parties, the public, who had supported campaign finance reform but never put it high on its list of most important issues, clamored for the passage of the so-called McCain–Feingold bill (or Shays–Meehan as the House version was known after sponsors Republican Christopher Shays and Democrat Marty Meehan). Using a little-known technique called a discharge petition, House Democrats were able to dislodge the bill from committee and bring it to a vote on the floor. Ultimately, the bill, titled the Bipartisan Campaign Reform Act (BCRA), passed and was signed into law by a reluctant President Bush in 2002.

While there were several provisions in BCRA, the most commonly discussed aspects dealt with soft money, nonparty electioneering and issue ads, and individual donation limits. Most notably, BCRA eliminated national party soft money, limited the use of issue advocacy ads within 60 days before a general election or 30 days before a primary except where the ad is funded by federally-regulated hard money, and raised individual donation limits to $2,000 per election (primary, general, and runoff) to be adjusted for inflation.[9] In addition, the donation limits to political parties as well as combined donation caps to parties and candidates increased.[10] Proponents argued that the law would shift more political money from unregulated issue ads and soft money to hard, regulated dollars fully disclosed to the public.

As with the 1974 FECA amendments, BCRA was immediately challenged in court again on First Amendment grounds. In *McConnell v. Federal Election Commission*, a divided 5–4 Supreme Court upheld all of the major provisions of BCRA.[11] Again, the majority judges were concerned about corruption, or the appearance of corruption, because of soft money donations to the candidates' political parties that would be spent in support of those candidates.

Regarding the ban on issue advocacy ads—referred to in BCRA as "election-eering communications"—the Court held that the ads were "'functionally equivalent' to express advocacy advertising and helped undermine public confidence in the electoral process."[12] Not surprisingly, the minority argued that there is no hard evidence of corruption and cited First Amendment protections in their dissent. Justice Scalia was most enraged:

> This is a sad day for the freedom of speech. Who could have imagined that the same court, which within the past four years, has sternly disapproved of restrictions on such inconsequential forms of expression as virtual child pornography, tobacco advertising, dissemination of illegally intercepted communication, and sexually explicit cable programming would smile with favor upon a law that cuts to the heart of what the First Amendment is meant to protect: the right to criticize government. For that is what the most offensive provisions of this legislation are all about. We are governed by Congress, and the legislation prohibits the criticism of members of Congress by those entities most capable of giving such criticism loud voice.[13]

Although BCRA and the *McConnell* verdict were major victories for reformers, only three election cycles after its passage seem to offer enough evidence that the law has failed. Even the justices in the majority in the *McConnell* decision did not believe that the law would fundamentally change the role of money in elections. "Money, like water, will always find an outlet," wrote Justices Stevens and O'Connor. "What problems will arise, and how Congress will respond are concerns for another day."[14]

Indeed, immediately after the passage of BCRA, new loopholes were evident. If you followed the 2004 presidential election, then you are probably familiar with a group called Swift Boat Veterans for Truth. This group questioned whether John Kerry deserved the medals of honor he received for his service in Vietnam. Swift Boat Veterans for Truth is a political group called a "527," which comes from the provision in the U.S. tax code that affords a tax-exemption for political organizations. Some political organizations register with the Internal Revenue Service under section 527, but structure their political activities in a way that avoids regulation by FECA and the Federal Election Commission. This allows the groups to raise and spend unlimited money on issue ads in support of campaigns as long as they do not expressly advocate the election or defeat of a candidate, coordinate with a candidate's campaign, or accept corporate or labor contributions.[15] Swift Boat Veterans for Truth was not the only 527 to emerge and spend millions of dollars in the presidential campaign. On the left, Americans Coming Together and MoveOn.org Voter Fund and, on the right, Progress for America, spent millions on advertising and voter mobilization efforts in the presidential election. Altogether, federal 527s spent $405 million on the 2004 presidential election.[16] In addition, more than a quarter of the funds raised by the 527s came from only 15 individuals who combined gave over $125 million.[17] Although 527s were less visible during the 2008 presidential election, they certainly were not absent. According to one source, 527s combined to spend roughly $200 million in 2008.[18]

The 527 organizations are not the only groups to exert more power in federal elections. While 527s have to disclose their donors, other tax-exempt organizations called "501(c)," again named after a provision in the tax code, do not. The 501(c) groups were estimated to spend between $70 and $100 million in connection with the 2004 election.[19] This amount grew to almost $200 million in 2008.[20] Like water, political speech found other outlets indeed.

Additionally, the constitutional future of BCRA is in doubt. In the summer of 2007, a more conservative Supreme Court, with the addition of Chief Justice John Roberts and Justice Samuel Alito, significantly curtailed restrictions on the use of issue advocacy ads that it had upheld in *McConnell*.[21] Although *McConnell* had upheld BCRA's ban on electioneering communications funded with unregulated corporate and labor contributions within 60 days of an election, in *Federal Election Commission v. Wisconsin Right to Life Inc.*, a 5–4 block of the Court narrowed what constitutes an electioneering communication. The Court held that Wisconsin Right to Life could run corporate-funded ads telling Wisconsin voters to contact Senator Russ Feingold to urge him to end a filibuster against the president's judicial nominees.

Since *McConnell*, other campaign finance cases have either been decided or loom on the horizon, which have or could undermine BCRA. In *Davis v. FEC*, the Supreme Court struck down the so-called "Millionaire's Amendment" to BCRA.[22] The purpose of the amendment was to help people who had to run against wealthy candidates who self-financed their campaigns. Under this amendment, individual contribution and party coordinated expenditure limits were raised when a candidate faced an opponent who, in the House, spent more than $350,000 of his own money on his campaign or, in the Senate, contributed $150,000 plus an amount equal to four cents times the state's eligible voting population. It is the *Davis* ruling that leads some to believe that the rescue funds provision of public financed campaigns, which I discuss momentarily, is unconstitutional.

While upsetting to those who want stricter regulations regarding campaign finance, the *Davis* case paled in comparison to the outrage that existed after another Supreme Court ruling on campaign finance, this one in *Citizens United v. FEC*.[23] In the case, on First Amendment grounds, the Court ruled that corporations and unions could not be prohibited from using treasury funds to broadcast "electioneering communications." As a result of *Citizens United*, many reformers predicted drastic consequences for democracy. "In effect, the Court was evoking a core civil right to advance corporate power," write Radhika Balakrishnan and James Heintz. "This is a dangerous precedent, one that will undermine the obligation of the government to respect and protect human rights by giving corporations full reign to advance their own interests in the democratic – yet increasingly plutocratic – United States."[24]

It is not clear that the Court is finished eliminating provisions within BCRA. The next threat is likely to be the ban on soft money. Until this point anyway, the Supreme Court has upheld the ban on soft money. However, not everyone is convinced that the prohibition will stand. After the Court affirmed a lower court ruling in June of 2010 upholding the ban on soft money, Rick Hasen, a vocal proponent of strict campaign finance laws, said, "This is only temporary good news for those who think the soft-money ban is an important anticorruption component of federal campaign finance law."[25] Hasen believes that a different case with a different set of circumstances may convince the Court to overturn the soft money ban.

The Concerns of Campaign Finance Reformers

The Court's recent rulings on campaign finances case, especially *Citizens United*, has obviously alarmed campaign finance reformers who have several concerns regarding the role of money in elections.

The Amount of Money in the System

Most simply, reformers believe that too much money is entering the political arena. In 2008, Barack Obama and John McCain combined to spend $1.1 billion in the primary and general election campaigns; this figure does not include the substantial amount of money spent by candidates like Hillary Clinton and Mitt Romney during the nominating phase.[26] In the same year, candidate spending in congressional races totaled $1.23 billion.[27] The average member of the U.S. Senate spent $7.8 million on his or her campaign. According to political scientist Marjorie Randon Hershey, "If you had to raise that much money, you would need to collect about $25,000—what some people pay for a year in college—*every week* of your six-year term. If you went a week without asking for money, then you'd need to raise $50,000 the following week."[28]

Because such large amounts of money are needed to run for office, reformers worry that candidates must spend too much of their time raising money and not enough time solving problems and passing policy. According to one well-known study of congressional candidate Brian Baird's campaign in 1998, Baird spent 35 percent of his time between July and October fundraising, more than double the amount of time he spent on any other activity.[29] In addition to the amount of time candidates must spend fundraising, reformers worry that the candidate pool is weakened because quality potential candidates who either do not want to engage in the unpleasant activity of fundraising or cannot foot the bill themselves decide not to run. In other words, the amount of fundraising required means that Americans are getting to choose among the best fundraisers (or people who are independently wealthy), not the people with the best ideas for the country.

An Increasing Incumbency Advantage

The amount of money entering the political system raises an additional problem because challenger and incumbent spending is not even. For example, in 2010 the average senator raised $10.7 million compared to only $850,000 for the average challenger; in the House those figures were $1.4 million and $231,690, respectively.[30] It is extremely difficult, then, for most challengers to compete with already established incumbents who have superior name recognition. In Chapter 7, I discussed the view that redistricting is to blame for the lack of competitive elections in the House. Political scientist Alan Abramowitz disagrees. According to Abramowitz, it is the discrepancy in spending between incumbents and challengers that shoulders the majority of the blame. He believes the best way to increase competition in the House is not to change the redistricting process, but to provide challengers with substantially more money to spend on their campaigns.[31]

Money Buys Elections

The prevalent view among many citizens is that, if you have enough money, you can buy yourself a seat in the city council, the state legislature, Congress, or wherever. I remember getting a phone call from my dad immediately after the 2000 election. He was incensed about the outcome of an election, but not the one that I would have thought. Unlike many Americans who were displeased with the fact that a presidential popular vote winner lost the election, my dad was miffed by the outcome of the U.S. Senate election in New Jersey. In that election, Democrat Jon Corzine spent more than $60 million of his own money on his campaign. In the Democratic primary, he refused to debate the former governor of the state, Jim Florio, and instead plastered commercials all over the airwaves. In the general election, he outspent his Republican opponent, Bob Franks, by roughly 10 to 1 and only defeated Franks by 3 percentage points in a heavily Democratic state. In my dad's eyes, Corzine's wealth bought the election. Again, the worry is that the better fundraiser or the person who can spend the most on his campaign wins, not the best candidate.

Concern Over Corruption

The American public does not view politicians too positively. In fact, in one comparison of the honesty and ethical standards of people in various fields, members of Congress ranked only slightly above car salesmen and below lawyers and business executives.[32] The belief is that politicians' votes are for sale. A special interest group gives money to candidates who need that money in exchange for the candidates' support of one of the interest group's bills. Conversely, if an interest group does not want a bill to pass, then their contributions will keep that bill from passing. Even some politicians subscribe to this view. Former Arkansas Senator Dale Bumpers was once quoted as saying, "Every Senator knows I speak the truth when I say bill after bill after bill has been defeated in this body because of campaign money."[33] Indeed, in their rulings on constitutionality of campaign finance laws, the courts have regularly relied on the "combating corruption or the appearance of corruption" argument when upholding aspects of the laws.

Lack of Political Equality

A final concern of campaign finance reformers is that the current campaign finance system leads to inequalities between those with money to give and those who cannot. According to campaign finance reformers, the current system violates the principle of "one person, one vote" by giving some people more of a voice in the policymaking process than others. Campaign finance scholar Victoria Farrar-Myers sums up this view nicely:

> The electoral process is an important representational mechanism by which public officials are chosen and some sense of the public will is expressed. Underlying the views of regulation advocates are assumptions that each person in the nation has an equal interest in the public will and that the public will is an aggregation of those interests. The elected representative's job is to serve the interests of each of his or her electoral constituents equally. Regulation advocates' conception of representation, therefore, is, or may be, corrupted by individuals and groups that spend great amounts of money. Certainly, providing a quid pro quo in exchange for a campaign contribution distorts this representational process. But perhaps more significant is that the flow of money results in elected officials putting more emphasis, or at least appearing to put more emphasis, on the interests, wishes, and concerns of large contributions over other voters—that is, not all interests are served equally. Thus, the notion of equality so crucial for representation in the American political system is lacking without constraints on money in elections.[34]

The Favorite Solution: Publicly Financed Elections

Because of the above apprehensions, campaign finance reformers continue to push new ideas to lessen the influence of money. The most prominent solution floated by reformers today is to publicly finance all federal elections.[35] This system is currently in place, at least partially, at the presidential level, and several states, such as Arizona, Maine, and Connecticut, have implemented so-called "Clean Election Laws" that provide public financing for state legislative elections. In Chapter 3, I noted that public financing of judicial elections has been enacted in North Carolina, New Mexico, and Wisconsin. Occasionally, bills have been introduced in Congress that would approve public financing for all federal elections, but none have been signed into law. According to proponents of public funding, such a system would eliminate—or, at the very least, alleviate—many of the problems mentioned previously.

How does public financing of elections work? There are numerous models and it is important to distinguish between the public financing of presidential elections and proposals for congressional elections. In the case of presidential elections, different systems are in place for the primaries and the general election. In the primaries, major party presidential candidates can qualify for matching funds.[36] To do so, beginning in January of the year before the presidential election, they must raise at least $5,000 in 20 states in contributions of $250 or less. If a candidate qualifies, then the first $250 of each contribution the candidate receives will be matched by the federal government. In other words, if a candidate qualifies for matching funds and I give that person a $100 contribution, the federal government will also donate $100 to the campaign. However, there is a big catch if candidates accept matching funds. If they do so, then they are limited in the amount of their own money they can spend on campaigns. Perhaps more importantly, they are limited regarding how much money in total they can spend during the nomination process, and spending in each state is capped as well. In 2008, the limit was roughly $50 million, with an additional amount that could be used for fundraising expenses. Additionally, candidates who accepted matching funds were limited to spending, for example, roughly $1.5 million in Iowa, $2.2 million in South Carolina, and $1.2 million in Nevada. To continue receiving matching funds, a candidate must win at least 10 percent of the vote in two consecutive primaries.[37] The general election is more straightforward. If they choose to accept public funds, the Democratic and Republican candidates each receives the same amount (in 2008, roughly $84 million), and they cannot raise private contributions.[38]

Because no system is in place for congressional elections, it is impossible to know what the rules would be. However, the Fair Elections Now Act bill introduced in the 111th Congress provides one model. In a nutshell, under the bill candidates would qualify for public funding by raising a large number of small donations in amounts less than $100. In return, candidates for the House would receive $900,000 to be divided 40 percent for the primary and 60 percent for the general election. Qualified candidates in the Senate would receive $1.25 million plus another $250,000 per congressional district in their state, again with the funding split 40 percent for the primary and 60 percent for the general election.[39]

On paper, the idea of public financing is intriguing. Candidates would no longer have to spend massive amounts of time fundraising, the campaign season might be shorter, the influence of special interest groups might be less, and the significant fundraising advantage held by incumbents likely would be eliminated. However, not everyone is enamored with public financing and some argue that it might actually make elections even *less* competitive than they already are. First, I will discuss the problems with the current presidential election funding system, then I will mention some concerns scholars and practitioners have regarding a possible congressional public funding system.

Simply put, the public financing system for presidential campaigns is broken and any fix will require an enormous increase in money from an already strapped election fund. In *Buckley*, the Court made it clear that mandatory spending limits, both at the presidential and congressional levels, were unconstitutional. As a result, it is entirely voluntary for presidential candidates to opt to obtain matching funds in the primary or public financing in the general election. For several election cycles, virtually every serious presidential candidate accepted the matching funds and *every* Republican and Democratic presidential candidate took the federal money in the general election. Today, this is no longer the case. In fact, *accepting* either the matching or general election funds is a sign of a weak candidate.

The problem began in 1996 when Republican Steve Forbes, the editor-in-chief of *Forbes* magazine, chose to forego matching funds because of his enormous personal wealth. In 1996, Forbes spent roughly $38 million of his money on his campaign (in 2000, he spent more than $48 million). In each case, it did not make sense for him to accept the matching funds because the amount of money Forbes donated to his campaign was greater than the spending limit imposed by the matching fund.

Because of his personal wealth, Forbes might have been seen as an outlier. Candidates who did not have the money of Forbes still relied on the matching funds. That changed in 2000. After Bob Dole's loss to Bill Clinton in 1996, prominent Republicans immediately began to coalesce around George W. Bush, the governor of Texas at the time, to be their party's nominee in 2000. The Bush fundraising machine was unlike anything anyone had seen before and easily surpassed the spending limit that would have been placed on him in the primaries had he accepted matching funds. From there, it has only gotten worse. In 2004, Bush and Democrats John Kerry and Howard Dean all opted out of matching funds because they could raise more on their own. In 2008, Barack Obama and Hillary Clinton on the Democratic side and John McCain, Mitt Romney, and Rudy Giuliani on the Republican side all refused matching funds.[40] In particular, Obama and Clinton each raised well over $200 million.

Although several candidates had declined to receive matching funds before 2008, no one had refused the lump sum stipend in the general election. That changed in 2008 when Barack Obama, realizing that he could raise far more than the $84.1 million provided to his campaign through public financing, chose to forgo public money. Obama's move was certainly a smart one. In September alone, the Obama campaign raised $150 million, nearly twice the amount he would have received under public financing.[41]

It is clear that the only way the public financing system for presidential campaigns will be able to survive is if the amount of money provided to candidates increases substantially. Serious candidates can raise far more money on their own than they will obtain if they accept matching funds in the primaries or public financing in the general election. Unless a considerable alteration is made regarding how presidential campaigns are financed, it is not realistic to think that the kind of change needed to make public financing attractive to presidential candidates is possible. The current system is financed by citizens who check a box on their tax returns to make a $3 donation to an election fund. The system is already woefully underfinanced, as only approximately 10 percent of the public checks the box. In the 2004 election, a *total* of about $400 million was available in the election fund for both the primaries and the general election. That amount was easily outraised by the Obama campaign alone in 2008.

The public financing of congressional elections will suffer from the same problem as the presidential system; unless the government supplies money, the system will be woefully underfunded. However, even if funding is provided, it is not clear that public funding of congressional elections would improve democracy. The traditional argument in favor of publicly funded congressional elections is that it would help level the playing field between incumbents and challengers. Incumbents have several advantages over challengers, one of which is that they are able to raise money more easily. Incumbents already have a campaign staff in place and a list of previous donors that are not available to most challengers. Moreover, since incumbents are likely to win, donors may be more apt to give money to their campaigns. Public financing alleviates these problems.[42]

Public financing could make congressional elections more competitive, although the evidence for this at the state legislative level is decidedly mixed,[43] and it is possible that it would have the opposite effect.[44] Most incumbents enter an election with a huge advantage over their opponents; they have greater name recognition. The only way for challengers to increase their name recognition is to spend money. If a public financing system is in place that too severely constrains spending, then challengers will not be able to compete with incumbents. In fact, Abramowitz argues that a public financing system with low spending ceilings would likely decrease competition for House seats.[45]

In order for public financing of congressional elections to improve competition, they would have to be funded at a level that seems unrealistic. First, such a system would have to benefit incumbents enough for them to decide to opt into the system. Because of the Court's ruling in *Buckley*, candidates cannot be forced to accept public funding. It would make no sense for incumbents who can raise a few million dollars to opt into a system that gives them less. Some states include so-called "rescue funds," which provide additional money to candidates whose opponents decline the public money. However, as I note in chapter 3, rescue funds have been under attack in the courts and the Supreme Court is likely to hear a case regarding the constitutionality of the funds. If the Court determines that rescue funds are unconstitutional, something many consider to be a strong possibility given its ruling in *Davis v. FEC*, then the future of public financed elections would be seriously threatened. Second, it is difficult to see what incentive incumbents, who would have to pass such a law, would have for setting a high level of funding. Why would the majority support something that could ultimately end up costing them their jobs? Third, while the public generally supports the concept of public funding, it would likely bristle at the costs of an effective system, especially if that system forced cuts in spending to other popular programs. Fourth, while public financing is attractive because it essentially eliminates the need for candidates to fundraise, which might encourage qualified people who are turned off by the prospect of having to raise money to run, studies at the state level find that public financing did not increase the number of challengers.[46] Finally, it does not eliminate or even significantly curtail independent spending. If anything, independent spending is only likely to increase as recent presidential elections illustrate. One might argue that public financing lessens the concern about corruption because interest groups will not be able to contribute directly to candidates. If politicians are influenced by campaign contributions, then it is tough to believe that independent spending, even though an indirect influence, does not affect politicians. Likewise, it is tough to believe that a $5,000 contribution, which is the current donation cap political actions committees can give to candidates, would be enough money to influence a member of Congress in the first place.

A Controversial Solution

The problem with most of the campaign finance reforms that scholars and practitioners have proposed is that they either do little to improve many of the serious problems with campaign finance—and, in some cases, may make the problems worse—or are based on faulty assumptions. BCRA's lack of success illustrates the futility of the current paradigm of campaign finance reform; tweaking here or there will not change much.

It seems to me that perhaps we are attacking the problem from the wrong end. Instead of placing further restrictions on campaign donations to candidates, parties, and other political organizations, we should consider eliminating contribution restrictions entirely. Under my proposed law, individuals or organizations who wish to donate money to candidates, political parties, or political action committees must disclose any contributions of, say, greater than $250—that's it.[47] Further, I would eliminate the distinction between express advocacy and issue advocacy. The sponsor of any commercial that clearly identifies a candidate for office should be required to disclose the source(s) of the funding for the ad, but the commercial can be broadcast at any time whether it is 60 days before the election or on election day. While most campaign reformers will cringe (or worse) when reading this paragraph, I am not alone in suggesting that contribution restrictions should be eliminated.[48]

Before getting into the advantages of lifting the contribution restrictions, let me first justify why the disclosure requirement is so important. First, it makes the process transparent, something that is essential in a well-functioning democracy. As I will argue momentarily, concerns about vote buying are overstated, but disclosure makes this problem even less of a concern. Second, disclosure provides voters with valuable information when evaluating campaign ads or deciding how to vote. The first thing I tell my students when teaching them critical thinking skills is to consider the source of the argument. Knowing the source (or who is funding the source) goes a long way in helping a person evaluate the credibility of the claim. Additionally, being aware of who donates to what candidates is an important cue when voting. If I am antiunion but I know that unions have contributed heavily to a congressional candidate's campaign, then I can be reasonably sure that I would not support that candidate.

Not everyone agrees with the view that disclosure should be required. After all, the *Federalist Papers*—the most important set of essays in American history— were written under a pseudonym. A disclosure requirement may limit speech by keeping people who would have otherwise spoken (or donated money) anonymously from doing so because of a perceived violation of privacy or fear of some sort of retaliation. For instance, a corporation may think twice about giving money to a candidate who is opposed to same-sex marriage for fear of public backlash. Indeed, Target Corporation, which is generally thought of as having gay-friendly policies, faced exactly this situation when it donated money for a campaign commercial supporting a 2010 Minnesota gubernatorial candidate who opposed same-sex marriage. In my mind, these possibilities do not trump the advantages of requiring disclosure. Given the importance of a transparent electoral process, I would argue that government has a compelling interest to require disclosure. Moreover, the decision is not between transparency and speech—people can still say whatever they want—but between transparency and *anonymous* speech. Limiting freedom of expression to promote transparency is a tough call; limiting anonymous freedom of expression to promote transparency is not.

Now that I have defended the disclosure requirement, let us turn to how removing campaign contribution limits could potentially make American elections more democratic. Recall that in Chapter 1 I argued that democracy is enhanced by competitive elections and when citizens are not constantly barraged by excessively long campaign seasons. Removing contribution restrictions would possibly make campaigns more competitive and not require candidates to start fundraising for their next campaign immediately after they are sworn into office.

At different points in this book, I have discussed reasons why the overwhelming majority of today's elections for Congress are so uncompetitive; front or center is the inherent fundraising advantage that incumbents have over challengers, which is only exacerbated by contribution restrictions. Why do contribution restrictions benefit incumbents at the expense of challengers? Incumbents have a list of donors already in place, who they can immediately call on for help; few challengers have such a luxury. As I noted when discussing public financing of elections, most challengers have to overcome an enormous hurdle that most incumbents do not: name recognition. The only way to efficiently increase name recognition is by spending money. Challengers face a problem, though, because most have little chance of defeating an incumbent. As a result, it is difficult for them to convince a large number of people to contribute to their campaigns. A vicious cycle occurs. Challengers cannot raise money because they are unlikely to win; they are unlikely to win because they have trouble raising the necessary money. The $2,400 individual contribution limit and the $5,000 PAC contribution limit aggravate this problem because challengers have to convince many people, not just a few, that their candidacy is viable. If the contribution limits were eliminated, challengers would be able to raise more money more quickly. A few donors who believe strongly in a challenger could essentially finance her campaign. Some may argue that a candidate who cannot raise money from a significant number of voters is not electable to begin with, but elections are decided by the number of votes a candidate receives, not the number of donations. Strong candidates who receive significant financial support from a small number of donors will be able to get their message to the people, which will likely translate into a large number of votes.

However, one could raise a logical question. It is certainly possible that a donor to a challenger would give significantly more money if no contribution limit existed, but couldn't the same be said for donors to incumbents? In fact, the probability of incumbents receiving a large donation is greater because they have more donors to begin with. What is interesting, though, is that the incumbency advantage has grown since regulations were enacted. Furthermore, additional spending by incumbents is likely to have only a marginal effect on the election; the law of diminishing returns sets in. Think of it this way. The Coca Cola Company has universal name recognition among consumers. Coke has to advertise to remain in the minds of consumers, but new advertisements for Coke will not increase consumer recognition of the product. On the other hand, FUZE does not have nearly the recognition among consumers that Coke has, so advertisements for FUZE will improve consumer recognition. In other words, FUZE gets more bang for their buck in advertising than Coke does. The same goes for challengers and incumbents. In fact, studies find that increased incumbent spending has virtually no impact on the outcome of an election, evidence that, while candidates must have money to win, having money cannot simply buy an election.[49]

A rallying cry of reformers is that too much money is spent on elections. It is odd that reformers would make such a claim when empirical studies clearly indicate that voters' knowledge about an election increases as spending increases.[50] This argument becomes even stranger when one considers that the reformers are trying to level the playing field between incumbents and challengers. The problem is not that too much money is in the system; the problem is that *too little* money is being spent by most challengers. Recall the discrepancies in incumbent and challenger spending that I noted earlier in the chapter.

"Competitive campaigns are unavoidably expensive," writes congressional scholar Gary Jacobson. "There is simply no way for most non-incumbent candidates to capture the attention of enough voters to make a contest of it without spending substantial sums of money."[51]

However, I do not want to overstate the argument regarding competition. Eliminating campaign donations will not *guarantee* competitive elections, only make them more likely than under the current campaign finance rules. Also, my argument here is more theoretical than empirical. There are some empirical studies of how campaign contributions limits influence competition at the state level, although admittedly the findings have been far from conclusive and the studies have suffered from methodological problems.[52] There is still much more empirical work needed to get a clear picture of the effects of contribution limits on electoral competition.

A second advantage of eliminating restrictions on campaign contributions is that the campaign season would shorten considerably. With the current limits, congressional candidates are forced to fundraise virtually nonstop and presidential candidates have to show fundraising viability years before the first vote is actually cast in a primary or caucus. The ability to raise more money quickly means that incumbents and challengers will not have to begin fundraising so early. As a result, voters will likely become less fatigued with the length of campaigns. Furthermore, the ability of candidates to raise money quickly will lessen the amount of time that candidates must spend on fundraising, allowing them to concern themselves with actually solving problems facing the country.

Even if all of this is true—that no contribution limits will lessen the incumbency advantage, shorten the campaign season, and allow incumbents and challengers to focus on substantive issues—reformers would ask: at what cost? Two arguments in particular drive the efforts of reformers: combating corruption and promoting political equality.

Campaign Finance Reform is Needed to Combat Corruption

Perhaps the strongest argument in favor of contribution limits—simply because it is the argument that the Supreme Court has used to defend the constitutionality of such limits—is that donations to candidates can be capped to prevent corruption or the appearance of corruption. With the number of times I have heard people claim that money buys politicians' votes, it must be true. Only it is not.

Although the institution of Congress is portrayed as a body whose members' votes are for sale, the fact is that cases of corruption, related to campaign finance donations, are few and far between. That is not to say that no politician has never traded votes for dollars, but to assume that all of Congress is corrupt because one or two members have been corrupt is analogous to assuming that because I have caught one or two students plagiarizing their papers, the entire class must have done so. Concern about corruption in

Congress made headlines with the convictions of former Congressmen Randy "Duke" Cunningham, Bob Ney, and William Jefferson. These cases were about personal bribes, however, not corruption because of campaign contributions. More recently, former Illinois Governor Rod Blagojevich is accused of soliciting campaign donations for his support of bills. It is important to note, however, that such quid pro quo deals are still *illegal* even without contributions limits. And interestingly in the Blagojevich case, it was not individuals that were trying to buy off the former governor, but the governor who was allegedly threatening them if they did not contribute to his campaign by withholding support for bills that were important to the individuals.

Moreover, to show that money influences a politician's vote, one would have to find evidence that contributions cause legislators to vote in ways that they otherwise would not have—for example, a congressman who is ideologically opposed to raising the minimum wage but votes in favor of an increase because he received a contribution from the Committee on Political Education (COPE), the AFL-CIO's political action committee. Yet, empirical research finds little evidence that campaign contributions influence the votes of members of Congress.[53] Instead, members' personal preferences as well as those of their constituents or political parties drown out the effects of campaign contributions.[54] The fact that contributions have little influence on a member of Congress should not be surprising, given that most individuals and organizations donate to candidates who have similar ideological beliefs. EMILY's List is simply not going to donate money to prolife candidates with the hopes of persuading them to back abortion rights. Likewise, the NRA's PAC will refuse to give donations to candidates who do not support Second Amendment rights. Some might argue the effects of campaign contributions may not be direct, but indirect instead. In other words, money might not buy votes, but it buys access to the member of Congress where the member could be persuaded to support the organization's position. But, as Bradley A. Smith, the former chairman of the Federal Election Commission, writes, "The fact is, the vast majority of campaign contributors never seek access, and legislators meet regularly with people who have never made contributions. Nor does every contributor who seeks access get it."[55] Smith also points out that while reformers argue that corruption is rampant because of campaign contributions, they are hard-pressed to point out any specific members of Congress who have been corrupted by contributions. Additionally, if the influence of money was so great, then we might expect that public policy would not reflect the wishes of the people, but numerous studies at both the federal and state level find that public preferences are generally translated into policy.[56]

A critic might respond that, "Of course corruption is not a problem in Congress *because the contribution limits in place keep corruption from occurring.*" If contribution restrictions are removed, then corruption will become widespread. The only way to test such a claim is to do an analysis of campaign contributions and corruption at the state level where some states have no restrictions on the amount of money that a person or organization can donate to a candidate. To my knowledge, no one has conducted such a study. Yet, I am unaware of any widespread corruption that exists in state legislative campaigns because of unlimited donations. If that were the case, one would think the media would cover it regularly, especially given the media's tendency to report on such subjects. In other words, corruption certainly does not appear to be any more pronounced or rampant at the state level where in some cases no limitations on contributions exist than it does at the federal level where such limitations do exist.

Finally, some readers might argue that I am inconsistent with my arguments. Recall in Chapter 3 that I made the case against judicial elections, and one of the reasons I provided was because of the conflict of interest that arises with such elections. However, there is a great difference between a judge who is supposed to impartially interpret the law and a politician whose job is to represent the wishes of her constituents. If politicians are receiving money from individuals and organizations with similar ideological views—and, as I said, they are—then it is difficult to argue that a conflict of interest exists.

Campaign Finance Reform is Needed to Promote Political Equality

While the Court has primarily relied on the "corruption or appearance of corruption" justification, some justices have invoked the *Baker v. Carr* decision and its progeny when upholding contribution restrictions. Recall that in *Baker v. Carr* the Supreme Court established the notion of "one person, one vote." As I noted earlier, campaign finance reformers claim that unlimited restrictions violate "one person, one vote," because it allows some people to have a greater voice than others.

It is easy to see why promoting political equality is such an enviable cause. After all, who doesn't want to protect the little guy against the "fat cats" in a battle for political influence (except for the fat cats of course!). Indeed, I have argued throughout this book that the idea of "one person, one vote" is essential in a model democracy. The problem is that "one person, one vote" has nothing to do with campaign finance reform. Again, the criterium is "one person, one *vote*," not "one person, one *dollar*." Equality is protected by the fact that every person's vote counts the same. We are not giving large donors ten votes, small donors five votes, and nondonors one vote. Whether you have contributed money or not, on election day your voice is equal.

Furthermore, campaign finance restrictions do nothing more than create "faux political equality." "The proponents of greater regulation appeal chiefly to equality," writes Dennis Thompson, "just as each citizen has an equal right to vote, so each citizen should have an equal opportunity to support a candidate. . . . To the extent that fund raising is not regulated, economic inequalities are translated into political inequalities. Some citizens . . . thereby gain unfair advantage over others."[57] But this argument is flawed on two accounts. First, the current contribution cap does not guarantee equality. Few people have the resources to donate $2,400 to one candidate, much less multiple candidates (unless I sell a lot of books, I certainly do not). In other words, unless you make the contribution limit low, like $5, inequalities based on money are always going to exist. Second, why is it that we are only concerned about equal opportunity as it relates to money? Some people have more political influence than others regarding a wide range of activities. Not every person can publish a letter to the editor or an op-ed piece. Political pundits get a voice that the average person does not have. Some people are asked to give political speeches, while others are not, and, of the people who get asked, some are more persuasive than others. I could go on and on. In short, it is impossible to create a system where political influence is truly equal.

Additionally, the above quote assumes that contributor money controls the issue agenda in campaigns or in Congress, but it is far from clear that it actually does. In the most influential study on agenda setting, John Kingdon argues that it is the president and the media, far more so than Congress, that sets the issue agenda.[58] Moreover, why would candidates for office want to highlight an unpopular issue with their constituents? Even if an organization raised the profile of an issue through independent spending, it is not clear why a candidate would take an unpopular position on the issue.

Finally, in perhaps the most cited statement of the *Buckley* decision, the Supreme Court rejected the idea that the equalization of speech was a compelling government interest. "The concept that the government may restrict the speech of some elements in our society in order to enhance the relative voice of others is wholly foreign to the First Amendment, which was designed to secure the widest possible dissemination of information from diverse and antagonistic views."[59]

If one is concerned about the political inequity created by money, there may be hope on the horizon. The rise of the Internet may provide those without financial resources a strong voice in an election. The Internet, according to election law lawyer Lee Goodman, "will serve as a powerful 'democratizer' of American politics."[60] Money will never cease to matter in elections, but the Internet may make it matter less.

A Brief Word on *Citizens United*

Because of the controversy surrounding the *Citizens United* case mentioned earlier in this chapter, a brief word is needed regarding the decision. After the verdict, many of my friends assumed that I would be happy with the decision because the ruling opened the door to allow more money into the system. However, my feeling about *Citizens United* is one of ambivalence. On the one hand, I do not necessarily agree that a corporation or labor union has the same rights to free speech as individuals. Corporations and unions are *comprised of* individuals whose right to speech should be protected. I am not persuaded that the corporation or unions themselves need protected speech.

That said, I am not convinced that the doomsday scenarios many predicted after the verdict will come to fruition. In a climate where corporations are not viewed positively by the majority of the public, there may actually be a back-lash if corporations spend large sums independently on candidates. Moreover, knowing that the potential backlash exists, corporations may be hesitant to spend significant amounts of money. If strict disclosure requirements are put in place (and, unfortunately at the time of this writing, Congress has been unable to do so), the effects of *Citizens United* may be muted. At this point, we simply do not know what the results of *Citizens United* will be. I should also be clear that the *Citizens United* ruling applies only to independent expenditures; corporations and unions still may not donate money directly to a candidate's campaign.

Scholars and practitioners will continue to discuss and debate campaign finance reform, but the truth is that any meaningful reform will be difficult to pass. Even BCRA, which has done little to allay the concerns of reformers, was passed only because a few cases of corporate corruption put campaign finance reform on the public's radar. Had Enron not occurred, it is likely that there would be no BCRA. Overhauling the campaign finance system is quite diffi-cult because incumbents benefit from the current system and there is little incentive for them to change it. Also, ideological divisions regarding the role of money in elections undermine support for campaign finance reform. Public financing, if funded at an appropriate level, might make elections more competitive and lessen the time candidates spend fundraising, but conserva-tives generally oppose such an idea because they believe in free markets and that public financing infringes on a person's right to free speech. Indeed, the Court has agreed that forcing candidates or individuals to limit campaign spending or independent expenditures is unconstitutional; there is no indica-tion that the Court will change its mind on this point any time in the near future. Additionally, as I have noted, the future of public financing systems may be threatened if the Court rules that rescue funds are unconstitutional. Liberals usually oppose reforms such as the one that I proposed here for the reasons already mentioned. Moreover, it would be difficult to sell the idea of eliminating contribution limits to the public as a whole, who already believe that Congress is corrupted by such contributions. All of this is disheartening for those who believe in the importance of the potential for competitive elec-tions in a democracy. Of all the subjects mentioned in this book, none have limited competition as much as discrepancies in campaign spending between incumbents and challengers. Because of disagreement over the best way to reform the system, the incumbency advantage is likely to continue well into the future.

Chapter 11

Conclusion: Moving Toward a Model Electoral Democracy

Revisiting the Criteria for a Model Electoral Democracy

Put forth in Chapter 1 were four criteria necessary for a model democracy that have guided my arguments throughout this book, all of which revolve around the concept of free and fair elections. To review, they are:

1 one person, one vote
2 the potential for competitive elections
3 transparency
4 rules that are not burdensome.

In this concluding chapter, I summarize how the claims I made in earlier chapters are consistent with these four criteria for a model democracy and briefly look at the prospects of reform.

One Person, One Vote

Citizens must have equal opportunities to vote and their votes should be weighted the same. Again, central to this criterion is the notion of "one person, one vote." Throughout the book I have argued in favor of reforms that are consistent with "one person, one vote." Crucial to upholding "one person, one vote" is making sure that each citizen in a state is using the same voting machine. It is well documented that some voting systems (for example, punch card ballots) are less accurate than others (for example, optical scanners). While it is not possible to guarantee that the probability of a person's vote counting will be the same for each voter because of human error, it is possible to maximize the likelihood that such a goal occurs by standardizing voting machines throughout the state. If people voting in a U.S. Senate election in one city are using punch card ballots and people voting in that same election in another city are using optical scanners, then the votes of the former will more likely be counted than the latter. In other words, "one person, one vote" is violated.

Standardizing voting equipment is only one way to promote the ideal of one person, one vote. Eliminating the Electoral College and enacting a national primary are also consistent with such a goal. As it stands, the Electoral College allows the vote of each person in a *state* to have his or her vote counted equally. However, the president is the only truly national figure that Americans elect and every person's vote is not counted the same nationwide under the Electoral College. Voters in states with low turnout have more influence than citizens voting in states with high turnout. Likewise, voters in states whose outcomes are in doubt have greater influence than states whose outcomes are clear before election day. The only way to promote "one person, one vote" in presidential elections, then, is to eliminate the Electoral College in favor of a popular vote election. Under such a system, every vote would count equally regardless of where the person lived. The same goes for a national primary. With a national primary, people voting in states that hold their primaries earlier in the season would not be more important than people voting in states that hold their primaries later in the season.

Recall that when discussing Electoral College reform I did not simply advocate a popular vote election, but a popular vote election with an instant runoff instead. Critics might contend that such a system, too, is inconsistent with "one person, one vote" because people now have the opportunity to cast more than one vote. But, such a system would not unfairly benefit one person at the expense of another. Every person would have the opportunity to cast the same number of votes; whether they actually do so would be up to the individual. Additionally, IRV has been upheld by the courts as not violating "one person, one vote."[1]

Another way to promote the idea of "one person, one vote" is to eliminate the barriers to voting that affect some people more than others. The goal should be to make the costs of participation as close to equal as possible. For example, same-day voter registration would benefit young or highly mobile people who might be disadvantaged by an early registration deadline. Likewise, extending the hours that the polls are open would make it easier, for example, for those with long commutes or multiple jobs to vote.

Lastly, the primary goal of redistricting should be to ensure equal populations between districts. Here is an area where the status quo promotes the idea of "one person, one vote" because the courts have been quite rigid in ruling that the other goals of redistricting cannot come at the expense of drawing equally populated (or as close to equal as possible) districts.

As noted in the preceding chapter, reformers often argue that restrictions must be placed on campaign contributions to guarantee the notion of "one person, one vote." I argued in favor of removing such restrictions, but do not believe that this position is inconsistent with the idea of "one person, one vote" because each person's vote is weighted equally whether they contributed to a campaign or not. For a more in-depth defense of this argument, see Chapter 10.

The Potential for Competitive Elections

Again, for a democracy to function well, citizens must have genuine options when voting. If all election outcomes are foregone conclusions, then fewer people will vote, making government less legitimate. Moreover, noncompetitive elections will likely increase polarization in government, threatening to make policy less representative of the wishes of the people. Likewise, without competitive elections, government accountability suffers. Accountability not only contributes to policy responsiveness, but promotes ethics in government as well. When accountability increases, so does honesty in government, as politicians who are corrupt are more likely to be removed from office or avoid corrupt practices in the first place.

I advocate two reforms in particular to generate elections that are more competitive than under the current system. First, redistricting should be conducted by a nonpartisan commission, which must follow guidelines that make drawing competitive districts a priority. As noted in Chapter 7, drawing competitive districts should not be the only goal—or even the primary goal if doing so creates malapportioned districts—and doing so does not guarantee competitive elections, but competition must be taken into consideration. As long as partisan politicians control the process, the only goals that will be advocated will be designed specifically to make elections uncompetitive.

Changing the redistricting process will help create more competitive districts, but it can only go so far toward reaching that goal. Instead, the second reform—eliminating campaign contribution limits—will likely prove to be more effective at creating competitive elections. The greatest obstacle that challengers must overcome is the advantage in name recognition that incumbents have. The most efficient way to lessen that advantage is for challengers to spend large amounts of money. Under current campaign finance rules, the fundraising ability of challengers is hampered. It is difficult for a challenger to compete with an incumbent, regarding fundraising, if the challenger cannot raise more than a few thousand dollars from an individual or political action committee. Eliminating campaign contribution restrictions does not guarantee a competitive election, but it makes one more likely because a challenger who appeals to a few wealthy donors will have the opportunity to raise the necessary money to wage a viable campaign.

Another reform that will create the potential for more competitive elections is for states to pass less restrictive ballot access laws. Voters must have a choice. Such legislation, too, will not necessarily lead to more competitive elections, but will lessen the number of uncontested races, which will at least create the conditions to hold elected officials accountable.[2] Moreover, increasing the number of candidates in a race creates greater uncertainty and gives voters more choices to express their dissatisfaction with incumbents.

Truthfully, none of these reforms will make all elections competitive. Incumbents will still have many other advantages that challengers do not. And, we would not want every election in the country to be competitive. Too much competition can lead to government instability and remove a great deal of institutional memory and experience from government. Indeed, this is one of many reasons why term limits for politicians are harmful. For a democracy to function properly though, more than a handful of congressional races out of several hundred have to be in play. Nonpartisan redistricting commissions, eliminating campaign contribution restrictions, and less restrictive ballot access laws will help to alleviate this problem.

Transparency

As mentioned in Chapter 1, voting should be private, but other aspects of elections should not. The reforms argued for in this book make American electoral democracy more visible to the public, allowing it to be more informed, thus lessening the opportunity for fraud or corruption. Chapter 6 argues for regular audits of election results, especially in instances where jurisdictions use electronic voting machines. Regular audits will provide important information regarding how accurately votes are counted, as well as make it more likely that fraud—if there is any—will be exposed.

Nonpartisan redistricting commissions also promote transparency. Instead of deals brokered in backrooms by politicians, the districting process would be conducted in the open and even provide the opportunity for citizen input.

If states allow for the initiative, then public hearings should be held on any qualifying initiative and proponents should be able to offer amendments. Such a reform would not only promote transparency, but encourage deliberation and compromise as well.

Finally, enforcing disclosure requirements for campaign contributions will lessen the opportunity for corruption and help citizens cast more informed votes. It is imperative, especially if contribution limits are eliminated, that people have an idea of where candidates' campaign money is coming from.

Rules That Are Not Burdensome

Several of the arguments made in this book are designed to lessen the costs of participating in elections. Voting for fewer elected officials and restricting the initiative process will make voting less overwhelming. Voters would be able to focus more extensively on a much smaller set of elections, which would hopefully improve their decision-making. If we are going to insist that government accountability is threatened when the number of elected officials is lessened, then we must make sure that the most important, reliable cue used by most voters—a candidate's party affiliation—is available (see Chapter 5). Eliminating nonpartisan elections will increase turnout, improve the quality of voting, and make election outcomes more representative of the electorate.

It is not just the number of decisions that Americans are asked to make that is problematic, but the number of *times* they are asked to make those decisions as well. Consolidating election dates (Chapter 2) will increase turnout (especially for local elections), making it more reflective of the eligible voting population. It will also lessen the fatigue of citizens who might have to go to the polls several times in one year. Moving to a national primary (Chapter 8) and making it easier for candidates to raise money by eliminating contribution restrictions (Chapter 10) lessen fatigue as well, because incorporating these changes will shorten the campaign season substantially.

Other Improvements to American Electoral Democracy

I have focused primarily on the four criteria for a model democracy just mentioned, but the reforms advocated in this book have the potential to improve American electoral democracy in other ways as well. Here are a few:

Expanding Voter Choice

Citizens are more apt to participate if they have a positive view of a candidate, the probability of which increases when citizens have more candidates from which to choose. As a result, states should pass laws making ballot access less stringent for third-party and independent candidates. Additionally, instant runoff voting (IRV) will allow citizens to vote both sincerely and sophisticatedly; people will no longer feel as though they are wasting a vote by supporting a candidate who has no chance to win. Finally, competitive elections expand voters' options because elections will not be foregone conclusions. Ultimately people may choose to vote for the incumbent, but they should do so because they believe the incumbent is the best candidate, not because that politician is the only candidate.

Critics might argue that expanding voter choice undermines the goal of making voting less burdensome. The greater the number of candidates—especially viable candidates—on the ballot, the more people have to research who is the best candidate. However, an increased number of candidates on the ballot will not be too burdensome. The number of legitimate candidates will quickly be pared down to just a few (remember the 2003 California gubernatorial recall). Also, given the single-member-district, first-past-the-post rules of American elections, it is unlikely that competitive elections will have more than two or three serious choices. We do not want election choices to be too onerous, but we *do* want voters to actually have a choice! Finally, if we eliminate many of the extraneous offices for which Americans are asked to vote, they could focus more closely on the remaining elections.

Another concern of some with expanding voter choice is that it may undermine the two-party system of government that many scholars of American politics believe is essential to an efficiently run government. For example, with multiple parties holding seats in government, it could lead to what is known as "partyocracy"—the domination of legislatures by a number of political parties, none of them strong enough to govern, yet none willing to let the other govern. However, arguments stating that reforms such as easier ballot access and IRV will weaken the U.S. two-party system are not convincing. There are numerous other aspects of U.S. elections and culture that will allow the two-party system to remain. Representation would still not be allocated proportionally. The United States does not have the kind of definite factions that exist in many European countries; unlike in some other countries, there is virtually universal support for capitalism and the central tenets of our Constitution. Holding party primaries allows dissident voices to compete for nominations within major parties. All of these protect a two-party system.

Increasing Voter Turnout

Some democratic theorists, such as Arend Lijphart, argue that high voter turnout is essential in a healthy democracy. I would not go as far as calling it essential—we should not increase voter turnout just for the sake of increasing voter turnout at the expense of other goals—but it is an important aspect of a sound democracy because it promotes government legitimacy and eliminates inequities in voter participation between the haves and have-nots. Several of the reforms supported herein will in fact increase voter turnout. Chapter 2 mentions many of these reforms including consolidating election dates, expanding the hours in which polls are open, and enacting same-day voter registration laws, and several other chapters contain proposals that will increase turnout as well. Abolishing the Electoral College and moving to a national primary would increase the number of people who can influence the outcome; the same goes for reforms that promote competitive elections. Other ideas, such as eliminating nonpartisan elections, simply designed ballots, and the use of optical scan voting machines, would not increase the number of people who turn out to vote on election day, but would lessen voter roll-off and the number of people whose votes are not counted.

Protecting Judicial Independence and Promoting Sound Public Policy

Eliminating judicial elections would allow judges to protect individual rights without the fear of rebuke from the electorate. Likewise, restricting the use of direct democracy will lessen the number of times that the courts must declare popular initiatives unconstitutional. Allowing the initiative only to deal with nonrevenue or nonexpenditure measures will keep the legislature's hands from being tied when dealing with budgetary matters and will help eliminate the income disparity in policies passed by initiative.

The Prospects for Reform

Now that the case for a model electoral democracy has been made, I should close with a few comments on the prospects for reform. In other words, what are the chances that this vision of democracy will be enacted?

The problem with election reform is that the people who write the rules are the same people who benefit from the status quo. Incumbents who have already won under the current rules are not likely to want to change the rules to lessen the probability of a future victory. Unless there is substantial pressure from the public (and on issues related to elections there usually is not), politicians are often reluctant to rock the boat. In other cases, because of ideological divisions, it may be difficult to obtain enough support to pass a reform. Additionally, some of the reforms advocated in this book, such as abolishing the Electoral College, would require a constitutional amendment, something that has only happened 27 times in more than 200 years. Even statutory changes may be difficult to implement because of separation of powers. A small majority in Congress may pass a reform bill only to have the president veto it. Finally, because of federalism, broad electoral reform is often hard to enact.

There are some reforms advocated in this book that, quite simply, are not likely to be enacted. It will be a long time before any substantial change to the Electoral College is made. Too many states have an interest in maintaining the status quo. And, although the National Popular Vote plan discussed in chapter 9 has had some success, I am not convinced that it can get enough states on board for it to be implemented.

While polls indicate that the public wants the Electoral College abolished, in other cases it is the public that is likely to resist the proposed reforms. It is tough to convince people to give up the vote, even when they do not understand the job descriptions of the offices for which they are voting. As much as judicial elections are frustrating, because of public support the real debate is not whether we should hold them, but what type of judicial election we should have (partisan, nonpartisan, or merit selection). Even the American Bar Association, one of the most vocal opponents of judicial elections, has given up hope for their elimination and has turned its attention instead to "improving" them. Again, because of public support, rules regarding the initiative process and the recall could possibly be tweaked, but abolishing direct democracy is unlikely to happen. In today's political climate, eliminating campaign contributions has about as much of a chance of occurring as me playing centerfield for the Cubs. If change is likely to come, it will come from the courts (e.g., *Citizens United*) and not the legislature. Incumbents would likely resist any campaign finance proposal that threatens their status as incumbents. Additionally, the public is deeply skeptical of the effects of campaign contributions on legislative behavior and is frustrated by the amount of money that already enters American elections; it would not support such a proposal. The fact that none of these changes are likely to happen—at least any time soon—does not mean that the debate about them should cease. Indeed, American history is full of examples of reforms that at one time seemed impossible, including voting rights for women and racial and ethnic minorities, direct election of senators, and the secret ballot, that ultimately came to fruition.

Other reforms that I call for have a much greater likelihood of enactment, and, to be sure, some already have been. Most states and localities have eliminated the use of punch card ballots and instead are employing optical scanners or electronic voting. As much as some people are opposed to the use of electronic voting, its use is inevitable. While many localities will continue holding their elections separately from those for federal office, there is evidence that some are consolidating their elections.[3] Though IRV may not be used on a widespread basis any time soon, an increasing number of localities have implemented it. The enactment of nonpartisan redistricting commissions has gained support on the eve of the next round of redistricting. A growing number of states are moving to make voter registration easier and remove barriers to voting.

There are other aspects of election reform on the horizon as well, although perhaps not the reform advocated here. For example, with the increased front-loading of presidential primaries, something is likely to change in the next presidential election cycle or two; whether that change is the enactment of a national primary is another matter. Whatever the case, the questions about what kind of electoral democracy the United States should have will not subside. I began this book by mentioning Robert Dahl's challenge to make democratic countries more democratic. It is my hope that this book has advanced the debate on how to best improve American electoral democracy.

Notes

1 Creating a Model Electoral Democracy

1. Gerber, *The Populist Paradox*, p. 3.
2. Dahl, *On Democracy*, p. 2.
3. Ibid., p. 31.
4. Ibid., p. 32.
5. Ibid., p. 37.
6. Thompson, *Just Elections*, p. 6.
7. Downs, *An Economic Theory of Democracy*.
8. Riker and Ordeshook, "A Theory of the Calculus of Voting."
9. Filer and Kenny, "Voter Turnout and the Benefits of Voting."
10. Westlye, "Competitiveness of Senate Seats"; Rosenstone and Hansen, *Mobilization, Participation, and Democracy in America*; Cox and Munger, "Closeness, Expenditures, and Turnout"; Wielhouwer and Lockerbie, "Party Contacting and Political Participation."
11. Kim, Petrocik, Enokson, "Voter Turnout among the American States"; Filer, Kenny, and Morton, "Redistribution, Income, and Voting"; Shachar and Nalebuff, "Follow the Leader."
12. Ansolabehere, Snyder, and Stewart, "Old Voters, New Voters, and the Personal Vote."
13. Griffin, "Electoral Competition and Democratic Responsiveness."
14. Alvarez and Hall, *Point, Click, & Vote*, p. 36.

2 Factors that Influence Voter Turnout

1. Crewe, "Electoral Participation," p. 232.
2. Boyd, "Decline of U.S. Voter Turnout."
3. Crewe, "Electoral Participation," p. 232.
4. Schier, *You Call This an Election?*
5. Wood, "Voter Turnout in City Elections."
6. Calculated by author from Georgia Secretary of State webpage and McDonald, "2008 General Election Turnout Rates." In a November 2004 Georgia runoff election for a statewide appellate court seat, turnout was only 6 percent. Rankin, "Bernes Wins Judicial Election."
7. Boyd, "Election Calendars and Voter Turnout"; Teixeira, *The Disappearing American Voter*; Norris, "Do Institutions Matter?"; Patterson, *Vanishing Voter*, p. 136; Jackman and Miller, "Voter Turnout in the Industrial Democracies."
8. Hajnal and Lewis, "Municipal Institutions and Voter Turnout in Local Elections"; Wood, "Voter Turnout in City Elections."

9. Hajnal and Lewis, "Municipal Institutions and Voter Turnout in Local Elections," p. 655.
10. Hajnal, Lewis, and Louch, *Municipal Elections in California*.
11. DeSipio, "United States."
12. Doppelt and Shearer, *Nonvoters*.
13. Verba, Schlozman, and Brady, *Voice and Equality*; Rosenstone and Hansen, *Mobilization, Participation, and Democracy in America*; Wolfinger and Rosenstone, *Who Votes?*
14. Hajnal and Lewis, "Municipal Institutions and Voter Turnout in Local Elections," p. 646.
15. See, for example, Citrin, Shickler, and Sides, "What if Everyone Voted?"; Gant and Lyons, "Democratic Theory, Nonvoting, and Public Policy"; Nagel and McNulty, "Partisan Effects of Voter Turnout in Senatorial and Gubernatorial Elections."
16. Hajnal and Trounstine, "Where Turnout Matters."
17. Gregory, "The High Cost of Low Turnout," Section 4, pg. 1.
18. Bailey, "The Heroic Presidency in the Era of Divided Government"; Jacobson, *The Politics of Congressional Elections*; Herrnson, *Congressional Elections*.
19. Wattenberg, McAllister, and Salvanto, "How Voting Is Like Taking an SAT Test."
20. Hajnal and Lewis, "Municipal Institutions and Voter Turnout in Local Elections," p. 662.
21. Schaffner, "Media Coverage."
22. Hajnal and Lewis, "Municipal Institutions and Voter Turnout in Local Elections," p. 656.
23. Gosnell, *Getting Out the Vote*; Lijphart, "Unequal Participation"; Wolfinger and Rosenstone, *Who Votes?*; Rosenstone and Hansen, *Mobilization, Participation, and Democracy in America*.
24. Powell, "American Voter Turnout." Powell conducted this study several years before the Motor Voter law went into effect. It is likely that automatic registration would increase voter turnout at a slightly lower rate today.
25. Rosenstone and Wolfinger, "The Effect of Registration Laws," p. 22.
26. Wayne, *Road to the White House*, p. 70.
27. Although Knack argues that the real effect of NVRA will take several election cycles to assess. Furthermore, some variants of NVRA that were implemented in the states before the bill's passage showed a modest increase in turnout rates. See Knack, "Election-day Registration"; Knack, "Does Motor Voter Work?"; Rhine, "Registration Reform and Turnout Change."
28. Rosenfield, "New Report Highlights Online Voter Registration."
29. United States Election Assistance Commission, "EAC Releases Data from 2008 Presidential Election."
30. Pillsbury, Johannesen, and Adams, *America Goes to the Polls*.
31. See, for example, Wolfinger and Rosentone, *Who Votes?*; Teixeira, *The Disappearing Voter*; Fenster, "The Impact of Allowing Day of Registration Voting"; Rhine, "An Analysis of the Impact of Registration Factors on Turnout"; Brians and Grofman, "Election Day Registration's Effect on U.S. Voter Turnout"; Knack, "Election-Day Registration"; Leighley and Nagler, "The Effects of Non-Precinct Voting Reforms on Turnout, 1972–2008."
32. Patterson, *Vanishing Voter*.
33. Demos: A Network for Ideas & Action, "Election Day Registration Helps America Vote." See also, Leighley and Nagler, "The Effects of Non-Precinct Voting Reforms on Turnout, 1972–2008."

34. Demos: A Network for Ideas & Action, "Election Day Registration Helps America Vote."
35. Demos: A Network for Ideas & Action, "Expanding the Vote."
36. Fund, *Stealing Elections*.
37. One problem with this idea is that it would be difficult for homeless people to register on the day of the election.
38. Gouras, "Secretary of State Wants to Do Away with Same-Day Voting."
39. Quoted in Fund, *Stealing Elections*, p. 141.
40. Schaffner, Streb, and Wright, "Teams Without Uniforms"; Schaffner and Streb, "The Partisan Heuristic in Low-Information Elections"; Squire and Smith, "The Effect of Partisan Information on Voters."
41. Pillsbury, Johannesen, and Adams, *America Goes to the Polls*.
42. Stein and Vonnahme, "The Cost of Elections."
43. Cemenska, et. al., *2009 Report on the 1972–2008 Early and Absentee Voting Dataset*.
44. DiCamillo, "The Continuing Growth of Mail Ballot Voting in California."
45. I use presidential election years only for an easier comparison to turnout.
46. Barreto, et al., "Do Absentee Voters Differ From Polling Place Voters?"
47. Fitzgerald, "Greater Convenience but Not Greater Turnout"; Oliver, "The Effects of Eligibility Restrictions and Party Activity"; Gronke, Galanes-Rosenbaum, and Miller, "Early Voting and Turnout"; Leighley and Nagler, "The Effects of Non-Precinct Voting Reforms on Turnout, 1972–2008."
48. Hansen, "Early Voting, Unrestricted Absentee Voting, and Voting by Mail"; Fitzgerald, "Greater Convenience but Not Greater Turnout."
49. Fitzgerald, "Greater Convenience but Not Greater Turnout"; Stein and Garcia-Monet, "Voting Early, but Not Often"; Richardson and Neeley, "Implementation of Early Voting"; Gronke, Galanes-Rosenbaum, and Miller, "Early Voting and Turnout"; Leighley and Nagler, "The Effects of Non-Precinct Voting Reforms on Turnout, 1972–2008."
50. Stein, "Early Voting."
51. Berinsky, Burns, and Traugott, "Who Votes By Mail?" Although, see Southwell and Burchett, "The Effects of All-Mail Elections," and Richey, "Voting by Mail" for slightly different perspectives.
52. Fund, *Stealing Elections*.
53. Stein, "Early Voting."
54. Hansen, "Early Voting, Unrestricted Absentee Voting, and Voting by Mail."
55. Barreto, et al., "Do Absentee Voters Differ From Polling Place Voters?" p. 229.
56. Alvarez and Hall, "Controlling Democracy."
57. Hansen, "Early Voting, Unrestricted Absentee Voting, and Voting by Mail."
58. Ibid.
59. McDonald, "The Return of the Voter."
60. Crigler, Just, and Buhr, "Cleavage and Consensus."
61. Franklin, "The Dynamics of Electoral Participation."
62. See Caltech/MIT Voting Technology Project, *Voting: What Is, What Could Be*.
63. Wolfinger, Highton, and Mullin, "How Postregistration Laws Affect the Turnout of Citizens Registered to Vote."
64. Crigler, Just, and Buhr, "Cleavage and Consensus."
65. Indeed, at least one study of Georgia's voter identification statute found that African Americans, Hispanics, and the elderly were less likely to have a DMV-issued photo identification. Hood and Bullock, "Worth a Thousand Words?"

66. *Crawford v. Marion County Election Board* 553 U.S. 181 (2008).
67. Indiana's photo identification law was again recently upheld, this time by the state's supreme court. The U.S. Supreme Court argued that the law did not violate the *federal* Constitution. However, a state intermediate appellate court held that the law violated the *state's* constitution. In *League of Women Voters v. Rokita* (2010), Indiana's Supreme Court disagreed.
68. Ornstein, "There's Value in Voter ID Requirement."
69. Ibid.
70. Even here, the laws differ by state. In Georgia, for instance, a felon may have his or her voting rights restored by the Governor or "other appropriate authority." In Virginia, the Governor can restore voting rights to some felons, but drug-related or violent crimes require a longer waiting time and additional documentation than others. Those convicted of election-related crimes or treason may never have their voting rights restored. For a detailed breakdown of the state's law regarding felon voting, see "Felon Voting Rights by State."
71. Manza and Uggen, "Punishment and Democracy," p. 497.
72. Chapman, "Too Many Ex-Convicts Aren't Able to Vote."
73. Uggen and Manza, "Voting and Subsequent Crime and Arrest."
74. Manza and Uggen, "Punishment and Democracy," p. 499.
75. *Simmons v. Galvin* 575 F.3d 24 (2009).
76. *Farrakhan v. Gregoire* 590 F.3d 989 (2010).
77. Project Vote, *Restoring Voting Rights to Former Felons*," p. 6.
78. Manza and Uggen, "Punishment and Democracy," p. 500.
79. Uggen and Manza, "Voting and Subsequent Crime and Arrest."
80. Lijphart, "Unequal Participation."
81. Ibid., p. 10.
82. Ibid., p. 11.
83. Katosh and Traugott, "Costs and Values in the Calculus of Voting."

3 The Offices We Elect

1. Wattenberg, *The Decline of American Political Parties*, p. 14.
2. It is not just people that we are voting for; as I discuss next chapter, voters in some states become additionally taxed by a number of initiatives that appears on the ballot.
3. "City Clerk Candidates."
4. The president can appoint judges during a congressional recess who do not need Senate confirmation.
5. Kozlowski, "Robed and Running," p. 35.
6. Berkson, "Judicial Selection in the United States."
7. Croley, "The Majoritarian Difficulty"; Berkson, "Judicial Selection in the United States." For more on the history of judicial elections, see Streb, "The Study of Judicial Elections," pp. 8–11.
8. Justice at Stake Campaign, "Poll of American Voters."
9. Lovrich and Sheldon, "Voters in Contested, Nonpartisan Judicial Elections."
10. Johnson, Schaefer, and McKnight, "The Salience of Judicial Candidates and Elections."
11. "Cash v. Quality," p. B8.
12. Squire and Smith, "The Effects of Partisan Information."
13. Dubois, "Voting Cues in Nonpartisan Trial Court Elections."
14. Lovrich and Sheldon, "Voters in Contested, Nonpartisan Judicial Elections."
15. As a side note, it always amazes me that so few judicial candidates turn in statements since the sample ballot is an important source of information for voters.

People may actually vote for a candidate simply because she had a statement and her opponent did not.

16. Streb, Frederick, and LaFrance, "Voter Rolloff in a Low-Information Context."
17. Hall and Bonneau, "Does Quality Matter?" See, also, Bonneau and Hall, *In Defense of Judicial Elections.*
18. Streb and Frederick, "Conditions for Competition in Low-Information Judicial Elections."
19. Glick and Emmert, "Selection Systems and Judicial Characterisitcs"; Choi, Gulati, and Posner, "Professionals or Politicians."
20. Justice at Stake Campaign, "What's Coming Up in 2005?"
21. Schouten, "States Act to Revise Judicial Selection."
22. Rankin, "Bernes Wins Judicial Election."
23. Goldberg, Holman, and Sanchez, *The New Politics of Judicial Elections*, p. 9.
24. Sample, Jones, and Weiss, *The New Politics of Judicial Elections*, 2006.
25. McClellan, "Merit Appointment versus Popular Election."
26. Heller, "Judicial Races Get Meaner."
27. Justice at Stake Campaign, "2004 State Supreme Court Election Overview."
28. *Citizens United v. FEC*, 130 S. Ct. 876 (2010).
29. Brennan Center for Justice, "Buying Time 2004."
30. Justice at Stake Campaign, "Poll of American Voters"; Justice at Stake Campaign, "Poll of State Judges."
31. Gibson, "Challenges to the Impartiality of State Supreme Courts"; Gibson, "New-Style Judicial Campaigns and the Legitimacy of State High Courts."
32. Bonneau and Cann, "The Effect of Campaign Contributions on Judicial Decisionmaking." Cann, "Justice for Sale? Campaign Contributions and Judicial Decisionmaking." Yet, even here one must be cautious to not make too much of these findings. First, they apply only to a small number of states (Georgia, Michigan, and Texas) and do not indicate that "justice is for sale" in every case.
33. Quoted in Krivosha, "Acquiring Judges by the Merit Selection Method."
34. See Boutrous and Hungar, "Ethical Issues after Election."
35. Blakenship only contributed $1,000 directly to Benjamin's campaign.
36. West Virginia law gave individual justices discretion over whether they should recuse themselves from a case.
37. Ortiz, "Constitutional Restrictions," p. 63.
38. Bonneau, "The Dynamics of Campaign Spending."
39. Streb and Frederick, "Judicial Reform and the Future of Judicial Elections."
40. Kennedy, "Speech to Hong Kong High Court."
41. Brace and Boyea, "Judicial Selection Methods and Capital Punishment in the American States."
42. Huber and Gordon, "Accountability and Coercion."
43. Hamilton, Madison, and Jay, *The Federalist*, p. 400.
44. Zakaria, *The Future of Freedom.*
45. Reynoso, "In Memoriam."
46. Because of the nature of the office, the rules of judicial elections are much different than the rules of elections for other offices. For example, many states have enacted laws that keep judicial candidates from attending political gatherings, receiving campaign contributions directly, and seeking endorsements. Judicial candidates are also expected to abide by canons based on the American Bar Association's (ABA) Model Code of judicial conduct. One such canon was the announce clause, which, in the *White* case, the Court declared to violate the First Amendment.

47. *Republican Party of Minnesota v. White* (O'Connor, concurring), p. 789.
48. Hall, "State Supreme Courts in American Democracy"; Hall, "Competition as Accountability in State Supreme Court Elections"; Streb, Frederick, and LaFrance, "Contestation, Competition, and the Potential for Accountability in Intermediate Appellate Court Elections."
49. Streb, Frederick, and LaFrance, "Contestation, Competition, and the Potential for Accountability in Intermediate Appellate Court Elections."
50. Schotland, "Financing Judicial Elections," p. 225.
51. Hall, "State Supreme Courts in American Democracy," p. 324.
52. Ruelas, "Judge an Unexpected Target."
53. Spence, *With Justice for None*, p. 263.
54. Ibid., p. 261.
55. Cheek and Champagne, "Political Party Affiliation in Partisan and Nonpartisan Elections."
56. Hall, "State Supreme Courts in American Democracy."
57. Streb, "Partisan Involvement in Partisan and Nonpartisan Trial Court Elections."
58. See, for example, Hall and Brace, "Toward an Integrated Model of Judicial Voting Behavior"; Brace and Hall, "Integrated Models of Judicial Dissent."
59. Liptak, "Judges Mix with Politics," B1.
60. Hamilton, Madison, and Jay, *The Federalist*, p. 396.
61. Gibson, "Challenges to the Impartiality of State Supreme Courts"; Gibson, "New-Style Judicial Campaigns and the Legitimacy of State High Courts."
62. Gibson, "New-Style Judicial Campaigns and the Legitimacy of State High Courts." p. 1298.
63. Bonneau, Hall, and Streb, "White Noise."

4 Direct Democracy

1. The referendum is also a form of direct democracy, but as I discuss later in the chapter, I do not focus on it here.
2. Cain and Miller ("The Populist Legacy") point out that scholars tend to combine the populists and progressives when discussing the development of the initiative process, but that the groups actually had different reasons for supporting the initiative. According to Cain and Miller, progressives were simply concerned with eliminating corruption that dominated the state legislatures at the time; they did not want to replace representative government altogether. Populists, on the other hand, were more concerned with substituting direct democracy for representative democracy. Cain and Miller argue that it is the populist vision that is more dominant today, which has dangerous consequences because representative government is undermined.
3. Signature requirements are generally higher for constitutional initiatives.
4. For excellent discussions of the various state rules regarding the initiative process, see Magleby, "Direct Legislation in the American States," pp. 224–228, or Tolbert, Lowenstein, and Donovan, "Election Law and Rules for Using Initiatives."
5. Ten states allow for the indirect initiative.
6. Bowler and Donovan, "The Initiative Process," p. 133.
7. Public Policy Institute of California, *Citizens' Initiative Process.*
8. Initiative and Referendum Institute, "National Survey."
9. *Buckley v. Valeo*, 425 U.S. 946 (1976).
10. *First National Bank of Boston v. Bellotti*, 435 U.S. 765 (1978).

11. Quoted in Tolbert, Lowenstein, and Donovan, "Election Law and Rules for Using Initiatives," p. 46.
12. *Citizens Against Rent Control (CARC) v. City of Berkeley*, 454 U.S. 290 (1981).
13. The numbers in the preceding paragraph were obtained from Bauer, *2008 Ballot Measure Overview*. Spending figures for 2010 ballot measures were not available at the time of this writing.
14. Gerber, *The Populist Paradox*; Owens and Wade, "Campaign Spending on California Ballot Propositions"; Smith, "Campaign Financing of Ballot Initiatives"; Magleby, *Direct Legislation*. Although, see Zisk, *Money, Media, and the Grassroots* for a competing view.
15. Cronin, *Direct Democracy*.
16. Quoted in McCuan, et al., "California's Political Warriors," p. 73.
17. Smith, *Tax Crusaders and the Politics of Direct Democracy*, p. 13.
18. Gerber, "Pressuring the Legislatures through the Use of Initiatives," p. 192.
19. Quoted in Cronin, *Direct Democracy*, p. 80.
20. Baker, "Tips for Voters," p. 23.
21. Magleby, "Direct Legislation in the American States."
22. Magleby, *Direct Legislation*.
23. Ibid.
24. Ibid., p. 128.
25. Broder, *Democracy Derailed*, p. 160.
26. Chavez, *The Color Bind*.
27. Ellis, *Democratic Delusions*.
28. Magleby, "Direct Legislation in the American States," p. 249.
29. Magleby, *Direct Legislation*, p. 129.
30. Lupia, "Shortcuts Versus Encyclopedias."
31. Karp, "The Influence of Elite Endorsements."
32. However, Garrett and McCubbins, "When Voters Make Laws," note that, in the case of local bond measures in Los Angeles and San Francisco, reliable voting cues were not always available to voters.
33. Bowler and Donovan, *Demanding Choices*.
34. Banducci, "Searching for Ideological Consistency."
35. Bowler and Donovan, *Demanding Choices*, p. xii.
36. Ibid., p. 165.
37. Cronin, *Direct Democracy*, p. 87.
38. Gamble, "Putting Civil Rights to a Popular Vote."
39. Ibid., p. 254.
40. Donovan and Bowler, "Direct Democracy and Minority Rights."
41. Hajnal, Gerber, and Louch, "Minorities and Direct Legislation."
42. Matsusaka, *For the Many or the Few*.
43. Donovan and Bowler, "An Overview of Direct Democracy."
44. Cronin, *Direct Democracy*, p. 92.
45. Magleby, *Direct Legislation*, p. 182.
46. Ellis, *Democratic Delusions*, p. 79.
47. Magleby, "Direct Legislation in the American States," p. 256.
48. National Conference of State Legislatures, "The Term Limited States." In six of those states, terms limits were either repealed by the state legislature or declared unconstitutional by the state supreme court.
49. Gerber, "Legislative Response to the Threat of Popular Initiatives."
50. Erikson, Wright, and McIver, *Statehouse Democracy*.
51. Lascher, Jr., Hagen, and Rochlin, "Gun Behind the Door?"
52. Erikson, Wright, and McIver, *Statehouse Democracy*, p. 247.

53. Magleby, *Direct Legislation*, p. 121.
54. Everson, "The Effects of Initiatives on Voter Turnout."
55. Magleby, *Direct Legislation*, p. 197.
56. Smith and Tolbert, *Educated by Initiative*.
57. Smith, "The Contingent Effects of Ballot Initiatives"; Smith, "Ballot Initiatives and the Democratic Citizen"; Bowler and Donovan, "Democracy, Institutions, and Attitudes"; Donovan, Tolbert, and Smith, "Political Engagement, Mobilization, and Direct Democracy"; Tolbert, Bowen, and Donovan, "Initiative Campaigns." Although Dyck, "Initiated Distrust," finds that direct democracy causes people to be less trusting of government.
58. Smith and Tolbert, *Educated by Initiative*, p. 70.
59. Schlozman and Yohai, "How Initiatives Don't Always Make Citizens," also note the conditional effects of initiatives on turnout, political knowledge, and efficacy.
60. Magleby, *Direct Legislation*, pp. 180–181.
61. Quoted in Broder, *Democracy Derailed*, p. 202.
62. Garrett and McCubbins, "When Voters Make Laws."
63. Cain and Miller, "The Populist Legacy," p. 33.
64. The proposition was on the ballot in 2004, a time when it was less clear about the state of the budget. At the time of this writing, California is in the midst of a budget crisis making it easier for voters to understand the budget implications.
65. Donovan and Bowler, "Responsive or Responsible Government?", p. 256.
66. Broder, *Democracy Derailed*.
67. See Schrag, *Paradise Lost*, for a particularly stinging critique of Prop. 13.
68. Broder, *Democracy Derailed*, p. 48.
69. Schrag, *Paradise Lost*, p. 12.
70. Tolbert, "Changing Rules for States Legislatures."
71. Donovan and Bowler, "Responsive or Responsible Government?"; Clingermayer and Wood, "Disentangling Patterns of State Indebtedness."
72. Donovan and Bowler, "Responsive or Responsible Government?"; Lascher, Jr., Hagen, and Rochlin, "Gun Behind the Door?"
73. Matsusaka, "Fiscal Effects of the Voter Initiative."
74. Donovan and Bowler, "Responsive or Responsible Government?", p. 264.
75. National Conference of State Legislatures, "Trends in Reform." It is important to note that scholars have conducted little empirical research on the effects that many of these reforms would have (see Gerber, "The Logic of Reform").
76. See Ellis, *Democratic Delusions*, pp. 39–42, for more on Mississippi's initiative process.
77. See Broder, *Democracy Derailed*, pp. 210–212, for more on the Commission's recommendations.
78. Cronin, *Direct Democracy*, pp. 5–6.
79. Cronin, *Direct Democracy*.
80. Ibid., p. 133.
81. Erikson, Wright, and McIver, *Statehouse Democracy*; Stimson, Mackuen, and Erikson, "Dynamic Representation."
82. Cronin, *Direct Democracy*, pp. 148–149.
83. Ibid., p. 155.
84. The person that almost solely funded the recall effort, Darrel Issa, was a congressman who unsuccessfully ran for governor in 1998 and initially threw his hat into the ring as a candidate to replace Davis if the governor were recalled. Issa ultimately dropped out of the recall replacement election.

85. CNN/USA Today/Gallup Poll, July 25–27, 2003.
86. The requirement is actually slightly more complex, as a certain number of signatures had to be obtained from each county.

5 Ballot Laws

1. Occasionally there are examples of write-in candidates winning elections. These occurrences are rare, however, and usually happen at local levels. Lisa Murkowski's apparent win in the 2010 Alaska Senate election is clearly an exception.
2. In some cases, such as Pennsylvania and Ohio, the Democratic Party was successful. In other states, like Florida and New Mexico, they were not. In all cases, however, Nader had to spend significant money to challenge the lawsuits.
3. Compiled by author from Dave Leip's Atlas of US Presidential Elections, http://uselectionatlas.org/, accessed on March 21, 2007. In 2000, when Nader was a more serious challenger, he failed to qualify in only three states (North Carolina, Oklahoma, and South Dakota). In 2008, Nader was not listed on the ballot in Georgia, Indiana, North Carolina, Oklahoma, and Texas.
4. Lewis-Beck and Squire, "The Politics of Institutional Choice."
5. Winger, "Institutional Obstacles to a Multiparty System," p. 165.
6. Collet and Wattenberg, "Strategically Unambititous," p. 230.
7. Ibid., p. 244.
8. First-past-the-post systems encourage a two-party system; they do not necessitate one. For example, Canada has a first-past-the-post system, but multiple competitive parties.
9. People could cast write-in votes for Nader, but appearing on the ballot makes candidates seem more legitimate (even if they have no chance of winning). Had Nader not appeared on most of the state's ballots in 2000, he still would have won votes, but not nearly the roughly three million he received.
10. Ansolabehere and Gerber, "The Effects of Filing Fees and Petition Requirements on U.S. House Elections."
11. Ibid., p. 260
12. Ibid.
13. Pomper, "Ethnic and Group Voting in Nonpartisan Municipal Elections"; Lorinkas, Hawkins, and Edwards, "The Persistence of Ethnic Voting in Urban and Rural Areas"; McDermott, "Voting Cues in Low-Information Elections"; McDermott, "Race and Gender Cues in Low-Information Elections"; Matson and Fine, "Gender, Ethnicity, and Ballot Information."
14. Although, special elections in the House because of a death or resignation are often nonpartisan.
15. Duncan, *The Progressive Movement*.
16. Schaffner, Streb, and Wright, "Teams Without Uniforms."
17. Dubois, *From Ballot to Bench*; Hall, "Voting in State Supreme Court Elections"; Streb, Frederick, and LaFrance, "Voter Rolloff in a Low-Information Context."
18. Schaffner and Streb, "The Partisan Heuristic in Low-Information Elections."
19. Schaffner, Streb, and Wright, "A New Look at the Republican Advantage in Nonpartisan Elections."
20. Ibid., p. 242.
21. Ibid.
22. McDermott, "Candidate Occupations and Voter Information Shortcuts," p.204.

23. Byrne and Pueschel, "But Who Should I Vote for County Coroner?"; Aspin and Hall, "Friends and Neighbors Voting in Judicial Retention Elections."
24. McDermott, "Candidate Occupations and Voter Information Shortcuts."
25. Nakinishi, Cooper, and Kassarjian, "Voting for a Political Candidate under Conditions of Minimal Information."
26. McDermott, "Candidate Occupations and Voter Information Shortcuts." See, also, Byrne and Pueschel, "But Who Should I Vote for County Coroner?" and Dubois, "Voting Cues in Nonpartisan Trial Court Elections." Although, see Klein and Baum, "Ballot Information and Voting Decisions," for evidence that incumbency status might not matter in state supreme court elections.
27. McDermott, "Candidate Occupations and Voter Information Shortcuts," p. 204.
28. Schaffner, Streb, and Wright, "Teams Without Uniforms"; Klein and Baum, "Ballot Information and Voting Decisions."
29. Brook and Upton, "Biases in Local Government Due to Position on the Ballot Paper"; Miller and Krosnick, "The Impact of Candidate Name Order on Election Outcomes"; Krosnick, Miller, and Tichy, "An Unrecognized Need for Ballot Reform." Although, see Matson and Fine, "Gender, Ethnicity, and Ballot Information," for a competing argument.
30. Krosnick, Miller, and Tichy, "An Unrecognized Need for Ballot Reform."
31. Ibid.
32. Krosnick, "In the Voting Booth, Bias Starts at the Top."
33. Krosnick, Miller, and Tichy, "An Unrecognized Need for Ballot Reform," see Table 4.1.
34. Ibid.
35. Ibid., p. 58.
36. Krosnick, "In the Voting Booth, Bias Starts at the Top," p. A19.
37. "Ballots Made to Order," p. B2.
38. Winger, "Ballot Access News."
39. For an excellent overview of the complexities of ballot design, see Norden, et al., *Better Ballots*. Such seemingly mundane issues as the type of font and whether all capital letters are used can influence how easy a ballot is to navigate.
40. Niemi and Herrnson, "Beyond the Butterfly," p. 317.
41. Kimball and Kropf, "Ballot Design and Unrecorded Votes."
42. Niemi and Herrnson, "Beyond the Butterfly."
43. In Rhode Island, the length of term of the president is not listed.
44. A person could argue that term length might be an important piece of information for voters to have because they need to know how long they might be "stuck" with the elected official. Longer term lengths, then, could make people take their votes for these offices more seriously. In other words, they might try to be more informed about the candidates, the longer the term is. The problem with this argument, however, is that by the time voters receive this information (when they are in the voting booth), it is too late to research the candidates' positions and qualifications.
45. Wattenberg, McAllister, and Salvanto, "How Voting Is Like Taking an SAT Test"; Kimball, Owens, and Keeney, "Residual Votes and Political Representation."
46. Niemi and Herrnson, "Beyond the Butterfly," pp. 320–321.
47. Ibid.
48. However, if anything, the movement seems to be away from the straight-ticket option. Missouri abolished straight-ticket voting in 2006; New Hampshire did so in 2007.

6 Voting Machines

1. National Commission on Federal Election Reform, *Final Report of the National Commission on Election Reform*, p. 50.
2. Caltech/MIT Voting Technology Project, *Voting: What Is, What Could Be*.
3. Ansolabehere and Stewart, "Residual Votes Attributable to Technology," p. 365.
4. Caltech/MIT Voting Technology Project, *Voting: What Is, What Could Be*; United States General Accounting Office, *Statistical Analysis of Factors*.
5. See Alvarez and Hall, *Electronic Elections*, chapter 4.
6. Alvarez and Hall, *Electronic Elections*, p. 21; Brace, "Nation Sees Drop in Use of Electronic Voting Equipment." At the time of this writing, the percentage of counties using different types of voting equipment in the 2010 midterm elections was not available. However, in an email to me dated April 30, 2010, Kimball W. Brace, the President of Election Data Services, an organization that actively tracks the use of voting equipment, indicated that he did not expect significant changes in 2010.
7. Brace, "Nation Sees Drop in Use of Electronic Voting Equipment."
8. Alvarez and Hall, *Electronic Elections*, p. 21.
9. Alvarez, Sinclair, and Wilson, "Counting Ballots and the 2000 Election," p. 39.
10. Brace, "Nation Sees Drop in Use of Electronic Voting Equipment."
11. Ibid.
12. Alvarez and Hall, *Electronic Elections*, p. 21.
13. Ansolabehere and Stewart, "Residual Votes Attributable to Technology," p. 373.
14. Brace, "Nation Sees Drop in Use of Electronic Voting Equipment."
15. Stewart, "Residual Vote in the 2004 Election."
16. Whether a person's vote is counted may also be a function of how local elections are administered. See Caltech/MIT Voting Technology Project, *Voting: What Is, What Could Be*.
17. Ibid., p. 21.
18. Ansolabehere and Stewart, "Residual Votes Attributable to Technology"; Knack and Kropf, "Voided Ballots in the 1996 Presidential Elections"; Ansolabehere, "Voting Machines, Race, and Equal Protection."
19. Ansolabehere and Stewart, "Residual Votes Attributable to Technology," p. 365.
20. Knack and Kropf, "Who Uses Inferior Voting Technology?" Although, see Ansolabehere, "Voting Machines, Race, and Equal Protection." He finds that, although heavily minority *counties* are not more likely to use punch card ballots, minority *voters* are more apt to do so.
21. Sinclair and Alvarez, "Who Overvotes, Who Undervotes, Using Punchcards?" See, also, Alvarez, Sinclair, and Wilson, "Counting Ballots and the 2000 Election."
22. Tomz and Van Houweling, "How Does Voting Equipment Affect the Racial Gap in Voided Ballots?"
23. Stewart, "Residual Vote in the 2004 Election."
24. Caltech/MIT Voting Technology Report, *Voting: What Is, What Could Be*, p. 21.
25. Knack and Kropf, "Voided Ballots in the 1996 Presidential Election."
26. Tomz and Van Houweling, "How Does Voting Equipment Affect the Racial Gap in Voided Ballots?"
27. Caltech/MIT Voting Technology Report, *Voting: What Is, What Could Be*, p. 21. See, also, Ansolabehere and Stewart, "Residual Votes Attributable to

Technology." Paper ballots also performed well in Knack and Kropf's study of voided ballots and the 1996 presidential election, although not as well as lever machines. Knack and Kropf, "Voided Ballots in the 1996 Presidential Election."

28. Caltech/MIT Voting Technology Report, *Voting: What Is, What Could Be*, p. 21.
29. Ansolabehere and Stewart, "Residual Votes Attributable to Technology."
30. Tomz and Van Houweling, "How Does Voting Equipment Affect the Racial Gap in Voided Ballots?"
31. Farrington, "Study."
32. The bill did not pass.
33. Tomz and Van Houweling, "How Does Voting Equipment Affect the Racial Gap in Voided Ballots?"; Knack and Kropf, "Voided Ballots in the 1996 Presidential Election."
34. Illinois recently implemented optical scan machines that informed voters if they had any undervotes on the ballot. The reform appeared to be quite unpopular, not only from county clerks who had little time to install and test the machines, but from voters who complained that the notification violates the right to a secret ballot. Many voters purposely do not vote for certain offices. Although a DRE machine can highlight privately any offices for which votes were not cast, with the optical scan machine the election judge often read the error in a voice that could be heard clearly by others in the room (Vock, "New Illinois Undervote Law Not Overly Loved.")
35. Caltech/MIT Voting Technology Report, *Voting: What Is, What Could Be*, p. 21. Ansolabehere and Stewart find the same result in their analysis of presidential elections, but note that the DRE machines have less error in gubernatorial and Senate elections. Ansolabehere and Stewart, "Residual Votes Attributable to Technology."
36. Caltech/MIT Voting Technology Report, *Voting: What Is, What Could Be*, p. 23.
37. Stewart, "Residual Vote in the 2004 Election," p. 168.
38. Alvarez and Hall, *Electronic Elections*, p. 25.
39. Ibid.
40. Herrnson, et al., "Early Appraisals of Electronic Voting."
41. Herrnson, et al., "Voters' Evaluations of Electronic Voting Systems." However, certain groups were more likely to need to request help when using the machines.
42. Stein, et al., "Voting Technology, Election Administration, and Voter Performance."
43. See, also, Ansolabehere and Stewart, "Residual Votes Attributable to Technology."
44. Barr, Bishop, and Gondree, "Fixing Federal E-Voting Standards," p. 21.
45. Brennan Center for Justice, *The Machinery of Democracy*, p. 24.
46. Ibid., p. 26.
47. See Fund, *Stealing Elections*, pp. 118–129.
48. Stewart, "Election Technology and the Voting Experience in 2008." The length of time waiting is not likely due to the fact that it takes people longer to vote using DREs (as I noted, studies find that people can vote on DREs as quickly as optical scan equipment), but because jurisdictions generally can buy fewer electronic machines.
49. Caltech/MIT Voting Technology Report, *Voting: What Is, What Could Be*, pp. 23–24.
50. Ibid., p. 23.

51. Quoted in Fund, *Stealing Elections*, p. 115.
52. Ibid., p. 114.
53. For a more detailed rebuttal of the concerns regarding the security of electronic voting, see Alvarez and Hall, *Electronic Elections*.
54. Stewart, "Assessment of Voting Systems," p. 263.
55. See Brennan Center for Justice, *The Machinery of Democracy*.
56. Norden, et al., *Post-Election Audits*, p. 31.
57. Data obtained from the homepage of VerifiedVoting.org (accessed on May 3, 2010). There are different models of audits, but discussion of these is beyond the scope of this chapter. If readers are interested, they should consult Norden, et al., *Post-Election Audits*. Also, I agree with Norden, et al., that audits should not just be conducted for in-person voting, but absentee and early voting as well.
58. Alvarez and Hall, *Point, Click, & Vote*, p. 27.
59. Alvarez and Hall, *Electronic Elections*, p. 71.
60. Alvarez and Hall, *Point, Click, & Vote*, p. 9.
61. Ibid., p. 16.
62. Brennan Center for Justice, *The Machinery of Democracy*.
63. Alvarez and Hall, *Point, Click, & Vote*, pp. 100–101.
64. Ibid., p. 86.
65. Ibid., p. 134.
66. Ibid., p. 49.
67. Ibid., p. 52. However, in their study of Internet voting during the 2004 Michigan Democratic primary, Prevost and Schaffner, "Digital Divide or Just Another Absentee Ballot?," do not find any evidence of bias base on race and other socioeconomic factors
68. Alvarez and Hall, *Point, Click, & Vote*, p. 10.
69. Ibid., p. 17.
70. Although there are variations of each system.
71. United States General Accounting Office, *Statistical Analysis of Factors*; Caltech/MIT Voting Technology Report, *Voting: What Is, What Could Be*.
72. Stewart, "Residual Vote in the 2004 Election."

7 The Redistricting Process

1. Barone and Ujifusa, *The Almanac of American Politics*, p. 186.
2. It is possible that districts will be redrawn before the new census if the Supreme Court declares the district plan to be unconstitutional. Also, with the mid-decade Texas redistricting discussed later in the chapter, it is possible that new district maps will be implemented before a new census is conducted.
3. It is quite possible that a state could actually have a net increase in population but lose representation because the state's population did not grow as quickly as other states' populations.
4. Davidson, Oleszek, and Lee, *Congress and Its Members*, p. 44.
5. Even a state with only one representative has a redistricting procedure in place, however, if the time comes when its representation increases.
6. For the purposes of this chapter, I am only concerned with the redistricting process for the US House of Representatives, not for state legislative or other local legislative districts.
7. For an overview of each state's redistricting process, see McDonald, "A Comparative Analysis of Redistricting Institutions in the United States."
8. Gelman and King, "Enhancing Democracy Through Legislative Redistricting," p. 541.

9. Another way to think of this discrepancy in representation is the following: Districts A and B each have five people who live in the district while District C has 100. Individuals in Districts A and B have enormous power over who the districts' representatives will be, but the citizens in District C have significantly less. Moreover, when voting on laws, each district's representative gets one vote meaning that the representatives from Districts A and B, representing a total of 10 people, can out vote the representative of District C, representing 100 people.

10. *Colegrove v. Green*, 328 U.S. 549 (1946).

11. *Baker v. Carr*, 369 U.S. 186 (1962).

12. The *Baker* case only applied to state assemblies. In 1964 in *Reynolds v. Sims*, the Court ruled that equal populations in districts were required for both chambers in a state's legislature. *Reynolds v. Sims*, 377 U.S. 533 (1964).

13. The justification for "one person, one vote" was different in *Wesberry* because the equal protection clause only applies to the states. Instead, the Court argued that Article I, Section 2 required that states draw their districts on the basis of equal representation. *Wesberry v. Sanders*, 376 U.S. 1 (1964).

14. States are permitted up to 1 percent population deviations for congressional districts if there is a valid state interest in doing so.

15. *Karcher v. Daggett*, 426 U.S. 725 (1983).

16. *Vieth v. Pennsylvania*, 195 F. Supp. 2nd 672 (M.D. Pa., 2002).

17. Arizona and Iowa use an explicit formula to determine if a district is compact.

18. See Stevens' dissenting opinion in *Miller v. Johnson*, 515 U.S. 900 (1995).

19. *Beer v. U.S.*, 425 U.S. 130 (1976).

20. Cain, MacDonald, and McDonald, "From Equality to Fairness," p. 7.

21. See, for example, *Jeffers v. Clinton*, 740 F. Supp. 585 (E.D. Ark. 1990).

22. However, there is a heated debate over whether majority–minority districts have improved representation for minorities because they have also led to the election of more conservative Republicans. As redistricting scholar Charles S. Bullock writes, "After 1994, Republicans received handsome rewards while black Democrats were becoming an increasing numerical force within the minority party. The replacement of moderate white Democrats with conservative Republicans, even with the addition of a few African American legislative seats, bodes ill for the ability of African American legislators to find the allies they need to achieve their policy goals." Bullock, "Affirmative Action Districts," p. 23. For further debate on the subject, see Shotts, "Does Racial Redistricting Cause Conservative Policy Outcomes?" and "Racial Redistricting's Alleged Perverse Effects," and Lublin and Voss's response ("The Missing Middle.").

23. See, for example, *League of United Latin American Citizens, et al. v. Rick Perry et al.*, 126 S. Ct. 2594 (2006). Although, see *Georgia v. Ashcroft*, 123 S.Ct. 2498 (2003) for a case where the Court allowed the dilution of minority populations. In *Ashcroft* the Court ruled that there are a variety of factors to promote minority interests in politics, and that packing minority populations in districts was but one.

24. *Miller v. Johnson*, 515 U.S. 900 (1995).

25. Thompson, *Just Elections*, p. 40.

26. Texas law requires that two-thirds of the members of the state House and Senate be present for a vote.

27. Texas Republicans precipitated the re-redistricting by refusing to compromise on a congressional map in 2001, throwing redistricting to the courts and giving Republicans the argument that the legislature should have the chance to exercise its authority in redistricting.

28. *Davis v. Bandemer*, 478 U.S. 109 (1986). The standard for declaring a partisan gerrymander to be unconstitutional is so high that it is unlikely that the Court will *ever* overturn a partisan gerrymander in a congressional district. The standard is "evidence of continued frustration of the will of a majority of voters or effective denial to a minority of voters of a fair chance to influence the political process." Quoted in Mann, "Redistricting Reform," p. 5.

29. McDonald, "Drawing the Line," p. 15.

30. Persily, "Forty Years in the Political Thicket," p. 80.

31. Cain, MacDonald, and McDonald, "From Equality to Fairness," p. 19.

32. Drawing competitive districts (i.e., those with roughly equal number of registered Democrats and Republicans) does not guarantee competitive elections because of other factors, including incumbency advantage. But it is more likely that competitive elections will emerge in competitive districts instead of noncompetitive ones.

33. Thompson, *Fair Elections*, p. 6.

34. In presidential elections, see Kim, Petrocik, and Enokson, "Voter Turnout Among the American States"; Filer, Kenny, and Morton, "Redistribution, Income, and Voting"; Shachar and Nalebuff, "Follow the Leader." In gubernatorial elections, see Patterson and Calideira, "Getting Out the Vote." For House elections, see Cox and Munger, "Closeness, Expenditures, and Turnout"; Cox, "Closeness and Turnout"; Caldeira, Patterson, and Markko, "The Mobilization of Voters in Congressional Elections"; Gilliam, "Influences of Voter Turnout." For state legislative elections, see Caldeira and Patterson, "Contextual Influences on Participation."

35. Filer and Kenny, "Voter Turnout and the Benefits of Voting."

36. Westlye, "Competitiveness of Senate Seats."

37. Rosenstone and Hansen, *Mobilization, Participation, and Democracy in America*; Cox and Munger, "Closeness, Expenditures, and Turnout"; Wielhouwer and Lockerbie, "Party Contacting and Political Participation."

38. Bauer and Hibbing, "Which Incumbents Lose in House Elections," p. 262 (emphasis in original). Not everyone buys this Downsian view of the relationship between competition and accountability (Buchler, "Competition, Representation, and Redistricting"; Brunell, "Rethinking Redistricting"). Prominent scholars of congressional elections have long argued that the lack of competitive elections does not affect representation because incumbents never feel safe no matter what their margin of victory (Fenno, *Home Style*; Mann, *Unsafe at Any Margin*). Cohen, "Perceptions of Electoral Insecurity," makes the same argument regarding state legislative elections. Additionally, Canes-Wrone, Brady, and Cogan, "Out of Step, Out of Office," find that ideologically extreme members of Congress still get punished by voters even though elections are not competitive.

39. Quoted in Hulse, "Mapping the Causes of Corruption,"

40. Abramowitz, Alexander, and Gunning, "Don't Blame Redistricting for Uncompetitive Elections," p. 87.

41. Jacobson, "Competition in U.S. Congressional Elections."

42. Broder, "No Vote Necessary"; Brownstein, "Close Races Go the Way of Rotary Phones."

43. Brownstein, "Close Races Go the Way of Rotary Phones," p. A13.

44. McDonald, "Drawing the Line on District Competition"; McDonald, "Redistricting and Competitive Elections"; Swain, Borrelli, and Reed, "Partisan Consequences of the Post-1990 Redistricting"; Cain, MacDonald, and McDonald, "From Equality to Fairness."

45. Abramowitz, Alexander, and Gunning, "Don't Blame Redistricting for Uncompetitive Elections"; Oppenheimer, "Deep Red and Blue Congressional Districts"; Glazer, Grofman, and Robbins, "Partisan and Incumbency Effects of 1970 Redistricting"; Erikson, "Malapportionment, Gerrymandering, and Party Fortunes in Congressional Elections." Jacoboson, "Competition in U.S. Congressional Elections," argues that redistricting is part of the reason for the decrease in competition in the House, but a small part.
46. Abramowitz, Alexander, and Gunning, "Don't Blame Redistricting for Uncompetitive Elections." See, also, Oppenheimer, "Deep Red and Blue Congressional Districts."
47. Gelman and King, "Enhancing Democracy Through Legislative Redistricting," p. 542.
48. Ibid., p. 541.
49. Brunell, "Rethinking Redistricting," p. 77. See, also, Brunell, *Redistricting and Representation.*
50. Barreto and Streb, "Barn Burners and Burn Out."
51. Brunell, Rethinking Redistricting," p. 83.
52. Ibid.
53. Cain, MacDonald, and McDonald, "From Equality to Fairness," p. 27.
54. Ibid., pp. 25–26.
55. Another issue is that even if district populations are equal today, tomorrow they may not be because people are constantly moving, dying, or being born, but redistricting is generally only done once every 10 years. Still, roughly equal district populations are needed to keep map drawers from drawing one district with, as an example, several million Republicans in it and several others with only a few thousand Democrats. District population will never be perfectly equal for long, but we have to begin some place.
56. Ansolabehere, Gerber, and Snyder, "Equal Votes, Equal Money."
57. Another way to think about this is that Wyoming has just as much influence over the passing of policy in the Senate than California, even though California has roughly 70 times the number of people as Wyoming.
58. *Georgia v. Ashcroft*, 539 U.S. 461 (2003).
59. Lublin and Voss, "The Missing Middle"; Bullock, "Affirmative Action Districts"; Epstein and O'Halloran, "Gerrymanders as Tradeoffs."
60. It is possible that, although minority incumbents may be reelected whether they represent a majority–minority district, minority representatives may have a more difficult time getting elected in the first place when they cannot rely on the incumbency advantage. However, the fact that so many black elected officials supported the Georgia plan may be an indication that this concern is not warranted.
61. Ansolabehere, Snyder, and Stewart, "Old Voters, New Voters, and the Personal Vote."
62. Griffin, "Electoral Competition and Democratic Responsiveness."
63. Ansolabehere, et al., "The Decline of Competition in U.S. Primary Elections."
64. I should point out that the Supreme Court disagrees with me. See the *Nader v. Schaffer* case discussed in the next chapter.
65. Thompson, *Just Elections*, p. 8.
66. Arizona Independent Redistricting Commission, "Proposition 106."
67. Thompson, *Fair Elections*, p. 41.
68. National Conference of State Legislatures, "Redistricting Commissions."
69. Arizona Independent Redistricting Commission, "Proposition 106."

70. For example, following part "E" in the Arizona redistricting plan might lead to unbiased districts in some states, but give one political party an advantage in another.

8 Presidential Primaries

1. Cook, *The Presidential Nominating Process*, p. 135.
2. This is not always the case, however, as some states require that a candidate receive a majority of the vote in the primary, otherwise the top two candidates will compete in a runoff at a later date.
3. Technically, the candidate is not officially nominated until the party's convention held during the summer, but in recent presidential elections it has been clear well before the convention which candidate had the most pledged delegates to win the nomination.
4. In caucuses, delegates at the first stage of the caucus are then sent to county, congressional district, and/or state conventions to represent a candidate. The later caucus rounds are mostly symbolic, however, as it is clear who will win the state's delegates after the first round of the caucus.
5. Cook, *The Presidential Nominating Process*, p. 13.
6. Johnson actually won the primary, receiving 49.5 percent of the vote to McCarthy's 42.4 percent, but his showing was especially weak for an incumbent. Shortly after McCarthy's strong showing in New Hampshire, Kennedy entered the race, no doubt another catalyst for Johnson's decision not to seek the nomination.
7. Kanthak and Morton, "Turnout and Primaries."
8. However, most of the empirical research finds little evidence for so-called malicious cross-over voting (Sides, Cohen, and Citrin, "The Causes and Consequences of Cross-over Voting"). Donovan, "The Limbaugh Effect," finds some evidence of cross-over voting in the 2008 Democratic primaries, but it is unclear whether this voting is sincere or malicious. He also notes that evidence of cross-over voting occurred before Limbaugh encouraged Republicans to do so.
9. *Nader v. Schaffer*, 429 U.S. 989 (1976).
10. See Kanthak and Williams, "Parties and Primaries," for a more thorough discussion of the *Nader* case.
11. Ibid., p. 13.
12. *California Democratic Party v. Jones*, 530 U.S. 567 (2000).
13. *Democratic Party v. Reed* 343 F.3d 1198 (2003).
14. *Washington State Grange v. Washington State Republican Party* 552 U.S. 442 (2008).
15. Sides, Cohen, and Citrin, "The Causes and Consequences of Cross-over Voting."
16. At one point the threshold was set at 20 percent in caucuses and 25 percent in primaries. These rules worked against Jesse Jackson in 1988 when Jackson received strong support, but regularly fell just short of the threshold. While Jackson won 19 percent of the popular vote, he obtained only 10 percent of the delegates (Wayne, *The Road to the White House*, p. 152). As a result, the threshold was lowered to 15 percent for both primaries and caucuses and it has remained that way since.
17. Buell and Sigelman, *Nominating the President*, p. 12.
18. Bartels, *Presidential Primaries and the Dynamics of Public Choice*.
19. Arbour, "Even Closer, Even Longer," p. 3.

20. Geer, "Rules Governing Presidential Primaries."
21. Wayne, *The Road to the White House*, p. 111.
22. Geer, "Rules Governing Presidential Primaries."
23. Republicans also have their version of superdelegates. In 2008, each state and the territories received three ex officio slots (one for the state party chair, and one each for the two national committee members). However, Republicans have substantially fewer superdelegates than Democrats.
24. Some states require that a candidate receive a majority of the vote in the primary to win the nomination. If a candidate fails to win a majority of the vote, then the candidates with the two highest vote totals enter into a runoff election, which is held on a separate day.
25. Lyndon, "Humphrey at 30% in Poll."
26. See, for example, Kifner, "Carter Campaigns in New Hampshire"; Ayres, "Carter's Candor Is Becoming an Issue."
27. Busch and Mayer, "The Front-Loading Problem," p. 24. (emphasis in original)
28. Although even the strategy of retail politics seems to be changing as candidates spent several million dollars advertising on television in these two states during the 2008 nomination season. For example, the Obama campaign spent more than $8 million on television ads in Iowa, while the Clinton and Romney campaigns each spent $6.5 million. "Economics."
29. Busch and Mayer, "The Front-Loading Problem," pp. 10–11.
30. Bill Clinton ran unopposed for the Democratic nomination.
31. Busch and Mayer, "The Front-Loading Problem," p. 4.
32. Although a state like Iowa held its caucus before February 5, it was not punished because technically the delegates were not awarded until after February 5.
33. Busch and Mayer, "The Front-Loading Problem," p. 33.
34. Burden, "The Nominations," p. 31.
35. Pillsbury and Johannesen, *America Goes to the Polls.*
36. McDonald, "2008 Presidential Nomination Contest Turnout Rates."
37. Wayne, *The Road to the White House*, p. 311.
38. A national primary that maintains delegates but holds all primaries and caucuses on the same day does not have this advantage.
39. Patterson, *Vanishing Voter*, p. 152.
40. Busch and Mayer, "The Front-Loading Problem," p. 23.
41. Abramson, et al., " 'Sophisticated Voting'."
42. See Geer, *In Defense of Negativity.*
43. There is another argument made against the national primary, which is that small states will be ignored by candidates and become irrelevant. Because the same argument is made against abolishing the electoral college, I address the problems with this argument in chapter 9.
44. Another argument against eliminating presidential primaries that will appeal to supporters of a two-party system is that removing the primary process may encourage more independent candidates. Under the current system, a candidate who runs in the primary and loses is unlikely to enter the general election as an Independent because they have run once and were rejected presumably by the people who should be most likely to support them. If the party elite chooses the nominee, then presidential aspirants who have been passed over may throw their hats into the ring in the general election because they believe that they can appeal to voters who never received the chance to nominate them.
45. Cook, *The Presidential Nominating Process*, p. 149.

46. See Hasen, "Too Plain for Argument?," for a discussion of the constitutional questions raised by a national law determining the nomination calendar.

9 The Electoral College

1. Initially it was the top five candidates, but the Twelfth Amendment changed the number of candidates to three.
2. It was not even clear that there should be only one executive, as many of the founders worried that a single executive would wield too much power.
3. Collier and Collier, *Decision in Philadelphia*, p. 297.
4. Ibid., p. 298.
5. The congressional plan had actually been supported and overturned several times during deliberations.
6. Collier and Collier, *Decision in Philadelphia*, p. 298.
7. Hardaway, *The Electoral College and the Constitution*, p. 13.
8. Quoted in Raskin, "Neither the Red States nor the Blue States but the United States," p. 188.
9. Collier and Collier, *Decision in Philadelphia*, p. 303.
10. Lutz, et al., "The Electoral College in Historical and Philosophical Perspective," p. 33.
11. Indeed, the founders did not view the Electoral College as sacrosanct, as it was amended almost immediately with the adoption of the Twelfth Amendment.
12. Schumaker and Loomis, "Reaching a Collective Judgment," p. 183.
13. In Christopher Collier's and James Lincoln Collier's exceptional book on the Constitutional Convention, *Decision in Philadelphia*, I see no evidence that promoting federalism was a goal of the founders when discussing the Electoral College.
14. Rakove, "Accidental Electors," p. A35.
15. Quoted in Edwards, *Why the Electoral College Is Bad for America*, p. 116.
16. Glenn, "The Electoral College," p. 7.
17. "Candidate Visit Map." The number of states that candidates did not visit would likely have been marginally higher if Barack Obama and Sarah Palin were not candidates for the presidency and vice-presidency, respectively. Obama was raised in Hawaii and Palin was the governor of Alaska, two states that are visited infrequently during most presidential campaigns, but that received visits in 2008.
18. Travel to a few other states was inflated. For example, Dick Cheney was the only candidate to visit Wyoming (he did so five times), but Wyoming is Cheney's home state.
19. Shaw, *The Race to 270*, pp. 86–87.
20. Ibid.
21. Edwards, *Why the Electoral College Is Bad for America*. See, also, Shaw, "The Effect of TV Ads."
22. Indeed, in 2008 none of the candidates made a single visit to Alabama.
23. Edwards, *Why the Electoral College Is Bad for America*.
24. Ibid., p. 96.
25. Ibid., p. 94.
26. Quoted in Ibid., p 95 (emphasis in original).
27. Ornstein, "No Need to Repeal the Electoral College."
28. Edwards, *Why the Electoral College Is Bad for America*, p. 124 (emphasis is original).
29. Raskin, "Neither the Red States nor the Blue States but the United States," p. 189.

30. To be fair, the likelihood of a recount would depend on the rules created by a popular vote election. For example, some states have provisions that trigger recounts automatically if the vote margin separating the candidates is within a certain percentage. If national legislation for a popular vote election included such a trigger provision of, say, 0.5%, then a national recount would be possible

31. Cigler, et al., "Changing the Electoral College," p. 87.

32. Lau and Redlawsk, "Voting Correctly."

33. By 1836, all states but South Carolina chose their electors through the popular vote. South Carolina did not use the popular vote to choose its electors until after the Civil War.

34. In 1800, Thomas Jefferson tied Aaron Burr in electoral votes, but no accurate count of the popular vote exists. Presidential scholar George Edwards argues that Nixon actually won the popular vote in 1960. See Edwards, *Why the Electoral College Is Bad for America*, pp. 48–51. Edwards also notes 15 other presidential races where a change of roughly 75,000 votes or less in several states would have led to a popular vote winner, electoral vote loser (p. 53).

35. Rakove, "Accidental Electors," p. A35.

36. Lind, "75 Stars."

37. Edwards, *Why the Electoral College Is Bad for America*, p. 119.

38. Hill and McKee, "The Electoral College, Mobilization, and Turnout"; McDonald, "The Return of the Voter"; Wolak, "The Consequences of Presidential Battleground Strategies for Citizen Engagement." Although, see Holbrook and McClurg, "The Mobilization of Core Supporters." Also, see Stein et al., "Citizen Participation and Electoral College Reform," for an argument that turnout would not increase under other presidential election systems.

39. Edwards, *Why the Electoral College Is Bad for America*.

40. Mellman, Electoral College Bias Probe." Mellman does indicate that which party benefits under the Electoral College may be time dependent. However, he argues that no consistent, systematic bias exists in favor of either party.

41. Schumaker, "Bush, Gore, and the Issues of Electoral Reform," p. 2.

42. One proposal that I do not examine, but emerged as a possible reform in the 1970s is the bonus plan. Under the bonus plan, 436 of the electoral votes (the House allocation plus the District of Columbia) would be decided state by state, as is currently the case. The remaining 102 electoral votes would go to the popular vote winner. This reform is an attempt to get around the problem of a popular vote winner/electoral vote loser scenario. Because it is no longer advocated strongly today (and because of space consideration), I do not discuss this proposal further.

43. In 2008, it appeared that North Carolina would become the third state to allocate their electors by district. The bill passed one house of the state legislature and was poised to pass the second and be signed into law by the governor. At the last minute, however, the North Carolina Democratic Party pulled its support for the bill at the request of the national Democratic Party. Republicans in California began to push for the state to allocate their electors by district. Although the Democratic Party thought they would benefit from a district plan in North Carolina, they would be hurt severely by such a plan in California. Democrats did not want to be on the record as supporting a district plan in North Carolina but then opposing one in California. The North Carolina example illustrates how difficult it is to actually reform the selection of electors. Ironically, had the Democrats continued to push the plan in North Carolina, it would have been detrimental to Barack Obama because he ended up winning the state.

44. There is some evidence, however, that a district plan would benefit the Republican Party because Democrats are more highly concentrated in districts. See Jacobson, "Competition in U.S. Congressional Elections."
45. Wayne, *The Road to the White House*, p. 323.
46. Schumaker and Loomis, "Reaching a Collective Judgment," p. 196.
47. There are two different versions of how a proportional plan would be enacted. First, the states could decide to allocate their electors proportionally. This plan would be the easiest to enact because each state could decide on its own to do so (similar to Nebraska and Maine deciding to allocate their electors by congressional district). Second, the electors would be abolished, but the Electoral College would remain intact. There would no longer be a formal vote among electors; instead each state would simply allocate its electoral votes proportionally. This plan would be much more difficult to enact because it would require a constitutional amendment.
48. Wayne, *The Road to the White House*, pp. 323–325.
49. One possibility would be to enact the system used in Louisiana. In Louisiana, all candidates from any party run in an election. If no candidate receives a majority of the vote, then the top two candidates face each other in a runoff. To enact this system at the presidential level would require the elimination of parties' primaries, something that they are unlikely to support. It could also lead to unmanageable numbers of candidates entering the race. A few dozen Democrats and Republicans might decide to run, not to mention a number of third-party and independent candidates, and all would be on the same ballot. The current presidential primary process weeds out almost all of these candidates making the decision in November much less onerous.
50. See the preceding chapter for how this process works.
51. Schumaker and Loomis, "Reaching a Collective Judgment," p. 194.
52. The Twenty-third Amendment, which gave the District of Columbia three electoral votes, technically was an amendment to the Electoral College. However, the Twenty-third Amendment simply added to the total number of electoral votes; it did not modify the structure of the Electoral College.
53. Nebraska has a unicameral legislature.
54. See the debate between Muller, "More Thoughts on the Compact Clause and the National Popular Vote" and Hendricks, "Popular Election of the President."
55. It is believed that the elector simply made a mistake when writing his or her vote. None of Minnesota's electors in 2004 admitted to voting for Edwards for president. Since electors in Minnesota cast secret ballots, it is unknown who cast the "faithless" vote.
56. Schumaker and Loomis, "Reaching a Collective Judgment," p. 201.
57. National Conference of State Legislators, "The Electoral College."
58. Levinson, "I Dissent!," p. B02.
59. Edwards notes seven elections that could have been decided by the House had roughly 53,000 votes or less changed in a few states. Edwards, *Why the Electoral College Is Bad for America*, p. 62.
60. The Twelfth Amendment stipulates that the Senate vote for the two vice-presidential candidates who received the most electoral votes instead of the top three candidates, as is the case in the House of Representatives.

10 Campaign Finance

1. Quoted in Witcover, *No Way to Pick a President*, p. 74.
2. In this chapter, I am only concerned with campaign finance law in federal elections.

3. For a good overview of the history of campaign finance laws before Federal Election Campaign Act (FECA), see Smith, *Unfree Speech*, ch. 2.
4. If a state's law required that a candidate receive a majority of the vote to win, then individuals could donate $1,000 to a candidate during the runoff election as well.
5. *Buckley v. Valeo*, 424 U.S. 1 (1976).
6. The Court also upheld the disclosure requirement and the public funding for presidential campaigns coupled with voluntary spending limits.
7. *Buckley v. Valeo*, 424 U.S. 1 (1976), p. 19.
8. Hershey, *Party Politics in America*, p. 235.
9. State and local parties can still accept soft money from unions and corporations up to $10,000.
10. Because of the provision adjusting for inflation, individuals who contributed money during the 2009–2010 election cycle were permitted to donate up to $2,400 per election to federal candidates, up to $30,400 per year to national party committees, and a combined total of up to $115,500 during the two-year period to all federal campaigns, parties, and other political committees.
11. *McConnell v. Federal Election Commission*, 124 S.Ct. 619 (2003).
12. Cigler, "Issue Advocacy Electioneering," p. 71.
13. *McConnell v. Federal Election Commission*, 124 S.Ct. 619 (2003), p. 3 of Justice Scalia's dissent.
14. Ibid., p. 118 of the majority opinion.
15. They cannot coordinate with a political party either.
16. Hershey, *Party Politics in America*, 12th ed., p. 237.
17. Ibid.
18. Hershey, *Party Politics in America*, 14th ed., p 219.
19. Hershey, *Party Politics in America*, 12th ed., p. 238.
20. Hershey, *Party Politics in America*, 14th ed., p 219.
21. *Federal Election Commission v. Wisconsin Right to Life Inc.*, No. 06–969 (2007).
22. *Davis v. FEC*, 128 S. Ct. 2759 (2008).
23. *Citizens United v. FEC* 130 S. Ct. 876 (2010).
24. Balakrishnan and Heintz, "Corporate Control of Our Democracy."
25. Quoted in Liptak, "Supreme Court Affirms Ban on Soft Money."
26. Hershey, *Party Politics in America*, 14th ed., p. 218
27. Ibid., p. 220
28. Ibid., p. 216 (emphasis in original).
29. Thurber and Long, "Brian Baird's 'Ring of Fire'," p. 188.
30. Opensecrets.org. "2010 Election Overview: Incumbent Advantage."
31. Abramowitz, "Incumbency, Campaign Spending, and the Decline of Competition in U.S. House Elections." See, also, Abramowitz, Alexander, and Gunning, "Don't Blame Redistricting for Uncompetitive Elections."
32. Barbour, et al., *Keeping the Republic*, p. 270.
33. Quoted in Smith, *Unfree Speech*, p. 51.
34. Farrar-Myers, "Campaign Finance," p. 47.
35. Another proposal that reformers advocate is free media time provided to candidates. Because this idea is essentially another version of public financing, I do not discuss it due to space limitations.
36. Minor party candidates may also qualify for matching funds, although they receive significantly less money than the Democratic or Republican candidates who qualify.

37. If candidates are on the ballot in more than one primary on a given day, they only have to win at least 10 percent in one primary. If candidates fail to win 10 percent of the vote in two consecutive primaries, then they must win 20 percent of the vote in a primary to requalify for matching funds.

38. Third parties may qualify for federal funds if the party's candidate received more than 5 percent of the vote in the previous election. The amount of money given to the third-party candidate is significantly less than the amount given to the Democratic and Republican candidates. For example, as the Reform Party candidate, Patrick Buchanan received $12.6 million in the 2000 presidential election based on Ross Perot's showing in the 1996 election. However, George W. Bush and Al Gore each received $67.6 million.

39. "Fair Elections Now Act Bill Summary."

40. John McCain originally indicated that he would accept matching funds. However, because the Republican field winnowed quickly, McCain's fund-raising grew substantially making it so that accepting matching funds would have actually limited his ability to spend.

41. Hershey, *Party Politics in America*, 14th ed., p. 218.

42. Another issue regarding public financing of congressional elections is who should qualify for such funds. Should every major party candidate receive it? How do we determine who qualifies for public funding in the primaries? What about third-party candidates? Certainly these questions can be answered, but it might take some tweaking to get the system to work efficiently.

43. Mayer and Wood, "The Impact of Public Financing on Electoral Competitiveness," Basham and Zelder, "Does Cleanliness Lead to Competitiveness?," and Malbin and Gais, "*The Day after Reform*," all find no evidence that publicly financed campaigns lead to more competitive elections. Donnay and Ramsden, "Public Financing of Legislative Elections," conclude that Minnesota's system of public financing of state legislative elections did make elections more competitive, but then go on to write that the system "promises more competitive campaigns, but does not go far toward creating them." (p. 362). Mayer, Werner, and Williams, "Do Public Funding Programs Enhance Electoral Competition?," find evidence that in some states public financing has led to more competitive state legislative campaigns, but in other states it has not.

44. Basham and Zelder, "Does Cleanliness Lead to Competitiveness?" find that competition in Maine's state legislative elections actually *decreased* in the first election cycle after the state enacted publicly financed elections. Although, see Mayer, Werner, and Williams, "Do Public Funding Programs Enhance Electoral Competition?" for a competing view.

45. Abramowitz, "Incumbency, Campaign Spending, and the Decline of Competition in U.S. House Elections," p. 52.

46. Mayer and Wood, "The Impact of Public Financing on Electoral Competitiveness"; Basham and Zelder, "Does Cleanliness Lead to Competitiveness?"; General Accounting Office, *Campaign Finance Reform*. Although, see Mayer's more recent work where he finds that publicly financed state legislative elections made it more likely that challengers would run against incumbents (Mayer, Werner, and Williams, "Do Public Funding Programs Enhance Electoral Competition?").

47. The disclosure of any donation smaller than that seems unnecessary; we would not, for example, want to discourage a child who simply wants to donate her allowance to a candidate that inspired her from doing so by forcing her to go through the process of disclosure.

48. See Smith, *Unfree Speech*, and Samples, *The Fallacy of Campaign Finance Reform*, for two particularly thorough arguments against restrictions on campaign contributions.
49. Jacobson, "The Effects of Campaign Spending in House Elections"; Abramowitz, "Incumbency, Campaign Spending and the Decline of Competition." Although, see Gerber, "Estimating the Effects of Campaign Spending," and Green and Krasno, "Salvation for the Spendthrift Incumbent" for a competing view.
50. Coleman and Manna, "Congressional Spending and the Quality of Democracy"; Jacobson, *The Politics of Congressional Elections*, 6th edition, pp. 132–133.
51. Jacobson, "Enough Is Too Much," p. 192.
52. See Stratmann, "Do Low Contribution Limits Insulate Incumbents from Competition?" for a nice overview of some of these studies.
53. See Ansolabehere, de Figueiredo, and Snyder, "Why Is There So Little Money in Politics?" for numerous studies that find no significant relationship between campaign contributions and roll-call votes. See, also, Ansolabehere, Snyder, and Ueda, "Did Firms Profit from Soft Money?"
54. See Davidson and Oleszek, *Congress and Its Members*, pp. 283–292.
55. Smith, *Unfree Speech*, p. 59.
56. See Stimson, Mackuen, and Erikson, "Dynamic Representation"; Bartels, "Constituency Opinion and Congressional Policy Making"; De Boef and Stimson, "The Dynamic Structure of Congressional Elections"; Erikson, Wright, and McIver, *Statehouse Democracy*, for a small sampling of studies.
57. Thompson, *Just Elections*, p. 106.
58. Kingdon, *Agendas, Alternatives, and Public Policies*.
59. *Buckley v. Valeo*, 424 U.S. 1 (1976), pp 48–49.
60. Goodman, "The Internet," p. 109.

11 Conclusion: Moving Toward a Model Electoral Democracy

1. *Stephenson v. Ann Arbor Board of City Canvassers*, File No. 75–10166 AW (1975).
2. Ansolabehere and Gerber, "The Effects of Filing Fees and Petition Requirements on U.S. House Elections."
3. Hajnal and Lewis, "Municipal Institutions and Voter Turnout in Local Elections."

Bibliography

Abramowitz, Alan I. "Incumbency, Campaign Spending, and the Decline of Competition in U.S. House Elections." *Journal of Politics* 53 (1991): 34–56.

Abramowitz, Alan, Brad Alexander, and Matthew Gunning. "Don't Blame Redistricting for Uncompetitive Elections." *PS* 34 (2006): 87–90.

Abramson, Paul R., John H. Aldrich, Phil Paolino, and David W. Rohde. "'Sophisticated Voting' in the 1988 Presidential Primaries." *American Political Science Review* 86 (1992): 55–69.

Alvarez, R. Michael, and Thad E. Hall. *Point, Click, & Vote: The Future of Internet Voting.* Washington, D.C.: Brookings Institution Press, 2004.

Alvarez, R. Michael, and Thad E. Hall. "Controlling Democracy: The Principal-Agent Problems in Election Administration." *The Policy Studies Journal* 34 (2006): 491–510.

Alvarez, R. Michael, and Thad E. Hall. *Electronic Elections: The Perils and Promises of Digital Democracy.* Princeton, NJ: Princeton University Press, 2008.

Alvarez, R. Michael, D.E. "Betsy" Sinclair, and Catherine H. Wilson. "Counting Ballots and the 2000 Election: What Went Wrong?" In *Rethinking the Vote: The Politics and Prospects of American Election Reform*, eds. Ann N. Crigler, Marion R. Just, and Edward J. McCaffery. New York: Oxford University Press, 2004.

Ansolabehere, Stephen. "Voting Machines, Race, and Equal Protection." *Election Law Journal* 1 (2002): 61–70.

Ansolabehere, Stephen, and Alan Gerber. "The Effects of Filing Fees and Petition Requirements on U.S. House Elections." *Legislative Studies Quarterly* 21 (1996): 249–264.

Ansolabehere, Stephen, and Charles Stewart III. "Residual Votes Attributable to Technology." *Journal of Politics* 67 (2005): 365–389.

Ansolabehere, Stephen, John de Figueiredo, and James M. Snyder, Jr. "Why Is There So Little Money in U.S. Politics?" *Journal of Economic Perspectives* 17 (2003): 105–130.

Ansolabehere, Stephen, Alan Gerber, and James M. Snyder, Jr. "Equal Votes, Equal Money: Court-Ordered Redistricting and Public Expenditures in American States." *American Political Science Review* 96 (2002): 767–777.

Ansolabehere, Stephen, James M. Snyder, Jr., and Charles Stewart III. "Old Voters, New Voters, and the Personal Vote: Using Redistricting to Measure the Incumbency Advantage." *American Journal of Political Science* 44 (2000): 17–34.

Ansolabehere, Stephen, James M. Snyder, Jr., and Michiko Ueda. "Did Firms Profit from Soft Money?" *Election Law Journal* 3 (2004): 193–198.

Ansolabehere, Stephen, John Mark Hansen, Shigeo Hirano, and James M. Snyder, Jr. "The Decline of Competition in U.S. Primary Elections, 1908–2004." In *The Marketplace of Democracy: Electoral Competition and American Politics*, eds. Michael P. McDonald and John Samples. Washington, D.C.: Brookings Institution Press, 2006.

Arbour, Brain. "Even Closer, Even Longer: What If the 2008 Democratic Primary Used Republican Rules?" *The Forum* 7 (2009). Available at www.bepress.com/forum/vol7/iss2/art3 (accessed May 25, 2010).

Arizona Independent Redistricting Commission. "Proposition 106." Available at http://www.azredistricting.org/?page=prop106 (accessed June 26, 2007).

Aspin, Larry T., and William K. Hall. "Friends and Neighbors Voting in Judicial Retention Elections: A Research Note Comparing Trial and Appellate Court Elections." *Western Political Quarterly* 42 (1989): 587–596.

Ayres, B. Drummond, Jr. "Carter's Candor Is Becoming an Issue in the Campaign." *New York Times*, January 26, 1976: A34.

Bailey, Michael E. "The Heroic Presidency in the Era of Divided Government." *Perspectives on Political Science* 31 (2002): 35–46.

Baker, Russell. "Tips for Voters." *The New York Times*, November 2, 1996: A23.

Balakrishnan, Radhika, and James Heintz. "Corporate Control of Our Democracy: *Citizens United v. Federal Election Commission*." *Huffington Post* July 12, 2010. Available at http://www.huffingtonpost.com/radhika-balakrishnan/corporate-control-of-our_b_643095.html (accessed July 15, 2010).

"Ballots Made to Order." *The Union Leader*, August 20, 2006: B2.

Banducci, Susan A. "Searching for Ideological Consistency in Direct Legislation Voting." In *Citizens as Legislators*, eds. Shaun Bowler, Todd Donovan, and Caroline J. Tolbert. Columbus: The Ohio State University Press, 1998.

Barbour, Christine, Gerald C. Wright, with Matthew J. Streb, and Michael R. Wolf. *Keeping the Republic: Power and Citizenship in American Politics*, 3rd edition. Washington, D.C.: CQ Press, 2006.

Barone, Michael, and Grant Ujifusa. *The Almanac of American Politics*, 1996. Washington, D.C.: National Journal, 1995.

Barr, Earl, Matt Bishop, and Mark Gondree. "Fixing Federal E-Voting Standards." *Communications of the ACM* 50 (2007): 19–24.

Barreto, Matt A., and Matthew J. Streb. "Barn Burners and Burn Out: The Effects of Competitive Elections on Efficacy and Trust." Paper presented at the annual meeting of the Midwest Political Science Association, Chicago, IL, April 12, 2007.

Barreto, Matt A., Matthew J. Streb, Mara Marks, and Fernando Guerra. "Do Absentee Voters Differ From Polling Place Voters? New Evidence from California." *Public Opinion Quarterly* 70 (2006): 224–234.

Bartels, Larry M. *Presidential Primaries and the Dynamics of Public Choice*. Princeton, NJ: Princeton University Press, 1988.

Bartels, Larry M. "Constituency Opinion and Congressional Policy Making: The Reagan Defense Build Up." *American Political Science Review* 85 (1991): 457–474.

Basham, Patrick, and Martin Zelder. "Does Cleanliness Lead to Competitiveness? The Failure of Maine's Experiment." In *Welfare for Politicians? Taxpayer Financing of Campaigns*, ed. John Samples. Washington, D.C.: Cato Institute, 2005.

Bauer, Anne. *2008 Ballot Measure Overview: Interests Spend Lavishly to Influence Voters on Hot-Button Issues.* National Institute on Money in State Politics, March 9, 2010. Available at http://www.followthemoney.org/press (accessed April 14, 2010).

Bauer, Monica, and John R. Hibbing. "Which Incumbents Lose in House Elections: A Response to Jacobson's 'The Marginals Never Vanished.'" *American Journal of Political Science* 33 (1989): 262–271.

Berinsky, Adam J., Nancy Burns, and Michael W. Traugott. "Who Votes By Mail? A Dynamic Model of the Individual-Level Consequences of Voting-By-Mail Systems." *Public Opinion Quarterly* 65 (2001): 178–197.

Berkson, Larry C. "Judicial Selection in the United States: A Special Report." *Judicature* 64 (1980): 176–193.

Bonneau, Chris W. "The Dynamics of Campaign Spending in State Supreme Court Elections." In *Running for Judge: The Rising Political, Financial, and Legal Stakes of Judicial Elections*, ed. Matthew J. Streb. New York: New York University Press, 2007.

Bonneau, Chris W., and Damon M. Cann. "The Effect of Campaign Contributions on Judicial Decisionmaking." Unpublished manuscript, 2009. Available at: http://ssrn.com/abstract=1337668.

Bonneau, Chris W., and Melinda Gann Hall. *In Defense of Judicial Elections.* New York: Routledge, 2009.

Bonneau, Chris W., Melinda Gann Hall, and Matthew J. Streb. "White Noise: The Unrealized Effects of *Republican Party v. White* on Judicial Elections." Unpublished manuscript, 2010.

Boutrous, Thomas J., Jr., and Thomas G. Hungar. "Ethical Issues after Election." In *State Judiciaries and Impartiality: Judging the Judges*, eds. Roger Clegg and James Miller. Washington, D.C.: National Legal Center for the Public Interest, 1996.

Bowler, Shaun, and Todd Donovan. *Demanding Choices: Opinion, Voting, and Direct Democracy.* Ann Arbor: University of Michigan Press, 1998.

Bowler, Shaun, and Todd Donovan. "Democracy, Institutions, and Attitudes about Citizen Influence on Government." *British Journal of Political Science* 32 (2002): 371–390.

Bowler, Shaun, and Todd Donovan. "The Initiative Process." In *Politics in the American States: A Comparative Analysis*, 8th edition, eds. Virginia Gray and Russell L. Hanson. Washington, D.C.: CQ Press, 2004.

Boyd, Richard W. "Decline of U.S. Voter Turnout: Structural Explanations." *American Politics Quarterly* 9 (1981): 133–159.

Boyd, Richard W. "Election Calendars and Voter Turnout." *American Politics Quarterly* 14 (1986): 89–104.

Brace, Kimball W. "Nation Sees Drop in Use of Electronic Voting Equipment for 2008 Election—A First." October 17, 2008. Available at http://www.electiondataservices.com/images/File/NR_VoteEquip_Nov-2008wAppendix2.pdf (accessed May 3, 2010).

Brace, Paul, and Brent D. Boyea. "Judicial Selection Methods and Capital Punishment in the American States." In *Running for Judge: The Rising Political, Financial, and Legal Stakes of Judicial Elections*, ed. Matthew J. Streb. New York: New York University Press, 2007.

Brace, Paul, and Melinda Gann Hall. "Integrated Models of Judicial Dissent." *Journal of Politics* 54 (1993): 914–935.

Brennan Center for Justice. "Buying Time 2004: Total Amount Spent on Judicial Advertising Peaks at $21 Million." Available at http://www. brennancenter.org/presscenter/releases_2004/pressrelease_2004_1118.html (accessed November 18, 2004).

Brennan Center for Justice. *The Machinery of Democracy: Voting System Security, Accessibility, Usability, and Cost.* New York: Brennan Center for Justice at NYU School of Law, 2006.

Brians, Craig Leonard, and Bernard Grofman. "Election Day Registration's Effect on U.S. Voter Turnout." *Social Science Quarterly* 82 (2001): 171–183.

Broder, David S. *Democracy Derailed: Initiative Campaigns and the Power of Money.* New York: Harcourt, Inc., 2000.

Broder, David S. "No Vote Necessary: Redistricting Is Creating a U.S. House of Lords." *Washington Post*, November 11, 2004: A37.

Brook, D., and G.J.G. Upton. "Biases in Local Government Elections Due to Position on the Paper Ballot." *Applied Statistics* 23 (1974): 414–419.

Brownstein, Ronald. "Close Races Go the Way of Rotary Phones, Newt Gingrich." *Los Angeles Times*, April 15, 2002: A13.

Brunell, Thomas L. "Rethinking Redistricting: How Drawing Uncompetitive Districts Eliminates Gerrymanders, Enhances Representation, and Improves Attitudes toward Congress." *PS* 34 (2006): 77–85.

Brunell, Thomas L. *Redistricting and Representation: Why Competitive Elections Are Bad for America.* New York: Routledge, 2008.

Buchler, Justin. "Competition, Representation, and Redistricting: The Case Against Competitive Congressional Districts." *Journal of Theoretical Politics* 17 (2005): 431–463.

Buell, Emmett, Jr., and Lee Sigelman. *Nominating the President.* Knoxville: University of Tennessee Press, 1991.

Bullock, Charles S., III. "Affirmative Action Districts: In Whose Faces Will They Blow Up?" *Campaigns and Elections* 16 (April 1995): 22–23.

Bullock, Charles S., III. "Two Generations of Redistricting: An Overview." *Extensions* (Fall 2004): 9–13.

Burden, Barry. "The Nominations: Technology, Money, and Transferable Momentum." *In The Elections of 2008*, ed. Michael Nelson. Washington, DC: CQ Press, 2005.

Busch, Andrew E., and William G. Mayer. "The Front-Loading Problem." In *The Making of the Presidential Candidates, 2004*, ed. William G. Mayer. Lanham, MD: Rowman & Littlefield, 2004.

Byrne, Gary C., and J. Kristian Pueschel. "But Who Should I Vote for County Coroner?" *Journal of Politics* 36 (1974): 778–784.

Cain, Bruce E., and Kenneth P. Miller. "The Populist Legacy: Initiatives and the Undermining of Representative Government." In *Dangerous Democracy? The Battle Over Ballot Initiatives in America*, eds. Larry J.

Sabato, Howard R. Ernst, and Bruce A. Larson. Lanham, MD: Rowman & Littlefield, 2001.

Cain, Bruce E., Karin MacDonald, and Michael P. McDonald. "From Equality to Fairness: The Path of Political Reform Since *Baker v. Carr*." In *Party Lines: Competition, Partisanship, and Congressional Redistricting*, eds. Bruce Cain and Thomas Mann. Washington, D.C.: Brookings Institution Press, 2005.

Caldeira, Gregory A., and Samuel C. Patterson. "Contextual Influences on Participation in U.S. State Legislative Elections." *Legislative Studies Quarterly* 7 (1982): 359–381.

Caldeira, Gregory A., Samuel C. Patterson, and Gregory A. Markko. "The Mobilization of Voters in Congressional Elections." *Journal of Politics* 47 (1985): 490–509.

Caltech/MIT Voting Technology Project. *Voting: What Is, What Could Be*. Pasadena, CA and Cambridge, MA: Caltech and MIT, 2001.

Candidate Visit Map. Available at http://www.cnn.com/ELECTION/2008/map/candidate.visits/index.html (accessed April 7, 2010).

Canes-Wrone, Brandice, David W. Brady, and John F. Cogan. "Out of Step, Out of Office: Electoral Accountability and House Members' Voting." *American Political Science Review* 96 (2002): 127–140.

Cann, Damon M. "Justice for Sale? Campaign Contributions and Judicial Decisionmaking." *State Politics and Policy Quarterly* 7 (2007): 281–297.

"Cash v. Quality." *Cleveland Plain Dealer*, March 5, 2003: B8.

Cemenska, Nathan, Jan E. Leighley, Jonathan Nagler, and Daniel P. Tokaji. *2009 Report on the 1972–2008 Early and Absentee Voting Dataset*. A report prepared for the Pew Charitable Trusts, 2009.

Chapman, Steve. "Too Many Ex-Convicts Aren't Able to Vote." *Chicago Tribune*, August 16, 2006.

Chavez, Lydia. *The Color Bind: California's Battle to End Affirmative Action*. Berkeley: University of California Press, 1998.

Cheek, Kyle D., and Anthony Champagne. "Political Party Affiliation in Partisan and Nonpartisan Elections." *Willamette Law Review* 39 (2003): 1357–1383.

Choi, Stephen J., G. Mitu Gulati, and Eric A. Posner. "Professionals or Politicians: The Uncertain Empirical Case for an Elected Rather than Appointed Judiciary." *Journal of Law, Economics, and Organization* 26 (2010):290–336.

Cigler, Allan J. "Issue Advocacy Electioneering: The Role of Organized Interests." In *Law and Election Politics*, ed. Matthew J. Streb. Boulder, CO: Lynne Rienner Publishers, 2005.

Cigler, Allan, Joel Paddock, Gary Reich, and Eric Uslaner. "Changing the Electoral College: The Impact on Parties and Organized Interests." In *Choosing a President: The Electoral College and Beyond*, eds. Paul D. Schumaker and Burdett A. Loomis. New York: Chatham House Publishers, 2002.

Citrin, Jack, Eric Shickler, and John Sides. "What if Everyone Voted? Simulating the Impact of Increased Turnout in Senate Elections." *American Journal of Political Science* 47 (2003): 75–90.

"City Clerk Candidates." *Northern Star*, April 2, 2009: 16.

Clingermayer, James, and B. Dan Wood. "Disentangling Patterns of States Indebtedness." *American Political Science Review* 89 (1995): 108–120.

Cohen, Jeffrey E. "Perceptions of Electoral Insecurity Among Members Holding Safe Seats in a U.S. State Legislature." *Legislative Studies Quarterly* 9 (1984): 365–369.

Coleman, John J., and Paul F. Manna. "Congressional Campaign Spending and the Quality of Democracy." *Journal of Politics* 62 (2000): 757–789.

Collet, Christian, and Martin P. Wattenberg. "Strategically Unamibitious: Minor Party and Independent Candidates in the 1996 Congressional Elections." In *The State of the Parties*, 3rd edition, eds. John C. Green and Daniel M. Shea. Lanham, MD: Rowman & Littlefield, 1999.

Collier, Christopher, and James Lincoln Collier. *Decision in Philadelphia: The Constitutional Convention of 1787*. New York: Ballantine Books, 1986.

Cook, Rhodes. *The Presidential Nominating Process: A Place for Us?* Lanham, MD: Rowman & Littlefield, 2004.

Cox, Gary W. "Closeness and Turnout: A Methodological Note." *Journal of Politics* 50 (1988): 768–775.

Cox, Gary W., and Michael C. Munger. "Closeness, Expenditures, and Turnout in the 1982 U.S. House Elections." *American Political Science Review* 83 (1989): 217–231.

Crewe, Ivor. "Electoral Participation." In *Democracy at the Polls: A Comparative Study of Competitive National Elections*, eds. David Butler, Howard R. Penniman, and Austin Ranney. Washington, D.C.: American Enterprise Institute for Public Policy Research, 1981.

Crigler, Ann N., Marion R. Just, and Tami Buhr. "Cleavage and Consensus: The Public and Electoral Reform." In *Rethinking the Vote: The Politics and Prospects of American Election Reform*, eds. Ann N. Crigler, Marion R. Just, and Edward J. McCaffery. New York: Oxford University Press, 2004.

Croley, Stephen P. "The Majoritarian Difficulty: Elective Judiciaries and the Rule of Law." *University of Chicago Law Review* 62 (1995): 618–714.

Cronin, Thomas E. *Direct Democracy: The Politics of Initiative, Referendum, and Recall*. Cambridge, MA: Harvard University Press, 1989.

Dahl, Robert. *On Democracy*. New Haven, CT: Yale University Press, 1998.

Davidson, Roger H., and Walter J. Oleszek. *Congress and Its Members*, 10th edition. Washington, D.C.: CQ Press, 2006.

Davidson, Roger H., Walter J. Oleszek, and Frances E. Lee. *Congress and Its Members*, 12th edition. Washington, D.C.: CQ Press, 2010.

De Boef, Suzanna, and James A. Stimson. "The Dynamic Structure of Congressional Elections." *Journal of Politics* 57 (1995): 630–648.

Demos: A Network for Ideas & Action. "Election Day Registration Helps America Vote." Available at www.demos.org (accessed January 4, 2007).

Demos: A Network for Ideas & Action. "Expanding the Vote: The Practice and Promise of Election Day Registration." Available at www.demos.org (accessed January 4, 2007).

DeSipio, Louis. "United States." In *Introduction to American Politics*, 2nd edition, eds. Mark Kesselman, Joel Krieger, and William A. Joseph. Boston, MA: Houghton Mifflin, 2000.

DiCamillo, Mark. "The Continuing Growth of Mail Ballot Voting in California in 2008." *The California Journal of Politics and Policy* 1 (2009): 1–6.

Donnay, Patrick D., and Graham P. Ramsden. "Public Financing of Legislative Elections: Lessons from Minnesota." *Legislative Studies Quarterly* 20 (1995): 351–362.

Donovan, Todd. "The Limbaugh Effect: A Rush to Judging Cross-Party Raiding in the 2008 Democratic Nomination Contests." *The Forum* 6 (2008). Available at www.bepress.com/forum/vol6/iss2/art6 (accessed May 25, 2010.)

Donovan, Todd, and Shaun Bowler. "Direct Democracy and Minority Rights." *American Journal of Political Science* 43 (1998): 1020–1025.

Donovan, Todd, and Shaun Bowler. "An Overview of Direct Democracy in the American States." In *Citizens as Legislators*, eds. Shaun Bowler, Todd Donovan, and Caroline J. Tolbert. Columbus: The Ohio State University Press, 1998.

Donovan, Todd, and Shaun Bowler. "Responsive or Responsible Government?" In *Citizens as Legislators*, eds. Shaun Bowler, Todd Donovan, and Caroline J. Tolbert. Columbus: The Ohio State University Press, 1998.

Donovan, Todd, Caroline J. Tolbert, and Daniel A. Smith. "Political Engagement, Mobilization, and Direct Democracy." *Public Opinion Quarterly* 73 (2009): 98–118.

Doppelt, Jack C., and Ellen Shearer. *Nonvoters: America's No Shows*. Thousand Oaks, CA: Sage Publications, 1999.

Downs, Anthony. *An Economic Theory of Democracy*. Boston, MA: Addison Wesley, 1957.

Dubois, Philip L. *From Ballot to Bench: Judicial Elections and the Quest for Accountability*. Austin: University of Texas Press, 1980.

Dubois, Philip L. "Voting Cues in Nonpartisan Trial Court Elections: A Multivariate Assessment." *Law and Society Review* 18 (1984): 395–436.

Duncan, Samuel John. *The Progressive Movement: Its Principles and Its Programme*. Boston: Small, Maynard, 1913.

Dyck, Joshua J. "Initiated Distrust: Direct Democracy and Trust in Government." *American Politics Research* 37 (2009): 539–568.

"Economics." The State of the News Media, 2008. Available at http://www.stateofthemedia.org/2008/narrative_localtv_economics.php?cat=2&media=8 (accessed May 25, 2010).

Edwards, George C., III. *Why the Electoral College Is Bad for America*. New Haven, CT: Yale University Press, 2004.

Ellis, Richard. *Democratic Delusions: The Initiative Process in America*. Lawrence: University Press of Kansas, 2002.

Epstein, David L., and Sharyn O'Halloran. "Gerrymanders as Tradeoffs: The Co-Evolution of Social Scientific and Legal Approaches to Racial Redistricting." Paper prepared for the Russell Sage Foundation sponsored conference of the Mobilizing Democracy Group of the American Political Science Association, New York, January 20–21, 2006.

Erikson, Robert S. "Malapportionment, Gerrymandering, and Party Fortunes in Congressional Elections." *American Political Science Review* 66 (1972): 1234–1245.

Erikson, Robert S., Gerald C. Wright, and John P. McIver. *Statehouse Democracy: Public Opinion and Policy in the American States*. New York, NY: Cambridge University Press, 1993.

Everson, David H. "The Effects of Initiatives on Voter Turnout: A Comparative State Analysis." *The Western Political Quarterly* 34 (1981): 415–425.

"Fair Elections Now Bill Summary." Available at http://www.fairelectionsnow. org/more/summary (accessed July 15, 2010).

Farrar-Myers, Victoria A. "Campaign Finance: Reform, Representation, and the First Amendment." In *Law and Election Politics: The Rules of the Game*, ed. Matthew J. Streb. Boulder, CO: Lynne Rienner Publishers, 2005.

Farrington, Brendan. "Study: Fla. Voting Machines Still Flawed." *Associated Press*, July 31, 2007.

"Felon Voting Rights by State." Washington, D.C.: Project Vote. Available at http://www.projectvote.org/images/publications/Felon%20Voting/felon_ voting_rights_by_state_05–11–2010.pdf (accessed July 1, 2010).

Fenno, Richard. *Home Style*. Boston, MA: Little, Brown, 1978.

Fenster, Mark J. "The Impact of Allowing Day of Registration Voting on Turnout in U.S. Elections From 1960 to 1992." *American Politics Research* 22 (1994): 74–87.

Filer, John E., and Lawrence W. Kenny. "Voter Turnout and the Benefits of Voting." *Public Choice* 35 (1980): 575–585.

Filer, John E., Lawrence W. Kenny, and Rebecca B. Morton. "Redistribution, Income, and Voting." *American Journal of Political Science* 37 (1993): 63–87.

Fitzgerald, Mary. "Greater Convenience But Not Greater Turnout: The Impact of Alternative Voting Methods on Electoral Participation in the United States." *American Politics Research* 33 (2005): 842–867.

Franklin, Mark N. "The Dynamics of Electoral Participation." In *Comparing Democracies II: New Challenges in the Study of Elections and Voting*, eds. Lawrence LeDuc, Richard G. Niemi, and Pippa Norris. Thousand Oaks, CA: Sage Publications, 2002.

Fund, John. *Stealing Elections: How Voter Fraud Threatens Our Democracy*. San Francisco, CA: Encounter Books, 2004.

Gamble, Barbara S. "Putting Civil Rights to a Popular Vote." *American Journal of Political Science* 41 (1997): 245–269.

Gant, Michael M., and William Lyons. "Democratic Theory, Nonvoting, and Public Policy: The 1972–1988 Presidential Elections." *American Politics Quarterly* 21 (1993): 185–204.

Garrett, Elizabeth, and Matthew D. McCubbins. "When Voters Make Laws: How Direct Democracy is Shaping American Cities." *Public Works Management & Policy* 13 (2008): 39–61.

Geer, John G. "Rules Governing Presidential Primaries." *Journal of Politics* 48 (1986): 1006–1025.

Geer, John G. *In Defense of Negativity: Attack Ads in Presidential Campaigns*. Chicago, IL: University of Chicago Press, 2006.

Gelman, Andrew, and Gary King. "Enhancing Democracy Through Legislative Redistricting." *American Political Science Review* 88 (1994): 541–559.

General Accounting Office. *Campaign Finance Reform: Experiences of Two States That Offered Full Public Funding for Political Candidates*. Washington, D.C., 2010.

Gerber, Alan. "Estimating the Effects of Campaign Spending on Senate Outcomes Using Instrumental Variables." *American Political Science Review* 92 (1998): 401–411.

Gerber, Elisabeth R. "Legislative Response to the threat of Popular Initiatives." *American Journal of Political Science* 40 (1996): 99–124.

Gerber, Elisabeth R. "Pressuring the Legislatures through the Use of Initiatives: Two Forms of Indirect Influence." In *Citizens as Legislators*, eds. Shaun Bowler, Todd Donovan, and Caroline J. Tolbert. Columbus: The Ohio State University Press, 1998.

Gerber, Elisabeth R. *The Populist Paradox*. Princeton, NJ: Princeton University Press, 1999.

Gerber, Elisabeth R. "The Logic of Reform: Assessing Initiative Reform Strategies." In *Dangerous Democracy? The Battle Over Initiatives in America*, eds. Larry J. Sabato, Howard R. Ernst, and Bruce A. Larson. Lanham, MD: Rowman & Littlefield, 2001.

Gibson, James L. "Challenges to the Impartiality of State Supreme Courts: Legitimacy Theory and 'New-Style' Judicial Campaigns." *American Political Science Review* 102 (2008): 59–75.

Gibson, James L. "'New Style' Judicial Campaigns and the Legitimacy of State High Courts." *Journal of Politics* 71 (2009): 1285–1304.

Gilliam, Franklin D., Jr. "Influences on Voter Turnout for U.S. House Elections in Non-Presidential Years." *Legislative Studies Quarterly* 10 (1985): 339–351.

Glazer, Amihai, Bernard Grofman, and Marc Robbins. "Partisan and Incumbency Effects of 1970 Redistricting." *American Journal of Political Science* 31 (1987): 680–707.

Glenn, Gary. "The Electoral College and the Development of American Democracy." *Perspectives on Political Science* 32 (2003): 4–8.

Glick, Henry R., and Craig F. Emmert. "Selection Systems and Judicial Characteristics: The Recruitment of State Supreme Court Judges." *Judicature* 70 (1987): 228–235.

Goldberg, Deborah, Craig Holman, and Samantha Sanchez. *The New Politics of Judicial Elections: How 2000 Was a Watershed Year for Big Money, Special Interest Pressure, and TV Advertising in State Supreme Court Campaigns*. Washington, D.C.: Justice at Stake Campaign, 2002.

Goodman, Lee E. "The Internet: Democracy Goes Online." In *Law and Election Politics: The Rules of the Game*, ed. Matthew J. Streb. Boulder, CO: Lynne Rienner Publishers, 2005.

Gosnell, Harold F. *Getting Out the Vote: An Experiment in the Stimulation of Voting*. Chicago, IL: University of Chicago Press, 1927.

Gouras, Matt. "Secretary of State Wants to Do Away with Same-Day Voting." *Associated Press*, January 18, 2007.

Green, Donald Phillip, and Jonathan Krasno. "Salvation for the Spendthrift Incumbent: Reestimating the Effects of Campaign Spending in House Elections." *American Journal of Political Science* 32 (1988): 884–907.

Gregory, Ted. "The High Cost of Low Turnout." *Chicago Tribune*, April 15, 2009. Section 4: 1, 7.

Griffin, John D. "Electoral Competition and Democratic Responsiveness: A Defense of the Marginality Hypothesis." *Journal of Politics* 68 (2006): 911–921.

Gronke, Paul, Eva Galanes-Rosenbaum, and Peter A. Miller. "Early Voting and Turnout." *PS* (2007): 639–645.

Hajnal, Zoltan L., and Paul G. Lewis. "Municipal Institutions and Voter Turnout in Local Elections." *Urban Affairs Review* 38 (2003): 645–668.

Hajnal, Zoltan, and Jessica Trounstine. "Where Turnout Matters: The Consequences of Uneven Turnout in City Politics." *Journal of Politics* 67 (2005): 515–535.

Hajnal, Zoltan, Elisabeth Gerber, and Hugh Louch. "Minorities and Direct Legislation: Evidence from California Ballot Propositions." *Journal of Politics* 64 (2002): 154–177.

Hajnal, Zoltan L., Paul G. Lewis, and Hugh Louch. *Municipal Elections in California: Turnout, Timing, and Competition*. San Francisco: Public Policy Institute of California, 2002.

Hall, Melinda Gann. "Voting in State Supreme Court Elections: Competition and Context as Democratic Incentives." *Journal of Politics* 69 (2007): 1147–1159.

Hall, Melinda Gann. "State Supreme Courts in American Democracy: Probing the Myths of Judicial Reform." *American Political Science Review* 95 (2001): 315–330.

Hall, Melinda Gann. "Competition as Accountability in State Supreme Court Elections." In *Running for Judge: The Rising Political, Financial, and Legal Stakes of Judicial Elections*, ed. Matthew J. Streb. New York: New York University Press, 2007.

Hall, Melinda Gann and Chris W. Bonneau. "Does Quality Matter? Challengers in State Supreme Court Elections." *American Journal of Political Science* 50 (2006): 20–33.

Hall, Melinda Gann, and Paul Brace. "Toward an Integrated Model of Judicial Voting Behavior." *American Politics Quarterly* 20 (1992): 147–168.

Hamilton, Alexander, James Madison, and John Jay. *The Federalist*. New York: The Macmillan Company, [1787–1788] 1948.

Hansen, John Mark. "Early Voting, Unrestricted Absentee Voting, and Voting by Mail." Report prepared for the Task Force on the Federal Election System, July 2001. Available at http://www.tcf.org/Publications/ElectionReform/NCFER/hansen_chap5_early.pdf (accessed August 6, 2007).

Hardaway, Robert M. *The Electoral College and the Constitution: The Case for Preserving Federalism*. Westport, CT: Praeger, 1994.

Hasen, Richard L. "'Too Plain for Argument?' The Uncertain Congressional Power to Require Parties to Choose Presidential Nominees Through Direct and Equal Primaries." *Northwestern University Law Review* 102 (2008): 253–263.

Heller, Emily. "Judicial Races Get Meaner." *The National Law Journal*, October 25, 2004. Available at http://www.law.com/jsp/article.jsp?id=1098217051328 (accessed August 6, 2007).

Hendricks, Jennifer S. "Popular Election of the President: Using or Abusing the Electoral College." *Election Law Journal* 7 (2008): 218–226.

Herrnson, Paul S. *Congressional Elections: Campaigning at Home and in Washington*, 4th edition. Washington, D.C.: CQ Press, 2004.

Herrnson, Paul S., Benjamin B. Bederson, Bongshin Lee, Peter L. Francia, Robert M. Sherman, Frederick G. Conrad, Michael Traugott, and Richard G. Niemi. "Early Appraisals of Electronic Voting." *Social Science Computer Review* 23 (2005): 274–292.

Herrnson, Paul S., Richard G. Niemi, Michael J. Hanmer, Peter L. Francia, Benjamin B. Bederson, Frederick G. Conrad, and Michael W. Traugott. "Voters' Evaluations of Electronic Voting Systems: Results from a Usability Field Study." *American Politics Research* 36 (2008) 580–611.

Hershey, Marjorie Randon. *Party Politics in America*, 12th edition. New York: Longman, 2007.

Hershey, Marjorie Randon. *Party Politics in America*, 14th edition. New York: Longman, 2010.

Hill, David, and Seth C. McKee. "The Electoral College, Mobilization, and Turnout in the 2000 Presidential Election." *American Politics Research* 33 (2005): 700–725.

Holbrook, Thomas M., and Scott D. McClurg. "The Mobilization of Core Supporters: Campaigns, Turnout, and Electoral Composition in United States Presidential Elections." *American Journal of Political Science* 44 (2005): 689–703.

Hood, M.V. III, and Charles S. Bullock III. "Worth a Thousand Words? An Analysis of Georgia's Voter Identification Statute." *American Politics Research* 36 (2008): 555–579.

Huber, Gregory A., and Sanford Gordan. "Accountability and Coercion: Is Justice Blind When It Runs for Office?" *American Journal of Political Science* 48 (2004): 247–263.

Hulse, Carl. "Mapping the Causes of Corruption." *New York Times Online*. Available at http://www.nytimes.com/2007/06/15/us/politics/15webhulse.html?ex=1185336000&en=dde506b1fa1eb6d6&ei=5070 (accessed July 23, 2007).

Initiative and Referendum Institute. "National Survey." Conducted by Portrait of America. April 29–May 1, 2001. Available at http://www.iandrinstitute.org/. (accessed February 22, 2007).

Jackman, Robert W., and Ross A. Miller. "Voter Turnout in the Industrial Democracies During the 1980s." *Comparative Political Studies* 27 (1995): 467–492.

Jacobson, Gary C. "Enough Is Too Much: Money and Competition in House Elections." In *Elections in America*, ed. Kay Lehman Schlozman. Boston, MA: Allen and Unwin, 1987.

Jacobson, Gary C. "The Effects of Campaign Spending in House Elections: New Evidence for Old Arguments." *American Journal of Political Science* 34 (1990): 334–362.

Jacobson, Gary C. *The Politics of Congressional Elections*, 6th edition. New York: Longman, 2004.

Jacobson, Gary C. "Competition in U.S. Congressional Elections." In *The Marketplace of Democracy: Electoral Competition and American Politics*, eds. Michael P. McDonald and John Sides. Washington, D.C.: Brookings Institution Press, 2006.

Johnson, Charles A., Roger C. Schaefer, and R. Neal McKnight. "The Salience of Judicial Candidates and Elections." *Social Science Quarterly* 49 (1978): 371–378.

Justice at Stake Campaign. "Poll of American Voters." Conducted by Greenberg, Quinlan, Rosner Research, Inc. October 30–November 7, 2001. Available at http://www.justiceatstake.org (accessed July 12, 2006).

Justice at Stake Campaign. "Poll of State Judges." Conducted by Greenberg, Quinlan, Rosner Research Inc. October 30–November 7, 2001. Available at http://www.justiceatstake.org (accessed July 12, 2006).

Justice at Stake Campaign. "2004 State Supreme Court Election Overview." Available at http://faircourts.org/files/JASElection2004Summary.pdf (accessed November 11, 2004).

Justice at Stake Campaign. "What's Coming Up in 2005?" Available at http://www.justiceatstake.org/contentViewer.asp?breadcrumb=3,538 (accessed January 14, 2005).

Kanthak, Kristin, and Rebecca Morton. "Turnout and Primaries." Paper presented at the annual meeting of the American Political Science Association, Philadelphia, PA, August, 28–31, 2003.

Kanthak, Kristin, and Jeffrey Williams. "Parties and Primaries: The First Electoral Round." In *Law and Election Politics: The Rules of the Game*, ed. Matthew J. Streb. Boulder, CO: Lynne Rienner Publishers, 2005.

Karp, Jeffrey A. "The Influence of Elite Endorsements in Initiative Campaigns." In *Citizens as Legislators*, eds. Shaun Bowler, Todd Donovan, and Caroline J. Tolbert. Columbus: The Ohio State University Press, 1998.

Katosh, John P., and Michael W. Traugott. "Costs and Values in the Calculus of Voting." *American Journal of Political Science* 26 (1982): 361–376.

Kennedy, Anthony M. "Speech to Hong Kong High Court." February 5, 1999.

Kifner, John. "Carter Campaigns in New Hampshire." *New York Times*, January 21, 1976: A29.

Kim, Jae-On, John R. Petrocik, and Stephen N. Enokson. "Voter Turnout among the American States: Systematic and Individual Components." *American Political Science Review* 69 (1975): 107–123.

Kimball, David C., and Martha Kropf. "Ballot Design and Unrecorded Votes on Paper-Based Ballots." *Public Opinion Quarterly* 69 (2005): 508–529.

Kimball, David C., Chris T. Owens, and Katherine M. Kenney. "Residual Votes and Political Representation." In *Counting the Votes: Lessons from the 2000 Presidential Election in Florida*, ed. Robert P. Watson. Gainesville: University of Florida Press, 2004.

Kingdon, John W. *Agendas, Alternatives, and Public Policies*, 2nd edition. New York: HarperCollins, 1995.

Klein, David, and Lawrence Baum. "Ballot Information and Voting Decisions in Judicial Elections." *Political Research Quarterly* 54 (2001): 709–728.

Knack, Stephen. "Does Motor Voter Work?" *Journal of Politics* 57 (1995): 796–811.

Knack, Stephen. "Election-Day Registration: The Second Wave." *American Politics Research* 29 (2001): 65–78.

Knack, Stephen, and Martha Kropf. "Who Uses Inferior Voting Technology?" *PS: Political Science and Politics* 35 (2002): 541–548.

Knack, Stephen, and Martha Kropf. "Voided Ballots in the 1996 Presidential Election: A County-Level Analysis." *Journal of Politics* 65 (2003): 881–897.

Kozlowski, Mark. "Robed and Running: Striking Prohibitions on Elected Judge's Political Speech Threatens Further Erosion of Public Faith in Their Capacity to Act Impartially." *Legal Times*, July 8, 2002: 35.

Krivosha, Norman. "Acquiring Judges by the Merit Selection Method: The Case for Adopting Such a Method." *Southwest Law Journal* 40 (1986): 15–21.

Krosnick, Jon A. "In the Voting Booth, Bias Starts at the Top." *The New York Times*, November 4, 2006: A19.

Krosnick, Jon A., Joanne M. Miller, and Michael P. Tichy. "An Unrecognized Need for Ballot Reform: The Effects of Candidate Name Order on Election Outcomes." In *Rethinking the Vote: The Politics and Prospects of American Election Reform*, eds. Ann N. Crigler, Marion R. Just, and Edward J. McCaffery. New York: Oxford University Press, 2004.

Lascher, Edward L., Jr., Michael G. Hagen, and Steven A. Rochlin. "Gun Behind the Door? Ballot Initiatives, State Policies, and Public Opinion." *Journal of Politics* 58 (1996): 760–775.

Lau, Richard R., and David P. Redlawsk. "Voting Correctly." *American Political Science Review* 91 (1997): 585–598.

Leighley, Jan E., and Jonathan Nagler. "The Effects of Non-Precinct Voting Reforms on Turnout, 1972–2008." A report prepared for the Pew Charitable Trusts, January 2009.

Levinson, Sanford. "I Dissent! The Constitution Got Us Into This Mess." *Washington Post*, December 17, 2000: B02.

Lewis-Beck, Michael S., and Peverill Squire. "The Politics of Institutional Choice: Presidential Ballot Access for Third Parties in the United States." *British Journal of Political Science* 25 (1995): 419–427.

Lijphart, Arend. "Unequal Participation: Democracy's Unresolved Dilemma." *American Political Science Review* 91 (1997): 1–14.

Lind, Michael. "75 Stars: How to Restore Democracy in the U.S. Senate (and End the Tyranny of Wyoming)." *Mother Jones* (January/February 1998): 44–49.

Liptak, Adam. "Judges Mix with Politics." *New York Times*, February 22, 2003: B1.

Liptak, Adam. "Supreme Court Affirms Ban on Soft Money." *New York Times*, June 29, 2010. Available at http://www.nytimes.com/2010/06/30/us/politics/30donate.html?_r=1 (accessed July 15, 2010).

Lorinkas, R.A., B.W. Hawkins, and S.D. Edwards. "The Persistence of Ethnic Voting in Urban and Rural Areas: Results from a Controlled Election Method." *Social Science Quarterly* 49 (1969): 891–899.

Lovrich, Nicholas P., Jr., and Charles H. Sheldon. "Voters in Contested, Nonpartisan Judicial Elections: A Responsible Electorate or a Problematic Public?" *Western Political Quarterly* 36 (1983): 241–256.

Lublin, David, and D. Stephen Voss. "The Missing Middle: Why Median-Voter Theory Can't Save Democrats from Singing the Boll-Weevil Blues." *Journal of Politics* 65 (2003): 227–237.

Lupia, Arthur. "Shortcuts Versus Encyclopedias: Information and Voting Behavior in California Insurance Reform Elections." *American Political Science Review* 88 (1994): 63–76.

Lutz, Donald, Philip Abbot, Barbara Allen, and Russell Hanson. "The Electoral College in Historical Perspective." In *Choosing a President: The Electoral College and Beyond*, eds. Paul D. Schumaker and Burdett A. Loomis. New York: Chatham House Publishers, 2002.

Lyndon, Christopher. "Humphrey at 30% in Poll, Widens Democratic Lead." *New York Times*, December 14, 1975: A1.

Magleby, David B. *Direct Legislation: Voting on Ballot Propositions in the United States.* Baltimore, MD: Johns Hopkins University Press, 1984.

Magleby, David B. "Direct Legislation in the American States. In *Referendums around the World: The Growing Use of Direct Democracy*, eds. David Butler and Austin Ranney. Washington, D.C.: American Enterprise Institute Press, 1994.

Malbin, Michael J., and Thomas L. Gais. *The Day after Reform: Sobering Campaign Finance Lessons from the American States.* Albany, NY: Rockefeller Institute Press, 1998.

Mann, Thomas E. *Unsafe at Any Margin: Interpreting Congressional Elections.* Washington, D.C.: American Enterprise Institute Press, 1978.

Mann, Thomas E. "Redistricting Reform." *The National Voter* (June 2005): 4–7.

Manza, Jeff, and Christopher Uggen. "Punishment and Democracy: Disenfranchisement and Nonincarcerated Felons in the United States." *Perspectives on Politics* 2 (2004): 491–505.

Matson, Marsha, and Terri Susan Fine. "Gender, Ethnicity, and Ballot Information: Ballot Cues in Low-Information Elections." *State Politics and Policy Quarterly* 6 (2006): 49–75.

Matsusaka, John G. "Fiscal Effects of the Voter Initiative: Evidence from the Last Thirty Years." *Journal of Political Economy* 103 (1995): 587–623.

Matsusaka, John G. *For the Many or the Few: The Initiative, Public Policy, and American Democracy.* Chicago, IL: University of Chicago Press, 2004.

Mayer, Kenneth R., and John M. Wood. "The Impact of Public Financing on Electoral Competitiveness: Evidence from Wisconsin, 1964–1990." *Legislative Studies Quarterly* 20 (1995): 69–86.

Mayer, Kenneth R., Timothy Werner, and Amanda Williams. "Do Public Funding Programs Enhance Electoral Competition?" In *The Marketplace of Democracy: Electoral Competition and American Politics*, eds. Michael P. McDonald and John Sides. Washington, D.C.: Brookings Institution Press, 2006.

McClellan, Madison. "Merit Appointment versus Popular Election: A Reformer's Guide to Judicial Selection Methods in Florida." *Florida Law Review* 43 (1991): 529–555.

McCuan, David, Shaun Bowler, Todd Donovan, and Ken Fernandez. "California's Political Warriors: Campaign Professionals and the Initiative Process." In *Citizens as Legislators*, eds. Shaun Bowler, Todd Donovan, and Caroline J. Tolbert. Columbus: The Ohio State University Press, 1998.

McDermott, Monika L. "Voting Cues in Low-Information Elections: Candidate Gender as a Social Information Variable in Contemporary United States Elections." *American Journal of Political Science* 41 (1997): 270–283.

McDermott, Monika L. "Race and Gender Cues in Low-Information Elections." *Political Research Quarterly* 51 (1998): 895–918.

McDermott, Monika L. "Candidate Occupations and Voter Information Shortcuts." *Journal of Politics* 67 (2005): 201–219.

McDonald, Michael P. "A Comparative Analysis of Redistricting Institutions in the United States, 2001–2002." *State Politics and Policy Quarterly* 4 (2004): 371–395.

McDonald, Michael P. "Drawing the Line: Redistricting and Competition in Congressional Elections." *Extensions* (Fall 2004): 14–18.

McDonald, Michael P. "Drawing the Line on District Competition." *PS* 34 (2006): 91–94.

McDonald, Michael P. "Redistricting and Competitive Elections." In *The Marketplace of Democracy: Electoral Competition and American Politics*, eds. Michael P. McDonald and John Sides. Washington, D.C.: Brookings Institution Press, 2006.

McDonald, Michael P. "The Return of the Voter: Voter Turnout in the 2008 Presidential Election." *The Forum* 6 (2008).

McDonald, Michael P. "2008 Presidential Nomination Contest Turnout Rates." Available at http://elections.gmu.edu/Turnout_2008P.html (accessed June 1, 2010).

Mellman, Mark. "Electoral College Bias Probe." *The Hill* May 27, 2008.

Miller, Joanne M., and Jon A. Krosnick. "The Impact of Candidate Name Order on Election Outcomes." *Public Opinion Quarterly* 62 (1998): 291–330.

Muller, Derek T. "More Thoughts on the Compact Clause and the National Popular Vote: A Response to Professor Hendricks." *Election Law Journal* 7 (2008): 227–232.

Nagel, Jack H., and John E. McNulty. "Partisan Effects of Voter Turnout in Senatorial and Gubernatorial Elections." *American Political Science Review* 90 (1996): 780–793.

Nakanishi, Masao, Lee G. Cooper, and Harold H. Kassarjian. "Voting for a Political Candidate under Conditions of Minimal Information." *Journal of Consumer Research* 1 (1974): 36–43.

National Commission on Federal Election Reform. *Final Report of the National Commission on Federal Election Reform*. Charlottesville: University of Virginia, 2001. Available at http://www.reformelections.org/ncfer.asp#finalreport (accessed May 17, 2007).

National Conference of State Legislatures. "The Electoral College." Available at http://www.ncsl.org/default.aspx?tabid=16555 (accessed April 7, 2010).

National Conference of States Legislatures. "The Term Limited States." Available at http://www.ncsl.org/Default.aspx?TabId=14844 (accessed April 15, 2010).

National Conference of State Legislatures. "Trends in Reform." Available at http:// www.ncsl.org/programs/legman/irtaskfc/sld019.htm (accessed May 15, 2005).

National Conference of State Legislatures. "Redistricting Commissions: Congressional Plans." Available at http://www.senate.leg.state.mn.us/departments/scr/redist/red2000/apfcomco.htm (accessed June 5, 2007).

Niemi, Richard G., and Paul S. Herrnson. "Beyond the Butterfly: The Complexity of U.S. Ballots." *Perspectives on Politics* 1 (2003): 317–326.

Norden, Lawrence, Aaron Burnstein, Joseph Lorenzo Hall, and Margaret Chen. *Post-Election Audits: Restoring Trust in Elections*. New York and Berkeley: Brennan Center for Justice at New York University Law School and Samuelson Law, Technology, & Public Policy Clinic at the University of California, Berkeley School of Law, 2007.

Norden, Lawrence, David Kimball, Whitney Quesenbery, and Margaret Chen. *Better Ballots*. New York: Brennan Center for Justice, 2008.

Norris, Pippa. "Do Institutions Matter? The Consequences of Electoral Reform for Political Participation." In *Rethinking the Vote: The Politics and Prospects of American Election Reform*, eds. Ann N. Crigler, Marion R. Just, Edward J. McCaffery. New York: Oxford University Press, 2004.

Oliver, J. Eric. "The Effects of Eligibility Restrictions and Party Activity on Absentee Voting and Overall Turnout." *American Journal of Political Science* 40 (1996): 498–513.

Opensecrets.org. "2010 Election Overview: Incumbent Advantage." Available at http://www.opensecrets.org/overview/incumbs.php (accessed November 22, 2010).

Oppenheimer, Bruce I. "Deep Red and Blue Congressional Districts: The Causes and Consequences of Declining Party Competitiveness." In *Congress Reconsidered*, 8th edition, eds. Lawrence C. Dodd and Bruce I. Oppenheimer. Washington, D.C.: CQ Press, 2005.

Ornstein, Norman. "No Need to Repeal the Electoral College." *State Legislatures Magazine* February (2001). Available at http://www.ncsl.org/programs/pubs/201elec.htm (accessed May 17, 2007).

Ornstein, Norman. "There's Value in Voter ID Requirement—If It's Done Properly." *Roll Call*, May 7, 2008.

Ortiz, Daniel. "Constitutional Restrictions of Campaign Finance Regulations: Introduction." In *Campaign Finance Reform: A Sourcebook*, eds. Anthony Corrado, Thomas E. Mann, Daniel Ortiz, Trevor Potter, and Frank J. Sorauf. Washington, D.C.: Brookings Institution Press, 1997.

Owens, John R., and Larry L. Wade. "Campaign Spending on California Ballot Propositions, 1924–1984: Trends and Voting Effects." *The Western Political Quarterly* 39 (1986): 675–689.

Patterson, Samuel C., and Gregory A. Caldeira. "Getting Out the Vote: Participation in Gubernatorial Elections." *American Political Science Review* 77 (1983): 675–689.

Patterson, Thomas E. *The Vanishing Voter: Public Involvement in an Age of Uncertainty*. New York: Alfred A. Knopf, 2002.

Persily, Nathaniel. "Forty Years in the Political Thicket: Judicial Review of the Redistricting Process since *Reynolds v. Sims*." In *Party Lines: Competition, Partisanship, and Congressional Redistricting*, eds. Bruce Cain and Thomas Mann. Washington, D.C.: Brookings Institution Press, 2005.

Pillsbury, George, and Julian Johannesen. *America Goes to the Polls: A Report on Voter Turnout in the 2008 Presidential Primary*. Boston, MA: Nonprofit Voter Engagement Network, 2008. Available at www.nonprofitvote.org (accessed June 23, 2010).

Pillsbury, George, Julian Johannesen, and Rachel Adams. *America Goes to the Polls: A Report on Voter Turnout in the 2008 Election*. Boston, MA: Nonprofit Voter Engagement Network, 2008. Available at www.nonprofitvote.org (accessed June 23, 2010).

Pomper, Gerald. "Ethnic and Group Voting in Nonpartisan Municipal Elections." *Public Opinion Quarterly* 30 (1966): 79–97.

Powell, G. Bingham, Jr. "American Voter Turnout in Comparative Perspective." *American Political Science Review* 80 (1986): 17–43.

Prevost, Alicia Kolar, and Brian F. Schaffner. "Digital Divide or Just Another Absentee Ballot." *American Politics Research* 36 (2008): 510–529.

ProjectVote. *Restoring Voting Rights to Former Felons.* April 2010. Available at http://www.projectvote.org/images/publications/Felon%20Voting/FelonRestoration-PolicyPaper2010.pdf (accessed July 1, 2010).

Public Policy Institute of California. *Citizens' Initiative Process.* October 2010. Available at http://www.ppic.org/content/pubs/jtf/JTF_InitiativeJTF.pdf (accessed November 8, 2010).

Rakove, Jack. "The Accidental Electors." *New York Times,* December 19, 2000: A35.

Rankin, Bill. "Bernes Wins Judicial Election; Appeals Court Race Long, Costly." *Atlanta Journal-Constitution,* November 24, 2004: 1D.

Raskin, Jamin B. "Neither the Red States nor the Blue States but the United States: The National Popular Vote and American Political Democracy." *Election Law Journal* 7 (2008): 188–195.

Reynoso, Cruz. "In Memoriam: Chief Justice Rose Elizabeth Bird." Available at http://www.law.stanford.edu/library/wlhbp/articles/BirdRose.pdf (accessed May 31, 2007).

Rhine, Staci L. "Registration Reform and Turnout Change in the American States." *American Politics Quarterly* 23 (1995): 409–426.

Rhine, Staci L. "An Analysis of the Impact of Registration Factors on Turnout in 1992." *Political Behavior* 18 (1996): 171–185.

Richardson, Lilliard E., and Grant W. Neeley. "Implementation of Early Voting." *Spectrum: The Journal of State Government* 69 (1996): 16–23.

Richey, Sean. "Voting by Mail: Turnout and Institutional Reform in Oregon." *Social Science Quarterly* 89 (2008): 902–915.

Riker, William H., and Peter C. Ordeshook. "A Theory of the Calculus of Voting." *American Political Science Review* 62 (1968): 25–43.

Rosenfield, Steven. "New Report Highlights Online Voter Registration." *electionlineWeekly,* April 1, 2010. Available at www.electionline.org (accessed April 5, 2010).

Rosenstone, Steven J., and John Mark Hansen. *Mobilization, Participation, and Democracy in America.* New York: Macmillan, 1993.

Rosenstone, Steven J., and Raymond E. Wolfinger. "The Effect of Registration Laws on Voter Turnout." *American Political Science Review* 72 (1978): 22–45.

Ruelas, Richard. "Judge an Unexpected Target." *Arizona-Republic,* November 1, 2004: A1.

Sample, James, Lauren Jones, and Rachel Weiss. *The New Politics of Judicial Elections, 2006: How 2006 Was the Most Threatening Year Yet to the Fairness and Impartiality of Our Courts—and How Americans are Fighting Back.* Washington, D.C.: Justice at Stake Campaign, 2007.

Samples, John. *The Fallacy of Campaign Finance Reform.* Chicago, IL: University of Chicago Press, 2006.

Schaffner, Brian F. "Media Coverage: The Local Effects of Deregulation." In *Law and Election Politics: The Rules of the Game,* ed. Matthew J. Streb. Boulder, CO: Lynne Rienner Publishers, 2005.

Schaffner, Brian F., and Matthew J. Streb. "The Partisan Heuristic in Low-Information Elections." *Public Opinion Quarterly* 66 (2002): 559–581.

Schaffner, Brian F., Matthew J. Streb, and Gerald C. Wright. "Teams Without Uniforms: The Nonpartisan Ballot in State and Local Elections." *Political Research Quarterly* 54 (2001): 7–30.

Schaffner, Brian F., Matthew J. Streb, and Gerald C. Wright. "A New Look at the Republican Advantage in Nonpartisan Elections." *Political Research Quarterly* 60 (2007): 240–249.

Schier, Steven E. *You Call This an Election? America's Peculiar Democracy.* Washington, D.C.: Georgetown University Press, 2003.

Scholozman, Daniel, and Ian Yohai. "How Initiatives Don't Always Make Citizens: Ballot Initiatives in the American States, 1978–2004. *Political Behavior* 30 (2008): 469–489.

Schotland, Roy A. "Financing Judicial Elections." In *Financing the 2000 Election*, ed. David B. Magleby. Washington, D.C.: Brookings Institution Press, 2002.

Schouten, Fredreka. "States Act to Revise Judicial Selection: Influence Worries Rise as Money Floods Races." *USA Today*, March 30, 2010. Available at http://www.usatoday.com/news/politics/2010-03-30-judges_N.htm (accessed July 6, 2010).

Schrag, Peter. *Paradise Lost: California's Experience, America's Future.* New York: The New Press, 1998.

Schumaker, Paul D. "Bush, Gore, and the Issues of Electoral Reform." In *Choosing a President: The Electoral College and Beyond*, eds. Paul D. Schumaker and Burdett A. Loomis. New York: Chatham House Publishers, 2002.

Schumaker, Paul D., and Burdett A. Loomis. "Reaching a Collective Judgment." In *Choosing a President: The Electoral College and Beyond*, eds. Paul D. Schumaker and Burdett A. Loomis. New York: Chatham House Publishers, 2002.

Shachar, Ron, and Barry Nalebuff. "Follow the Leader: Theory and Evidence on Political Participation." *American Economic Review* 89 (1999): 525–547.

Shaw, Daron R. "The Effect of TV Ads and Candidate Appearances on Statewide Presidential Votes, 1988–96." *American Political Science Review* 93 (1999): 345–361.

Shaw, Daron R. *The Race to 270: The Electoral College and the Campaign Strategies of 2000 and 2004.* Chicago, IL: University of Chicago Press, 2006.

Shotts, Kenneth W. "Does Racial Redistricting Cause Conservative Policy Outcomes? Policy Preferences of Southern Representatives in the 1980s and 1990s." *Journal of Politics* 65 (2003): 216–226.

Shotts, Kenneth W. "Racial Redistricting's Alleged Perverse Effects: Theory, Data, and 'Reality.'" *Journal of Politics* 65 (2003): 238–243.

Sides, John, Jonathan Cohen, and Jack Citrin. "The Causes and Consequences of Crossover Voting." In *Voting on the Political Fault Line: California's Experiment with the Blanket Primary.* Berkeley, CA: University of California Press, 2002.

Sinclair, D.E. "Betsy," and R. Michael Alvarez. "Who Overvotes, Who Undervotes Using Punchcards? Evidence from Los Angeles County." *Political Research Quarterly* 57 (2004): 15–25.

Smith Bradley, A. *Unfree Speech: The Folly of Campaign Finance Reform.* Princeton, NJ: Princeton University Press, 2001.

Smith, Daniel A. *Tax Crusaders and the Politics of Direct Democracy.* New York: Routledge, 1998.

Smith, Daniel A. "Campaign Financing of Ballot Initiatives in American States." In *Dangerous Democracy? The Battle Over Initiatives in America*, eds. Larry J. Sabato, Howard R. Ernst, and Bruce A. Larson. Lanham, MD: Rowman & Littlefield, 2001.

Smith, Daniel A., and Caroline J. Tolbert. *Educated by Initiative: The Effects of Direct Democracy on Citizens and Political Organizations in American States.* Ann Arbor: University of Michigan Press, 2004.

Smith, Mark A. "The Contingent Effects of Ballot Initiatives and Candidate Races on Turnout." *American Journal of Political Science* 45 (2001): 700–706.

Smith, Mark A. "Ballot Initiatives and the Democratic Citizen." *Journal of Politics* 64 (2002): 892–903.

Southwell, Priscilla L., and Justin I. Burchett. "The Effect of All-Mail Elections on Voter Turnout." *American Politics Quarterly* 28 (2000): 72–79.

Spence, Gerry. *With Justice for None.* New York: Penguin Books, 1984.

Squire, Peverill, and Eric R.A.N. Smith. "The Effect of Partisan Information on Voters in Nonpartisan Elections." *Journal of Politics* 50 (1988): 169–179.

Stein, Robert M. "Early Voting." *Public Opinion Quarterly* 62 (1998): 57–69.

Stein, Robert M., and Patricia M. Garcia-Monet. "Voting Early, but Not Often." *Social Science Quarterly* 78 (1997): 657–671.

Stein, Robert M., and Greg Vonnahme. "The Costs of Elections." Paper presented at the annual Midwest Political Science Meeting, April 22–25, 2010, Chicago, IL.

Stein, Robert M., Paul Johnson, Daron Shaw, and Robert Weissberg. "Citizen Participation and Electoral College Reform." In *Choosing a President: The Electoral College and Beyond*, eds. Paul D. Schumaker and Burdett A. Loomis. New York: Chatham House Publishers, 2002.

Stein, Robert M., Greg Vonnahme, Michael Byrne, and Daniel Wallach. "Voting Technology, Election Administration, and Voter Performance." *Election Law Journal* 7 (2008): 123–135.

Stewart, Charles III. "Assessment of Voting Systems." *Election Law Journal* 8 (2009): 261–265.

Stewart, Charles III. "Election Technology and the Voting Experience in 2008." Paper presented at the annual meeting of the Midwest Political Science Association, April 2–5, 2009.

Stewart, Charles III. "Residual Vote in the 2004 Election." *Election Law Journal* 5 (2006): 158–169.

Stimson, James A., Michael B. Mackuen, and Robert S. Erikson. "Dynamic Representation." *American Political Science Review* 89 (1995): 543–565.

Stratmann, Thomas. "Do Low Contribution Limits Insulate Incumbents from Competition?" *Election Law Journal* 9 (2006): 125–140.

Streb, Matthew J. "Partisan Involvement in Partisan and Nonpartisan Trial Court Elections." In *Running for Judge: The Rising Political, Financial, and Legal Stakes of Judicial Elections*, ed. Matthew J. Streb. New York: New York University Press, 2007.

Streb, Matthew J. "The Study of Judicial Elections." In *Running for Judge: The Rising Political, Financial, and Legal Stakes of Judicial Elections*, ed. Matthew J. Streb. New York: New York University Press, 2007.

Streb, Matthew J., and Brian Frederick. "Conditions for Competition in Low-Information Judicial Elections: The Case of Intermediate Appellate Court Elections." *Political Research Quarterly* 62 (2009): 523–537.

Streb, Matthew J., and Brian Frederick. "Judicial Reform and the Future of Judicial Elections." In *Running for Judge: The Rising Political, Financial, and Legal Stakes of Judicial Elections*, ed. Matthew J. Streb. New York: New York University Press, 2007.

Streb, Matthew J., Brian Frederick, and Casey LaFrance. "Contestation, Competition, and the Potential for Accountability in Intermediate Appellate Court Elections." *Judicature* 90 (2007): 70–78.

Streb, Matthew J., Brian Frederick, and Casey LaFrance. "Voter Rolloff in a Low-Information Context: Evidence from Intermediate Appellate Court Elections." *American Politics Research* 37 (2009): 644–669.

Swain, John W., Stephen A. Borrelli, and Brian C. Reed. "Partisan Consequences of the Post-1990 Redistricting for the U.S. House of Representatives." *Political Research Quarterly* 51 (1998): 945–967.

Teixeira, Ruy A. *The Disappearing American Voter*. Washington, D.C.: Brookings Institution Press, 1992.

Thompson, Dennis F. *Just Elections: Creating a Fair Electoral Process in the United States*. Chicago, IL: University of Chicago Press, 2002.

Thurber, James A., and Carolyn Long. "Brian Baird's 'Ring of Fire'": The Quest for Funds and Votes in Washington's Third District." In *The Battle for Congress*, ed. James A. Thurber. Washington, D.C.: Brookings Institution Press, 2001.

Tolbert, Caroline J. "Changing Rules for States Legislatures: Direct Democracy and Governance Policies." In *Citizens as Legislators*, eds. Shaun Bowler, Todd Donovan, and Caroline J. Tolbert. Columbus: The Ohio State University Press, 1998.

Tolbert, Caroline J., Daniel C. Bowen, and Todd Donovan. "Initiative Campaigns: Direct Democracy and Voter Mobilization." *American Politics Research* 37 (2009): 155–192.

Tolbert, Caroline J., Daniel H. Lowenstein, and Todd Donovan. "Election Law and Rules for Using Initiatives." In *Citizens as Legislators*, eds. Shaun Bowler, Todd Donovan, and Caroline J. Tolbert. Columbus: The Ohio State University Press, 1998.

Tomz, Michael, and Robert P. Van Houweling. "How Does Voting Equipment Affect the Racial Gap in Voided Ballots?" *American Journal of Political Science* 47 (2003): 46–60.

Uggen, Christopher, and Jeff Manza. "Voting and Subsequent Crime and Arrest: Evidence from a Community Sample." *Columbia Human Rights Law Review* 36 (2004): 193–215.

United States Election Assistance Commission. "EAC Releases Data from 2008 Presidential Election." Available at www.eac.gov/News/Press/eac-releases-data-from -2008-presidential election (accessed on November 6, 2009).

United States General Accounting Office. *Statistical Analysis of Factors That Affected Uncounted Votes in the 2000 Presidential Election*. Washington, D.C., 2001.

Verba, Sidney, Kay Lehman Schlozman, and Henry E. Brady. *Voice and Equality: Civic Volunteerism in American Politics*. Cambridge, MA: Harvard University Press, 1995.

Vock, Daniel C. "New Illinois Undervote Law Not Overly Loved by Voters and Clerks." *ElectionlineWeekly*, February 4, 2010.

Wattenberg, Martin P. *The Decline of American Political Parties, 1952–1956.* Cambridge, MA: Harvard University Press, 1998.

Wattenberg, Martin P., Ian McAllister, and Anthony Salvanto. "How Voting Is Like Taking an SAT Test: An Analysis of American Voter Rolloff." *American Politics Quarterly* 28 (2000): 234–250.

Wayne, Stephen J. *The Road to the White House, 2004: The Politics of Presidential Elections.* Belmont, CA: Thomson Wadsworth, 2004.

Westlye, Mark C. "Competitiveness of Senate Seats and Voting Behavior in Senate Elections." *American Journal of Political Science* 22 (1983): 253–283.

Wielhouwer, Peter W., and Brad Lockerbie. "Party Contacting and Political Participation, 1952–1990." *American Journal of Political Science* 38 (1994): 211–229.

Winger, Richard. "Institutional Obstacles to a Multiparty System." In *Multiparty Politics in America*, eds. Paul S. Herrnson and John C. Green. Lanham, MD: Rowman & Littlefield, 1997.

Winger, Richard. *Ballot Access News.* January 1, 2007. Available at http:// www. ballot-access.org/2007/010107.html (accessed March 15, 2007).

Witcover, Jules. *No Way to Pick a President: How Money & Hired Guns Have Debased American Elections.* New York: Farrar, Straus, and Giroux, 1999.

Wolack, Jennifer. "The Consequences of Presidential Battleground Strategies for Citizen Engagement." *Political Research Quarterly* 59 (2006): 353–361.

Wolfinger, Raymond E., and Steven J. Rosenstone. *Who Votes?* New Haven, CT: Yale University Press, 1980.

Wolfinger, Raymond E., Benjamin Highton, and Megan Mullin. "How Post-registration Laws Affect the Turnout of Citizens Registered to Vote." *State Politics and Policy* 5 (2005): 1–23.

Wood, Curtis. "Voter Turnout in City Elections." *Urban Affairs Review* 38 (2002): 209–231.

Zakaria, Fareed. *The Future of Freedom: Illiberal Democracy at Home and Abroad.* New York: W.W. Norton, 2003.

Zisk, Betty H. *Money, Media, and the Grassroots: State Ballot Issues and the Electoral Process.* Newbury Park, CA: Sage Publications, 1987.

Court Cases

Baker v. Carr, 369 U.S. 186 (1962).

Beer v. U.S., 425 U.S. 130 (1976).

Buckley v. Valeo, 424 U.S. 1 (1976).

California Democratic Party v. Jones, 530 U.S. 567 (2000).

Caperton, et al., v. A.T. Massey Coal Co. 129 S. Ct. 2252 (2009).

Citizens Against Rent Control (CARC) v. City of Berkeley, 454 U.S. 290 (1981).

Citizens United v. FEC 130 S. Ct. 876 (2010).

Colegrove v. Green, 328 U.S. 549 (1946).

Crawford v. Marion County Election Board, 553 U.S. 181 (2008).

Davis v. Bandemer, 478 U.S. 109 (1986).

Davis v. FEC, 128 S. Ct. 2759 (2008).

Democratic Party v. Reed, 343 F.3d 1198 (2003).

Farrakhan v. Gregoire, 590 F.3d 989 (2010).

Federal Election Commission v. Wisconsin Right to Life Inc., No. 06–969 (2007).

First National Bank of Boston v. Bellotti, 435 U.S. 765 (1978).

Georgia v. Ashcroft, 539 U.S. 461 (2003).

Jeffers v. Clinton, 740 F. Supp. 585 (E.D. Ark. 1990).

Karcher v. Daggett, 426 U.S. 725 (1983).

League of United Latin American Citizens, et al. v. Rick Perry, et al., 126 S. Ct. 2594 (2006).

League of Women Voters v. Rokita, No. 49S02–1001-CV-50 (2010).

McConnell v. Federal Election Commission, 124 S.Ct. 619 (2003).

Miller v. Johnson, 515 U.S. 900 (1995). *Nader v. Schaffer*, 429 U.S. 989 (1976).

Nader v. Schaffer, 429 U.S. 989 (1976).

Republican Party of Minnesota v. White 536 U.S. 765 (2002).

Reynolds v. Sims, 377 U.S. 533 (1964).

Simmons v. Galvin, 575 F.3d 24 (2009).

Stephenson v. Ann Arbor Board of City Canvassers, File No. 75–10166 AW (1975).

Vieth v. Pennsylvania, 195 F. Supp. 2nd 672 (M.D. Pa., 2002).

Washington State Grange v. Washington State Republican Party 552 U.S. 442 (2008).

Wesberry v. Sanders, 376 U.S. 1 (1964).

Index